Library of
Davidson College

THE UNIVERSITY OF MISSISSIPPI
Its First Hundred Years

LAMAR HALL

(School of Law)

THE UNIVERSITY OF MISSISSIPPI

Its First Hundred Years

SECOND EDITION

*(Originally published in 1949 under the title,
A History of the University of Mississippi)*

by
ALLEN CABANISS

UNIVERSITY & COLLEGE PRESS OF MISSISSIPPI
Southern Station, Box 5164
Hattiesburg, Mississippi 39401

378.75
M67c2

Copyright © 1971 by
The University and College Press of Mississippi
All rights reserved
Manufactured in the United States of America
Second edition

Library of Congress Catalog Card Number 79-156350
Standard Book Number 87805-000-0

78-1200

IN MEMORIAM
ALFRED HUME
(1866–1950)

Preface to Second Edition

DURING the academic session of 1948–1949 the University of Mississippi celebrated its hundredth anniversary. Part of that observance was publication of this book. A quarter of another century will soon elapse and I am preparing a narrative to cover the years 1948–1973. But drastic events since 1948 and my own intimate association with the University will, in the nature of things, necessitate considerable difference in kind as well as degree between the earlier and the future account. In the meanwhile it has seemed appropriate to reissue the older volume which has been out of print for fifteen years or more.

This second edition remains essentially the same as the first. Some corrections have been incorporated; a few additional statements have been inserted; and the title has been changed. The Introduction by Dean Pete Kyle McCarter and Epilogue by Chancellor J. D. Williams have been omitted; entirely useful for a centennial occasion, they have served their purpose. The volume stands, therefore, virtually as it was, a monument to a past that is over.

Walter Lord, in his eminently readable, but scantily documented, journalistic sketch, *The Past That Would Not Die* (New York: Harper and Row, 1965), p. 259, remarked: "Ole Miss's colorful past is lovingly recounted in James Allen Cabaniss, *A History of the University of Mississippi*." That statement is, of course, gratuitous, indeed inaccurate in employment of the adverb *lovingly*, but I do not intend here to pursue the implication. By the time I deal with the period 1948–1973, Lord's account, along with others, will fall into perspective. So, pending the hundred twenty-fifth anniversary, one may hope that this reissue will be an adequate memorial of the first hundred years.

ALLEN CABANISS

University, Mississippi
November 6, 1970

Preface to First Edition

THE "kind reader" will do me a great favor by studying this Preface before turning to the remainder of the book. For here I shall try to anticipate certain criticisms by suggesting the strictures which I have observed in writing a centennial history.

The preparation of the volume may have been a rash undertaking. In fact, I may have incurred the dismal fate wished upon his enemies by the patriarch Job, when he exclaimed, "Oh that . . . mine adversary had written a book" (Job 31:35). The source materials are so extensive that a process of selection was necessary—and that is always dangerous! Moreover, some half-legendary incidents in the history of the University have been omitted because they cannot be adequately documented. Finally, as in many other circumstances, so in the case of documentary evidence—

> *The evil that men do lives after them,*
> *The good is oft interred with their bones. . . .*

Especially is that true in the annals of student life; it is all too frequently a disciplinary matter which is recorded rather than an instance of merit.

In order to state the purpose of the book, it may be well to warn the reader what he is not to expect. First, he must not look for a definitive history of the University of Mississippi. Such a production would require more time, space, and expenditure than have been deemed feasible. Furthermore, it is quite probable that to devote so much attention to an American institution with only one century of existence behind it could not be justified.

Secondly, the volume is not intended to take the place of an historical catalogue, but to be a supplement to it. The curious reader will therefore look in vain for many names. Formerly the University published such a catalogue every ten years. The last, however, was that of 1909. A new one is overdue and may soon be prepared.

Thirdly, this is not a collection of reminiscences. It is not based on hearsay, but on documents, primarily the minutes of the Board of Trustees and those of the faculty. I am not unmindful of the passage of Scripture which says, "Remember the days of old, consider the years of many generations: ask thy father, and he will shew thee; thy elders, and they will tell thee" (Deuteronomy 32:7). But, as someone has noted, we forgot to ask our fathers until it was too late, and when we asked our elders they gave us conflicting reports. For that reason, I have consistently declined to listen to those who have wanted to tell me tales about the University.

Fourth, since I am not a graduate of the University, I have no personal memories about it and hence no ax to grind. I have attempted to approach the research in an objective, scientific, and unbiased manner, yet with sympathy and interest.

Fifth, the work was not done in an unhurried, leisurely fashion. It was done with the full realization that there was a "dateline" to be met. The task was assumed as late as December, 1946, shortly after I had come to the faculty of the University. There was no relaxation of primary duties such as a full teaching load and the supervision of three theses. Nor was there any secretarial assistance. The work should have been done over a much longer period of time. As a matter of fact, it was projected about 1927, but changes in the faculty and administration and the crises in the national and international spheres caused it to be neglected until just on the eve of the University centennial.

So much for what the study is not. Now, what is it? First of all, it is a simple, chronological *narrative*, the third of its kind, recounting the salient features of a century at the University of Mississippi. Its predecessors are John Newton Waddel, *Historical Discourse Delivered on the Quarter-Centennial of the University of Mississippi* (Oxford, Miss., 1873), and Chapter IX, "The University of Mississippi," in Edward Mayes, *History of Education in Mississippi* (Washington, 1899).

Next, it is an *institutional history*. Just as one sketches the history of the Holy Roman Empire by grouping the information around the succession of emperors, so in this treatment the main theme is the series of University chancellors. However, an attempt has been made to enrich the method by including enough material of broader interest to prevent the volume from becoming merely an account of administrative officials. I had originally planned to add chapters on student life, intellectual activity, the religious character of the University, its Southern quality, and its relation to Freemasonry, but was dissuaded. Most of the material is already in the book and the inclusion of such chapters would be repetitive and destroy the unity of the history as it is at present organized.

Lastly, it should be kept in mind that this is a *centennial history*. It is only one phase of the total celebration. Many important people, events, and circumstances are therefore omitted from consideration here, because they were dealt with in other parts of the hundred-year birthday anniversary. . . .

ALLEN CABANISS

University, Mississippi
November 6, 1948

Table of Contents

	Preface to Second Edition	vii
	Preface to First Edition	ix
I	Once Upon a Time	3
II	In the Beginning	13
III	Old Bullet and the Boys	21
IV	Before the War	35
V	The Years the Cankerworm Hath Eaten	55
VI	False Dawn	60
VII	By the Waters of Babylon	71
VIII	The Forgotten Chancellor	81
IX	The Majesty of the Law	100
X	How Firm a Foundation	108
XI	A New Age	121
XII	A Troubled Era	129
XIII	The Good Old Days	135
XIV	Nightmare and Restoration	145
XV	The University Comes of Age	152
	Notes	163
	Bibliographical Note	197
	Index	201

THE UNIVERSITY OF MISSISSIPPI
Its First Hundred Years

CHAPTER I

Once Upon a Time

TO the coldly scientific mind the University of Mississippi may be located in the vicinity where longitude 89°44′21″ is intersected by latitude 34°22′12″."[1] But sentimental hearts will express the same fact in a different manner. They will say:

> 'Way down South in Mississippi, there's a spot that
>   ever calls,
> Where among the hills enfolded stand old Alma
>   Mater's halls,
> Where the trees lift high their branches to the
>   whispering Southern breeze,
> There Old Miss is calling, calling to our hearts'
>   fond memories.[2]

An earlier historian sought to enhance the glamor of the place by intimating as not improbable that Hernando de Soto and his paladins had traversed this very spot in the spring of 1541 on their way to search for the golden cities of Cibola.[3] Whether this be true or not, the real tale is fascinating enough.

When Mississippi was officially erected into a territory (April 7, 1798), the Congressional statute provided that the same rights and privileges be accorded it as were granted in the Ordinance of 1787 for the government of the Northwest Territory.[4] This ordinance carried the memorable statement that "religion, morality and knowledge being necessary to good government and the happiness of mankind, schools and the means of education shall forever be encouraged." To accomplish such a worthy end, later action authorized the donation of certain public lands (usually two townships) to the legislatures of states formed out of the Northwest Territory for the use of a university.[5] It was to be expected that Mississippi would receive the benefit of this generosity.

Through a misunderstanding, Jefferson College at Washington (in the Mississippi Territory), a private corporation, received on February 20, 1812, the grant of one township from Congress.[6] Hence, three years later, March 3, 1815, only one additional township was reserved for the territory from the lands formerly belonging to the Creek Indians.[7] This township was in the Alabama Territory when that was separated from Mississippi (March 3, 1817). Therefore, after Mississippi became a state (December 10, 1817), another act of Congress (February 20, 1819) was necessary so that the township would be within the limits of Mississippi. The land was "vested in the legislature of the said state, in trust, for the support of a seminary of learning therein...."[8]

In an address to the state legislature, November 7, 1821, Governor George Poindexter called attention to the necessity of selecting the thirty-six sections (23,040 acres). Later the same month the legislature authorized the Governor to do this. Two years afterwards, December 23, 1823, Governor Walter Leake reported the accomplishment of the duty. In addition, he suggested that permission be sought from Congress to sell part of the lands.[9]

No significant action was taken on Governor Leake's suggestion, so it was reiterated in a message of January 4, 1825. The legislature, however, deemed itself competent to dispose of the lands without consulting Congress and proceeded at that session to allow the leasing. This action was amended once and supplemented twice by 1830.[10]

The leasing began immediately and continued until 1833. In that year it was found that the revenue was very small and that the lands were deteriorating. The legislature thereupon, March 2, 1833, provided for the sale of the seminary lands.[11] Notes for thirty-five and a half sections, in the amount of $277,332.52, to bear ten per cent interest, were taken and placed for collection and investment in the Planters' Bank, a reckless venture undertaken by the state in 1830.[12] As the notes became due the state auditor was to collect them and invest the proceeds in the stock of the bank.[13] The sordid story of that debacle is not a credit to the state.

Collection of the notes was carelessly neglected. Fourteen months after full payment was due, if not indeed overdue, Governor Alexander G. McNutt, in an urgent message, January 8, 1839, warned the legislators that "unless the University is speedily established, or the law providing for the collection of the fund changed, a large portion of it may be lost." He intimated that many of the notes were under protest and that some of the holders were either dead or had removed beyond the jurisdiction of the state.[14] But the Governor's voice was of one crying in the wilderness. Later in the following month the legislature cut itself even further loose from the property by transferring its stock to the Mississippi Railroad Company and surrendering its director in the Planters' Bank.[15]

In 1840 McNutt once more invoked speedy action on the seminary fund. In 1841 a committee of the House of Representatives indicated the precarious condition of the fund. Still the legislature hesitated.[16] At long last, however, but too late, on July 26, 1843, the legislature passed an act providing for the adequate protection of the remainder of the fund.[17]

Meanwhile, the Planters' Bank had failed in 1840. With it went the amount of $127,639.00, which had been collected from the sale of the lands granted by Congress and invested in the stock of the bank.[18] The amount uncollected through heedless negligence was also beyond recovery, chiefly because of the statute of limitations.[19] But even now carelessness was not at an end. The bank was put in liquidation in 1844. The following year an additional sum of $10,222.00 was collected, paid into the bank, and consequently lost![20]

What the total loss was no one knows. The uncertain element of interest and renewals prevented the establishment of the precise amount. The day the act was passed to protect the fund, July 26, 1843, there were deposited in the state treasury in principal and interest only $61,718.05 of the once munificent endowment.[21]

During all this ruinous financial activity hardly a regular session of the legislature passed without the Governor's urgently pressing the matter of the speedy founding of the "seminary," but these requests of Governors Gerard C. Brandon, Hiram G. Runnels, John A. Quitman, and Charles Lynch had been ignored.[22] Indifference, laxity, the frontier suspicion of education, and some feeling that education was not a function of the state were factors contributing to this failure. Finally, on January 7, 1840, Governor McNutt made his appeal. His message reveals the more positive reason for the unfortunate delay: there was a bitter sectional antagonism between the northern and the southern parts of the state which made itself felt in the legislature in relation to the location of the proposed university.[23]

Governor McNutt, however, did achieve results. A committee appointed to study the matter reported a bill, which was passed on February 20, 1840, authorizing the selection of seven sites to be considered for a university.[24] Reports of the virtues and faults of each site were discussed. The legislature in joint assembly proceeded to ballot on January 26, 1841. Of the towns under consideration, six were in the northern or central part of the state, Louisville, Kosciusko, Brandon, Oxford, Middleton, and Monroe Missionary Station, while only one, Mississippi City (in Hancock county on the Coast), was in the southern section.

As the balloting progressed, the town receiving the lowest number of votes was dropped from the list. On the sixth ballot only Oxford and Mississippi City remained. Oxford won by a vote of fifty-eight to fifty-seven.[25] It was a strictly sectional vote and one so bitterly contested that it, together with other elements of dissension, almost threatened to split the state, the old aristocratic section, centering about Adams and Wilkinson counties, seriously discussing the possibility of seceding to form a new state or to join Louisiana.[26] As late as 1846 attempts were still being made to change the proposed location.[27] The result of this continuing bitterness was apparent during the first session of the University, 1848-1849, in the fact that of the eighty students who matriculated most were from the northern and central counties. The southernmost county represented was Copiah with one student. Two were present from Jackson in Hinds county.[28] The following year one student came from Pass Christian (Harrison county) on the Coast. It was not until the third year of the University, 1850-1851, that any students from the southwestern counties were present. In that year there were one from Vicksburg (Warren county), one from Natchez (Adams county), and two from Woodville (Wilkinson county).[29] Since the War Between the States the issue of sectionalism within the state has not been very troublesome.

Needless to say, after the selection of a site, nothing further could be accomplished toward actually beginning a university for some years yet. Three years later, realizing the disastrous situation of the seminary fund, the legislature responded to the plea of Governor Albert G. Brown and passed the act (February 24, 1844) constituting "a body politic and corporate by the name and style of the 'University of Mississippi'. . . ."[30]

The original Board of Trustees appointed under this act was made up of thirteen of the most eminent men of the state. It was somewhat unevenly distributed sectionally, six being residents of north Mississippi. Of the other seven, two were from the old Natchez region, four from the central part of the state, and one from the Coast (from Mississippi City, which had been Oxford's rival for the site of the new university). Of those who were to achieve more than local fame there were John A. Quitman, twice Governor of Mississippi (1835-1836, 1850-1851) and for many years Grand Master of Masons of the state (1826–1837, 1840, 1845, 1846); William L. Sharkey, Provisional Governor after the surrender of the Confederate armies (1865); Francis L. Hawkes, twice elected bishop in the Protestant Episcopal Church (but never consecrated); Jacob Thompson, Secretary of the Interior in President Buchanan's cabinet; James M. Howry, Grand Master of Masons (1852); and John Newton Waddel, chancellor of the University (1865–1874) and the first chancellor of the Southwestern Presbyterian University (1879–1888), then at Clarksville, Tennessee. Other original Trustees were J. Alexander Ventress, called by action of the legislature "the Father of the University of Mississippi," Alexander M. Clayton, William Y. Gholson, Pryor Lea, Edward C. Wilkinson, John J. McCaughan, and A. H. Pegues.

The first meeting of the Board was in Jackson, January 15, 1845. An election of officers was held in order to achieve permanent organization, a set of by-laws was prepared, the seal was adopted, and an attempt was made to ascertain the amount of money in the fund. The seal is of some interest. The original description provided that it should "have the words, 'University of Mississippi,' engraved around the margin, with an Eye in the centre."[31] The adept will immediately recognize a Masonic symbol, the all-seeing eye. Much later two unsuccessful attempts were made to change the emblem.[32] Except for immaterial details, however, the Masonic character of the seal has remained the same from the earliest days to the present.

At this initial meeting of the Board William Nichols was consulted as the architect and a committee of the Board was appointed to make a contract for the building materials.[33] Nichols was later officially employed.[34] Meanwhile, the Trustees had accepted two half-sections of land lying immediately west of the town of Oxford, which had been deeded to the state by James Stockard and his wife, Sarah, and John D. Martin and his wife, Sarah, on December 8, 1841. Each half-section had been given in consideration of ten dollars and the gift was conditional on the establishment of a state university on the property.[35]

Lafayette county, where the University was to be located, was a part of the cession made by the Chickasaw Nation at the treaty of Pontotoc Creek (1832). Sale of the lands began at once. The county was created by act of the legislature, February 9, 1836.[36] On June 22 of that same year the officials (the Board of Police) accepted for a county seat the donation of fifty acres from three speculators, John Chisholm of Alabama, John D. Martin, and John J. Craig, and declared that it should be known as the town of Oxford.[37]

The name *Oxford* is attributed to Thomas Dudley Isom, one of the earliest white settlers, whose daughter, Sarah McGehee, later became the first woman on the faculty of the University (1885–1905).[38] He hoped even then that the town would become the home of a seminary of learning.[39] The village was incorporated on May 11, 1837.[40] A year later there were two hotels, six stores, and two schools. Arrangements were in progress for the building of two churches. This pleasant frontier region was a veritable "fairy land [of] park-like forests and waving native grasses. . . ."[41]

Here in the little out-of-the-way village of less than a thousand souls, on property given by town and county, construction of the new University was begun. The cornerstone of the first building, now called the "Lyceum" and at present occupied chiefly by the administrative offices, was laid with Masonic ceremonies, July 14, 1846. The principal address was delivered by William F. Stearns of Holly Springs, later to become the University's first professor of law.[42] (The custom of having the Masonic Grand Lodge lay the cornerstone of all major structures on the campus continued until 1912.)

The Trustees now directed their attention to the educational program to be put into effect. At their meeting on April 27, 1847, a resolution was adopted providing for the appointment of a committee whose duty it would be "to correspond with the Faculties of various Colleges and Universities in the United States and elsewhere, and others conversant with literary institutions on the subject of laws and regulations for the government and internal police of litterary institutions, to mature a plan of education, to limit the number and define the duties of Professors, and report to the Board . . ." at a later meeting.[43] The committee made a preliminary report on January 11, 1848.[44] Another report was made a month later.[45] On the basis of these it was thereupon decided that the faculty should consist of five members: the president, who was also to serve as professor of mental and moral philosophy, rhetoric, evidences of Christianity, logic, and political economy; a professor of ancient and modern languages; a professor of pure and mixed mathematics; a professor of natural philosophy and astronomy; and a professor of chemistry, geology, and mineralogy.[46] Notice was to be made in the press that these instructors would be elected at a meeting of the Board the following July and applications for the positions were invited.[47]

When the Trustees convened in Oxford in July, a more detailed plan was worked out involving some variations from the one adopted earlier.[48] The academic session was to last ten months. Each professor was to teach two classes. The president was to instruct his lower-division students in mental and moral philosophy, logic, and belles-lettres, and his upper-division students in political economy and international law. It was also finally agreed that he should teach the evidences of Christianity.[49] The professor of mathematics and astronomy was at liberty to divide his instructions between the upper and lower divisions as might appear proper to him. The same liberty was allowed the professors of natural science (chemistry, geology, mineralogy, botany, and natural philosophy), of ancient languages (Latin, Greek, and Hebrew), and of modern languages (French, Spanish, and German).

Approximately one hundred eighty men were applicants for these positions, distributed as follows: for the presidency, seventeen; for the professorship of mathematics and astronomy, sixty; for that of natural science, thirty; and for that of ancient languages, about seventy.[50] Out of this number the Board selected George Frederick

Holmes as president;⁵¹ Albert Taylor Bledsoe, professor of mathematics and astronomy;⁵² John Millington, professor of natural science;⁵³ and John Newton Waddel, an erstwhile Trustee, professor of ancient and modern languages.⁵⁴ It will be noted that although five professorships were planned only four professors were appointed. The secretary of the Board was then ordered to notify these men of their election and request them to move to Oxford as soon as they could so that the University might be opened on the first Monday of November.⁵⁵

The president of the Board was authorized to advertise the forthcoming opening in six newspapers of the state.⁵⁶ It was then resolved that the Trustees retain the right to remove any faculty member at any time upon sufficient cause, as well as to alter the mode of instruction and division of the different courses to be taught by the professors.⁵⁷

The University duly opened for its first session on Monday, November 6, 1848. The Board of Trustees "met pursuant to adjournment" to attend the installation of the faculty in the chemistry lecture-room of the Lyceum building. The address was delivered by Jacob Thompson for the Trustees, followed by "an elaborate and chaste oration" by President Holmes for the faculty, ". . . and thereupon the institution was declared open for the reception of students. . . ." ⁵⁸

The next day the Board adopted and authorized the printing and distribution of the "Laws and Regulations of the University of Mississippi," proposed by the faculty. The use of firearms was forbidden; the course of study was strictly defined; the times of the classes were prescribed; and the rules of discipline were enumerated.⁵⁹

It may be appropriate here to discuss a matter about which there has been some question, namely, the relationship the University bears respectively to the Federal government and to the state. Reporting an address delivered in Jackson in 1875 by Chancellor A. P. Stewart, a newspaper account said: "He desired . . . to show that the University was not a State institution, but a *creation* of the National Government. ..." [60] This position was virtually repeated by Edward Mayes, himself a former chancellor, who wrote: "The University of Mississippi was, in effect, founded by the Congress of the United States. ..." [61]

But in his statement Mayes contradicts his own earlier point of view in which he held that "in all the history of the University, although a large endowment came to it from the United States, no one has ever maintained that it is a Federal institution." [62] He, of course, ignores the fact that Stewart had clearly enunciated just such a position a mere dozen years previously. Mayes, however, goes on to say of the University that it "is but a part of the State machinery ... its *creature*, with its very existence subject to the arbitrary will of the State. ..." [63]

The latter view is undoubtedly the true one. Beyond the granting of the land the Federal government has never been concerned about the University. It has never attempted to exercise any authority over it. Indeed, the original phraseology, which specified the *support* of a seminary of learning, not the establishment of one, presupposes the founding of the institution by some other power. On the other hand, the state has always made its authority felt in regard to the University. The first appropriation of funds by the legislature, fifty thousand dollars, was an outright grant without reference to the seminary fund.[64] Even the property on which the institution stands came not from the national government but from the state, to which it had been deeded by local citizens. The state therefore has the legal, though not the moral, right "to throttle the institution ..., whenever it gets ready to do so." [65]

(How hollow the preceding paragraph sounds after the crisis of 1962–1963 should be obvious to everyone, but from the vantage point of 1948 it was accurate.)

CHAPTER II

In the Beginning

HERE to the new University amid the wooded hills flocked eighty boisterous young Mississippians. Eight were local students from Oxford, nine were from elsewhere in Lafayette county, and all the rest with one exception were from other parts of the state, chiefly from the more northerly counties. It is worthy of note that of these eighty students one was even then from Memphis, Tennessee, a city which has supported the University for a century.[1]

The sight that presented itself to these students and others has been described by one of the first faculty members:

"The campus, which was of great natural beauty, . . . began from a level spot facing east, and sloping gently and regularly for several hundred yards in that direction. . . . The Lyceum was an imposing structure of the height of three stories, and with a front portico supported by six large and handsome columns. It contained, on the first floor, two rooms, and a large chemical theatre for lectures, and a laboratory running back, of large dimensions. In the second story was, in front, a fine room devoted to a collection of shells and geological and mineral specimens of great value and beauty; and besides this room, were four [at first only two] rooms for lecture and recitation purposes. The third floor was occupied at that time by the Library and similar rooms, corresponding to those of the second story." [2]

This building was flanked on either side by a three-story dormitory, each having thirty-six rooms. Just beyond each dormitory was a three-story faculty house, each with twelve rooms, constituting a double residence sufficient for the four families.[3] "The University campus," continues the professor, "possesses as great attractions of natural beauty as any location of similar nature and for similar purposes. The beautiful inclination of the grounds, and the grand old oaks which tower above and overshadow the campus, make the spot one to endear the University to those who have been privileged to enjoy its priceless advantages." [4]

All this, however, was but a rude clearing in the midst of a virgin forest, and to the sensitive, temperamental young president "the campus seemed more like an unexplored wilderness than the location of a university...." [5] George Frederick Holmes, born in British Guiana, August 21, 1820, had been reared in England, where for a time he attended the University of Durham. At an early age he had migrated to Canada and thence to South Carolina, where he was admitted to the bar. In 1846 he was professor of ancient languages in the University of Richmond and the following year professor of history and political economy in the College of William and Mary. In the summer of 1848 he had been elected president of the new state University of Mississippi. The fact that he was only twenty-eight years of age when he came here was undoubtedly a handicap for the presiding officer of a faculty whose members were considerably older than he.[6]

He was recognized by his colleagues as "a polished scholar and gentleman," but was entirely lacking in disciplinary and administrative ability.[7] His wide range of intellectual interests and attainments may be illustrated by a later incident in his life. In 1857 he applied for a position on the faculty of the University of Virginia, but there was some ambiguity as to the subject he wished to teach. When asked by the Board of Visitors to be more explicit, his reply was, "Oh, it does not matter particularly. I prefer not having the chair of law, as I am a little rusty in that." [8]

Other characteristics were probably irritating to those associated with him. In his manner of dress he was slovenly and is reputed not to have looked in a mirror since 1847.⁹ He was moreover violently prejudiced and exceedingly iconoclastic toward American heroes and practices.¹⁰ For instance, when he was asked if he were an Episcopalian, his answer was unnecessarily tactless: "Sir, I was born under the allegiance of George III, christened by the Bishop of York, confirmed by the Archbishop of Canterbury. I am a communicant of the Established Church of England, and have an utter contempt for that church in this country." ¹¹

Another member of the first faculty, Albert Taylor Bledsoe, had had, and was yet to have, a restless, stormy career. Born in Frankfort, Kentucky, November 9, 1809, he had gone to the United States Military Academy at West Point in 1825. Being graduated in 1830 and commissioned as a second lieutenant, he had served a while at frontier posts as far west as Fort Gibson (Indian Territory), but resigned in 1833.

For a short time Bledsoe studied law with his maternal uncle, Samuel Taylor, in Richmond, Virginia, and then accepted appointment as tutor in mathematics at Kenyon College, Gambier, Ohio. There he became interested in theology and in 1835 was ordained to the Protestant Episcopal ministry. That same year he became professor of mathematics at Miami University, Oxford, Ohio, where he fell under the influence of a colleague, William H. McGuffey, of the McGuffey Reader fame. Both had to resign under pressure the following year because of dissension with the rest of the faculty.

For the remainder of 1836 Bledsoe served as rector of Grace Episcopal Church, Sandusky, Ohio. A succession of pastorates followed: assistant minister, Christ Church, Cincinnati; rector in Hamilton, Ohio; and assistant to the bishop of Kentucky. But in 1838 he returned with his family to Springfield, Illinois, and took up the practice of law. In 1839 he was at his own request divested of clerical office and restored to the status of a layman.

In Springfield he came into friendly contact with Abraham Lincoln. For a while (1843-1844) he had rooms in the Globe Tavern, where the Lincolns were living. Mrs. Bledsoe aided Mrs. Lincoln in a neighborly manner after the birth of Robert Todd. Bledsoe himself was the one who succeeded in averting a duel by suggesting the use of broadswords when Lincoln was challenged by James Shields. But by now he had remained too long in one place.

So the wandering began again. In 1844 he went to Cincinnati to practice law, but his wife's health was bad. The traveling therefore continued. He practiced law for a time in the national capital, but by 1847 was back in Springfield, where he was living when he was elected to the faculty of the University of Mississippi to teach mathematics and astronomy, and later natural philosophy, although his primary interests were theology and metaphysics.[12]

John Millington, the third member of the faculty, was the oldest. His fame as a scientist was international. Like Holmes, he was of English origin, having been born near London, May 11, 1779. Financial straits had prevented his receiving a degree from Oxford, so after studying law he was admitted to the English bar in 1803. From law he turned successfully to engineering, being associated for a time with John L. McAdam. He also gained a medical degree, although the time and place are unknown.

From 1805 to 1825, when he resigned, he was a fellow of the Royal Society of Arts, serving as an officer of the society from 1821 until his resignation. In 1820 he became a charter member, later officer and life member, of the Royal Astronomical Society, and in 1823, a fellow of the Linnean Society of London. The Royal Institution made use of his services (1815-1829) as lecturer in natural philosophy and professor of mechanics (some of the manuscript notes for these courses are in the library of the College of William and Mary). He also served on the first faculty of the University of London. By means of these associations he came into close contact with such eminent British scientists as Michael Faraday and Sir Humphrey Davy.

About 1830 he went to Mexico as the chief engineer and superintendent of an English mining concern. While there his wife died. He then toured the United States and settled in Philadelphia, where he opened a scientific supply shop. In 1835 the College of William and Mary called him to the chair of chemistry, natural philosophy, and engineering, a position he held until 1848, when he was elected to the University of Mississippi.

His selection at the advanced age of sixty-nine to the latter office was apparently influenced by his possession of some scientific apparatus which he offered for use at the University of Mississippi. This was purchased by the Board of Trustees in 1851 or 1852. Several pieces bearing his initials are still extant. He is said to have been the first one of the new faculty to report for duty.[13] Millington's temperament, as well as Waddel's, served as the counterpoise to Holmes's irascible sensitivity and Bledsoe's blunt and restless energy. He was friendly, lovable, guileless, charitable. Waddel says, "He took for granted that men were what they professed to be." [14]

Reserving fuller consideration of John Newton Waddel until later, it is now in order to consider the activity of the first academic session of the new University. The preparation and publication of a statement of entrance requirements had not been possible until just on the eve of the opening. As a consequence the young students were unprepared for college studies. Moreover, no provision had been made for securing textbooks and a great deal of time was lost before this situation was relieved. In the emergency, Waddel went to Holly Springs, in near-by Marshall county, where a classical school (St. Thomas Hall) had been in operation. There he found a meager store of books and other supplies for sale. These sufficed for the time.[15]

Classes, however, met regularly and the professors delivered their lectures. Millington performed a number of elementary but colorful experiments which fascinated his students. The immaturity of the students is indicated by the reaction of one who, after serious study had begun, plaintively inquired of Millington, "Doctor, when are you going to do some more of your tricks?" [16]

There was no class beyond that of sophomore. But in addition to the reguluar work, the instructors found it necessary to spend a great portion of the week tutoring the students privately in order to supply deficiencies in their preparation for college.[17] With all the expenditure of time and energy, it was soon discovered that the life of the students was still not fully occupied. Two literary societies, the Hermaean and Phi Sigma, were organized for debates, orations, and the reading of original essays. All the students were required to belong to one of them as they were considered a definite part of the academic life of the University.[18]

Still time weighed heavily upon the students. Soon the strangeness of their new situation wore off, and when it did it may be said without undue exaggeration that "all hell broke loose." Waddel, the clergyman, said, ". . . rarely, if ever, was an institution of learning attended by a body of students so disorderly and turbulent as those of that first session proved to be. . . ." Admitting that some of the young men were serious and gentlemanly, he wrote that "the large body of the students were idle, uncultivated, viciously disposed, and ungovernable." This he attributed to their lack of preparation and their conception that "college life was only a scene of fun and frolic." In his opinion, "nothing saved the University from utter and speedy ruin . . . but the sternest and most rigid exercise of discipline." [19]

Waddel's devastating indictment was substantiated by Bledsoe, the West Pointer, who at the end of the session was constrained by the year's experience to deliver an address on the educational consequences of the total depravity of mankind! In it he referred to the disorderliness of the first students. He ascribed this to their idea "that College life is a sort of farce or comedy in which each actor is expected to display the brilliancy of his parts, and to signalize his genius in freaks of mischief and scenes of dissipation." He served notice that hereafter steps would be taken to prevent young men from coming here "to waste the prime of life in idleness, and to squander their parents' money in dissipation; ... we cannot permit them to enact their obscene comedies in this holy temple of learning, nor to set their cloven feet upon the tender germs of Science, which has been so beneficently planted in this fair region of the South." [20]

The turbulence shocked the people of the state, causing a visit of some of the Trustees in order to inquire into it and insist that the faculty enforce more severely the rules of discipline.[21] The minutes of the faculty meetings of that session record incident after incident which bear out the statements of Waddel and Bledsoe. Drunkenness was particularly prevalent, although the law forbade the sale of liquor within five miles of the University. The statute was circumvented by importations in wagons carrying cotton to market and by the laxity with which a prescription could be secured which would allow it to be obtained from druggists for "medical" purposes.[22] Expulsion followed if a student were caught in a drunken condition.[23] That was also the penalty for "circulating false and calumnious reports," [24] for "very profane swearing in the presence of the Faculty," [25] and for numerous other offenses. By the end of the session it was reported to the Board of Trustees that of the eighty students who had enrolled five had been expelled, eight had been suspended, twelve had withdrawn "voluntarily by request," and eight were "absent on leave," leaving only forty-seven who actually finished the school term! [26]

It had been such a hectic session that, after enduring four months of it, President Holmes abandoned the place some time between March 3 and 10, 1849.[27] Waddel charitably attributed this action to Holmes's illness and that of his child and said that he returned to Virginia for medical counsel.[28] This is the usually accepted view, but it is also obvious that the strain was proving too much and Holmes needed some relief from it.[29] He apparently did intend to return, but failed to communicate with his colleagues or the Trustees. Bledsoe, as senior in point of election to the faculty, became acting president for the remaining four months of the session. Under his sterner administration the year was brought to a close "smoothly and delightfully," terminating "in as perfect order and quiet as ever reigned in any College." [30]

The Board of Trustees assembled on Monday, July 9, 1849, and continued in session through Thursday, July 12.[31] The freshman class was examined before the Board on Monday and the sophomores on Tuesday. On Thursday the first annual commencement of the University was held in the Presbyterian church of Oxford. Two addresses were delivered "in the presence of the students and a large auditory," one by Alexander M. Clayton of Holly Springs, president of the Board, and another by Bledsoe to which reference has already been made. A little over two-thirds of Clayton's address to the two literary societies is a remarkable summary of the course of Western civilization. In the last third he presented his ideal of a liberal, well-rounded, useful education, and thereby set a lofty standard for the new University.[32]

CHAPTER III

Old Bullet and the Boys

OTHER business was transacted at the meeting of the Board at the end of the first session of the University. The Trustees gratefully accepted a donation of books for the library by Jacob Thompson;[1] the long absence of President Holmes was deemed a voluntary abandonment of his office, which was thereupon declared vacant;[2] at seven o'clock the morning of July 11, 1849, Augustus B. Longstreet was elected president by the unanimous vote of the eight Trustees present;[3] and a chapter of the rules and regulations of the University was entirely recast so as to secure better discipline by a more minute accounting of the college hours.[4]

Although Holmes left in March, the Board continued his salary until April 15.[5] Holmes's action, already alluded to, is something of a mystery. The uncertainty is heightened by his own recollection of it after the lapse of almost half a century. He intimated that he stayed through the entire session in the performance of his duty and only then made a trip to South Carolina to spend the vacation with relatives. Toward the end of the summer he was stricken with typhoid fever. Fearing that he would be unable to return to the University in time for the opening in the autumn, he had written a letter to the Trustees explaining his situation and promising to hasten back as soon as his health would permit. The letter was entrusted to a young friend who unfortunately forgot to deliver it. Upon his recovery, Holmes set out by stage-coach to Oxford, "only to find, on reaching the latter place, that his position had been assigned to someone else." He thereupon returned to South Carolina.[6] Years later, in 1888, an alumnus of the class of 1872 saw him on the chautauqua platform at Piedmont, Georgia, and reported, "I was anxious to meet Dr. Holmes, first president of my Alma Mater. . . . But when I introduced myself as a former student of the University of which he had been the first president he assumed the air of haughty indifference." [7]

Be that as it may, the school now had a new president. Augustus Baldwin Longstreet, born in Augusta, Georgia, September 22, 1790, already had behind him an eventful and noteworthy career. Having been prepared for college at Willington Academy, South Carolina, under the Reverend Moses Waddel, father of John Newton Waddel, he had finished Yale in 1813. In emulation of his idol, John C. Calhoun, the older Waddel's brother-in-law, he studied law at Litchfield, Connecticut, under Judges Tapping Reeve and James Gould. From 1815, when he was admitted to the bar, until 1838, he conducted a successful practice of law in Georgia, serving for a while as a circuit judge, by which title he was known for the rest of his life. An ardent nullifier, states' rights man, and admirer of Calhoun, he ran for political office but failed to secure election. A series of sketches, "Georgia Scenes," first published in various papers from 1832 to 1835, gave him his real claim to fame.

In 1838 Longstreet was admitted to the Methodist ministry on probation and was finally ordained an elder in 1844. His pro-slavery attitude led him to take an important part in the division of the Methodist church into its northern and southern branches. In late 1839 he was appointed president of Emory College (now Emory University), Oxford, Georgia, an institution of the Methodist church. Here he stayed until the commencement of 1848, taking an active share in all the turbulent controversies of the time.

Meanwhile other events were happening in connection with the University of Mississippi. At the meeting of the Board of Trustees in February, 1848, it was agreed to invite applications for the proposed faculty to be elected at the July meeting.[8] Longstreet's name did not appear among the seventeen applicants, but he had been approached privately in regard to the matter, apparently by J. N. Waddel, the son of his old teacher, and Jacob Thompson, both members of the Board at that time.[9] Longstreet was favorable and signified his willingness to accept, although not making a formal statement. As he said, "I was immediately impressed with the opinion that I could serve God and my country better at the head of a state institution than at the head of a sectarian institution." He was encouraged in his decision by friends with whom he discussed it.[10] He therefore resigned from Emory with a flourish that spring. It was understood there that he would go to the Mississippi institution.[11]

But when the Mississippi Trustees came to vote in July, 1848, there ensued a stormy altercation among them over the propriety of having a clergyman on the faculty and of having the subject of the evidences of Christianity in the curriculum. One Trustee had already resigned over the issue and two others carried on the battle, but they were overwhelmingly defeated.[12] The discussion, however, was sufficient to prevent Longstreet's election by one vote,[13] although Waddel, a minister, was appointed to the faculty two days later.[14] Longstreet uncharitably and without warrant attributed his defeat to Roman Catholic influence.[15]

After his resignation from Emory, Longstreet spent five or six months in desultory pastoral activity, preaching here and there as occasion demanded. He was then called to the presidency of Centenary College, Jackson, Louisiana, a school belonging to the Methodist conferences of Mississippi and Louisiana, taking up his duties in February or March, 1849.[16] Much of his time was devoted to further writing, but his work proved so discouraging that after five months he resigned at the commencement. While packing to return to Georgia, he received the news of his election to the University of Mississippi.[17] He accepted but did not proceed immediately to his new place. He visited in Georgia, where Waddel saw him and confirmed the information under the erroneous impression that he was the first to let Longstreet know about it.[18]

Longstreet moved to Mississippi in September, 1849,[19] and began a period of activity which Waddel calls one of "unparalleled prosperity for the University."[20] He had two initial difficulties to confront. The first was the justly notorious reputation for poor discipline and order which the infant University had gained; the other, the widespread apprehension that this was a "regularly organized infidel Institution."[21] The latter was the result of the difference already alluded to among the Trustees. "The confidence of the citizens of the State had received a shock so violent, . . . that it was slow in returning."[22] This is indicated by the fact that for the second academic session, 1849–1850, Longstreet's first, there were four matriculates fewer than for the opening year.

"The people of the State, however, soon discovered that there was [now] at the helm a Master Spirit, and, year by year, the patronage steadily increased. . . ."[23] His second year, 1850–1851, a hundred thirty-five students were enrolled; the following year, one hundred forty-seven. There was a slight recession in the term of 1852–1853: only a hundred thirty-one attended. But enrollment jumped to one hundred sixty-two in 1853–1854; to one hundred seventy-nine in 1854–1855; and the following year, Longstreet's last, it reached a total of two hundred thirty-two students.[24] Hence, as Waddel puts it, "vigilant without being offensive; . . . solicitous for their highest intellectual and moral advancement; . . . eminently self-possessed . . . ," governing "without any ostentatious display of the machinery of government . . . ," possessing, "in a remarkable degree, the faculty of swaying the student-body during exciting scenes . . . ," Longstreet on the surface had the school running smoothly.[25]

Not entirely so, of course, for the animal spirits of the young Mississippians were—and are—irrepressible, no matter how stern the discipline, no matter how condign the punishment. There were instances of reprehensible visits to the village of Oxford in disguise as late as midnight or after.[26] The difficulty some students had in getting up at sunrise in the chill winter for devotions provoked the charge of "repeated absences from prayers without excuse."[27] There was the playful but boisterous mischief of shooting fire-crackers in the dormitories at Christmas-time.[28] Even "eccentricities in dress" had to be rebuked.[29] But perhaps the most surprising bit of daring occurred one day when an irresponsible youth threw a rock at President Longstreet himself. The student, immediately stricken with remorse, acknowledged his guilt before the faculty, which thereupon resolved that the president administer to him a reprimand "in presence of the whole of the students at evening-prayer on tomorrow," a somber Friday the thirteenth of late 1850.[30] About three months later a learned wag (perhaps Longstreet himself?) commemorated the incident in macaronic verse printed in a Holly Springs newspaper and signed "University:"

"OLD BULLET" ET PUERI

One night in anno fifty one,
Haec plan a pueris was begun,
    Gaudenter.
Intentis was agere pell-mell
Some porcos into the College well
    Violenter.
Pueri Colligunt in a group
And sequuntur porcos with a whoop,
    Multi sunt.
"Old Bullet" venit in a run,
"Habeam," inquit, "multum fun
    Dum ludunt."
Boys continue porcos agere
Intenti they some fun habere,
    Obliti "Bullet."
Adeunt the well many in numero
And catch a porcum by the tail O!
    Multum pull it.
"Old Bullet" jacet on the ground,
Cum ejus oculis he looks around
    Videre pueros.

Then one E pueris eum spies,
And "video old Judicem" loudly cries
Observat nos.
Tunc M. exclamat, "give me a brick
Enim d—n him, he deserves a lick—
Bullet look out!"
Sed "Bullet" capiens the alarum
From the well fugit harum scarum
Omnes shout.
My tale nunc venit to an end,
Sed to the moral your attention lend,
Benigne.
Quum in campum you take a spree,
Be sure to look behind every tree
Studiose.[31]

One prank provoked a reaction of sinister proportions. One day in April, 1852, Colonel James Brown, a local citizen and Trustee, was on the campus for a called meeting of the Board.[32] While he was in the meeting some students slily cut off his horse's tail. Brown was indignant. To "Judge" Longstreet, the writer of "Georgia Scenes," the incident must have appeared more ludicrous than serious, but suppressing his own wry humor, he dutifully made an inquiry, perhaps only half-hearted, to ascertain the identity of the youthful culprits. Failing in this, he later "delivered a general lecture to the students . . . in severe terms of reprobation." [33]

But the affair was not ended. At the meeting of the Board in July, a resolution was passed requesting information from the faculty "whether any & if any, what action was taken . . . in relation to the malicious mischief perpetrated on the horse of Col Brown. . . ." President Longstreet replied in a note citing his procedure. The Trustees were not satisfied and another resolution was adopted to the effect "that though at the time of the injury committed on the horse of Col Brown the Faculty might not have had sufficient evidence to proceed against any one or more of the students, yet in our opinion, they now have sufficient testimony to justify such proceeding & they are hereby required to investigate the matter immediately & to report the result to this board." [34]

The previous year, which had witnessed the first graduating class of the University, a number of the students had asked permission from the Board to use a University building for a party to honor the seniors at the commencement. The Trustees had graciously acceded to this request.[35] Now, before the meeting in July, 1852, there appeared a committee of students making a similar request. But this time the Trustees were adamant: "We think it due to the Board of Trustees that the indignity offered to one of its members & through him to the Board, Should be wiped out as far as possible. . . ." [36]

That night, July 13, 1852, the student body assembled and adopted the following resolution: "That we the students of the University of Mississippi disclaim & disavow the indignity offered to Col Brown in April last." The apology was duly presented next morning to the Board, which then reluctantly granted the use of the rooms for the commencement ball. Still the insult rankled and later that same day the entire faculty was summoned to appear before the Board to answer why "the government of the University has been too lax during the last Session. . . ." [37]

It is one of the minor ironies of history that on the following day the immortal Jefferson Davis, who only a year later would become Secretary of War in the cabinet of President Franklin Pierce, was to stand before the literary societies of the University and declare, "If I am competent to form an opinion in a case where I am certainly not free from prejudice, there is enough of talent, enough of energy in the youth of Mississippi to warrant the expectation that they will reach the highest degree of attainment, and in their day and generation, as circumstance may permit, fill the brightest pages of their country's history." [38]

A statement of truly prophetic insight! This most illustrious of the sons of Mississippi was wiser than all the sensitive Trustees wearing their honor on their sleeves. For circumstance did permit and most of those very students less than a dozen years later followed the Stars and Bars into battle against a greater foe than the Trustees and faculty.

The quieter side of University life is reflected in the following letter:

University of Mississippi
Sept. 30th—54

Friend Tom,

I sit down to write after having finished my Studies to write you a few lines. I expect that you have come to the conclusion ere this that I have but little regard for my word as I promised to write to you as soon as I arrived here, but Tom I have been busily engaged ever since I have been here and have had but little time for writing letters, as it takes me all my time with hard studying to prepare for my recitations, and on Saturday eve we attend our Society & on Sunday we are all compeled to attend church, but if you will excuse me for not writing soner I will endeavor to be more punctual in future and will be prompt in answering all your letters on reception. I arrived here in about forty hours from the time I left Jackson. I came up in the Stage with Messers A. T. & F. A. Wolfe, Thomson, McGowen & Hames and we had quite a lively time of it and found Oxford to be a very prety town it has several nice buildings the court-house and several very fine churches. The college buildings are situated one mile from town they are all large and fine buildings located in a large oak grove that is perfectly level, the college buildings themselves look almost like a town, they have also a very good library considering the age of the institution and a very fine set of apparatus. And besides what they now have, have sent to Germiny for a telascope which will cost a thousand dollars. We have two fine societies the Hermean and Phisigma they both have each a large hall finely furnished in which they are enlarging yearly, the two societies are rivals of each other and carry on most of their business in secret; their object is each to furnish the best orators on commencement day. I have joined the Phisigma. We have some very fine speakers in college belonging to both societies. I have formed acquaintance with most of the boys at the University. I fine them to be a collection of the most intelligent boys of the State. We have now about one hundred and twenty five students in the University and they are coming in every day. I passed an examination in a few days after my arrival here I applied for the Junior Class but failed as I was not prepared in French and I was also deficient in Mathematics that is in Burdan in Geometry I was very well prepared and was not able to enter regular I entered irregular and expect to bring the studies up in which I am deficient. My course of studies are as follows: I am reciting in Burdan with the Sophomores that is in the latter part of it we are reading Juvenel, Greek the Antigone of Sophicles the Eingles [?] branches Moral Philosophy and Chemistry and will commence logic soon. I will recite in Analetical geometry in a few days & also French. I assure you that I have no time to be idle. I have enjoyed my self very well since I have been here. I attended last night a Levee given by the President to the Students there were several very handsome and finely accomplished young ladies there I heard some of the sweetest music on the piano accompanied with some of the best singing that I ever heard. I have not received any letters from home since I left but have been looking for several days with the most intense anxiety and still hope that I will get one by the next male a letter would be received by me now with great possible delight. It is getting late and I must bring my letter to a close. Give my respects to all inquiring friends my love to all the girls and don't fail to write immediately, and give me in detail an account of matters and things in general.

       I remain
       Yours truly
       R. P. WILLING[39]

In the administration of the University a certain amount of friction was arising. Financially Judge Longstreet was independent. Even after the ruthless devastation of war and Reconstruction, he is said, at his death in 1870, to have left about twenty-five thousand dollars in cash and the same amount in real estate. In Mississippi he continued his inveterate and shrewd business habits, both buying and selling land and always accumulating. He was indeed so methodical in these transactions that he has left a manuscript concerning them, his "History of My Land Purchases in Lafayette County, Mississippi." By 1854 there was inevitable criticism of his apparent neglect of University duties, at which he indignantly threatened to resign. One citizen of Oxford deemed this as mere bluff and complained, ". . . old Longstreet is making money too fast for him to be induced to resign." [40]

There was another cause of dissension. Both Longstreet and Waddel were clergymen and felt it incumbent on themselves to attend their ecclesiastical meetings of conference and presbytery. They also engaged in a certain amount of pastoral activity, which seemed to imply neglect of the functions of a University professor.[41] The Board therefore enacted a ruling that faculty members would have to account for their absences from academic duties and have their pay reduced proportionately.[42] Longstreet considered this an intolerable outrage, but reported some of his own absences during the session of 1854–1855, "which were deemed satisfactory to the Board and on motion they were excused." [43] At the same time Longstreet filed a protest, in which he was joined by the other faculty members, asserting that the rule made the professors "mere automata" and was "derogatory to their position as officers of the college. . . ." In response the Board prepared and adopted a long defense of its own action, but acceded to the pressure and repealed the "disrespectfull and offensive" legislation.[44]

The Judge also found it difficult long to remain out of politics. In the early years of the 1850's an ominous portent appeared in the rise of the American or "Know-Nothing" party. For a while, to the delight of the moribund Whiggery, it seemed to threaten the Democratic party, of which Longstreet was an ardent member. So many Methodists were turning to the new movement that in mid-1855, he addressed several open letters to the Know-Nothing clergymen. Some of these were reprinted as campaign literature by the Democratic executive committee of Louisiana. An answer not long in forthcoming appeared over the signature of the Reverend William Winans, for years one of the outstanding Methodist ministers of

Mississippi. It was probably Winans who as a Trustee had originally secured the presidency of Centenary College for Longstreet. In 1849 he had run unsuccessfully on the Whig ticket for the state legislature.[45] Longstreet replied to Winans in a bitter letter and for a moment the issue languished. What the Trustees thought of the venture of their employee is uncertain.[46]

Meanwhile significant developments were taking place at the University. A new building, the chapel, was completed in 1853. This building, still in use, is the second oldest yet remaining on the campus. It now provides offices and rooms for the religious organizations of the University. By 1854, of the original faculty only Waddel remained. Millington had resigned in 1853 to go at the advanced age of seventy-four to the chair of chemistry and toxicology in the new Memphis Medical School. The following year Bledsoe went to the University of Virginia. The occasion of his leaving was marked by the Board's conferring on him the first honorary degree (that of Doctor of Laws) in the history of the institution.[47] There had been some serious dissension among the students in regard to Bledsoe. The class of 1851 had prepared a petition for the Board of Trustees requesting his removal, while the class of 1852 had countered by a request for his continuance in office. The Board simply filed both communications without action.[48]

The chair of law and governmental science was established in 1854. The first incumbent was William F. Stearns of Holly Springs, who had delivered the address at the laying of the cornerstone of the first building of the University. L. Q. C. Lamar, one of Longstreet's sons-in-law, later an Associate Justice of the national Supreme Court, served as adjunct professor of mathematics from 1850 to 1852, when he returned temporarily to Georgia to practice law. He was succeeded by Jordan M. Phipps, one of the members of the first graduating class of the University (1851), who held the position until 1858, when he was promoted to a full professorship.

But by far the most important change was the advent of Frederick

A. P. Barnard to succeed Bledsoe.[49] Although the loss of the latter was deemed irreparable, in time Barnard came to hold a place of peculiar favor with the Trustees.[50] The faculty now had a scholar of first rank. But now it also had three prima donnas instead of two: the old Judge, aware of his notoriety and financial independence, accustomed to having his way in the affairs of the University by the mere threat of resignation; Waddel, certain that without the slightest effort on his part Divine Providence had decreed his association with the University and had even vouchsafed him a premonition of it in Mobile, Alabama, as far back as 1841, long before the school was a reality;[51] and now Barnard, with his extensive scientific learning, increasing fame, incredible Yankee energy, bitter sensitiveness to criticism, and unfortunate ability for making enemies. A clash of the Olympians was in the making—or was it only a tempest in a teapot a-brewing?

All three were clergymen active in the affairs of their churches. Longstreet had been a leader in the formation of Southern Methodism; Waddel, an Old School Presbyterian, was serving as pastor of the local church; and Barnard, already in deacon's orders, was soon to be made a priest of the Protestant Episcopal Church, December 2, 1855. Even as a deacon he had the pastoral care of St. Peter's, Oxford.

At Longstreet's invitation Barnard undertook a laborious investigation of the situation in regard to the seminary fund and how it had been so negligently squandered by the state. In this and other ways he came into exceedingly favorable contact with Jacob Thompson, the most eminent Trustee.[52] He received an invitation to attend the British Association for the Promotion of Science, opening in Glasgow, September 12, 1855. The Board authorized him leave for that purpose provided he would return by November 1.[53]

Barnard's reputation was thus growing by leaps and bounds at the University and would quite naturally provoke a degree of jealousy. One of Longstreet's sons-in-law, a physician in Oxford, Henry R. Branham, began a family campaign urging the Judge to resign.[54]

Others perhaps added their voices to Branham's. The latter was convinced that Barnard was "intriguing to get Judge Longstreet away...." [55] Much later when Longstreet was questioned on this matter, he made no attempt either to deny or confirm the possibility.[56] It was also believed that Barnard, an ardent Whig, was in reality a Know-Nothing and hence opposed to Longstreet, the extreme Democrat.[57]

The Judge was beginning to groom Waddel as his successor in the presidency, to which Waddel feigned great reluctance—feigned, because he certainly showed no hesitancy in accepting when he was chosen as head of the institution after the War Between the States.[58] He moreover accepted a similar office in the Presbyterian Synodical College, LaGrange, Tennessee, in July, 1860. He had at the same time permitted the discussion of his name in connection with Davidson College and later was not loath to become the chancellor of Southwestern Presbyterian University, Clarksville, Tennessee.[59] In any case even Barnard acquiesced in the assumption that Waddel would in time succeed Longstreet.[60] This three-way by-play is all the clearer when one recalls the rather ambiguous description of Waddel which Longstreet had written: "The reputation of Dr. Waddel never suffered from change of time, place, or society, but ... grew brighter and broader at every move.... This certainly is a remarkable fact; for if there be any occupation in which merit is no guarantee of popularity, it is that of an instructor of youth...." [61] The conclusion is all but inescapable that Waddel's seniority was being deliberately but vainly played off against the encroaching importance of Barnard.

Finally, at a called meeting of the Board in Oxford, Thursday, July 10, 1856, Longstreet delivered a report proposing amendments to the rules and regulations of the University, in which he included his own resignation.[62] The report was laid on the table and nothing was done until Monday morning, July 14, when the Trustees unanimously requested him to withdraw the resignation.[63] The following day the Board conferred on him the degree of Doctor of Divinity.[64] Another day elapsed. Then on Thursday, July 17, the Trustees resolved to "accept the resignation of President Longstreet with the greatest reluctance, and tender him the assurances of their very high regard, and their earnest wishes for his future welfare." [65]

So ended the term of the second president of the University of Mississippi, a most remarkable man, "lawyer, politician, orator, judge, farmer, business man, patron of medical education, teacher, scholar, college president, author, newspaper editor, preacher, musician, naturalist, carpenter, artisan, sportsman. . . . And whatever he did, he did well, not with the greatest distinction, to be sure, but with something far above mediocrity." [66]

CHAPTER IV

Before the War

THE trustees, the day after they accepted Judge Longstreet's resignation, granted Barnard a leave of absence until October 1, 1856.[1] The latter went immediately to Albany, New York, to attend the inauguration of the Dudley Observatory and be present at the annual meeting of the American Association for the Advancement of Science. On the very day of the inauguration he received the news that he had on August 19 been elected president of the University.[2] He returned to Mississippi as quickly as possible.[3]

Barnard has said that he was not an avowed candidate for the office and was surprised to know that he was considered as a competitor for the position.[4] This does not entirely accord with the later account given by Eugene W. Hilgard, the assistant state geologist. His version stated that Barnard had gained the implacable enmity of Lewis Harper, professor of geology and state geologist, who had issued a libelous pamphlet at the time when the election to the vacancy was pending. Barnard was informed by a telegram sent by Hilgard and L. Q. C. Lamar, then an Oxford attorney, whereupon he prepared a circular and authorized its distribution, at the same time inciting "his friends in the Board of Trustees to redoubled exertion by the declaration that as the failure of his election would be interpreted by the public as the effect of Harper's pamphlet and as a *quasi* endorsement of the latter by the board, such failure would of necessity result in his withdrawal from the University."[5]

Frederick Augustus Porter Barnard, of whom some information

has already been given, was born in Sheffield, Massachusetts, May 5, 1809. At the youthful age of fifteen he entered Yale, where his record in mathematics was exceptional. He also became proficient at reading French, Spanish, and Italian. After teaching two years in the Hartford, Connecticut, Grammar School, he became a tutor at Yale in 1830. A year later he resigned because of impending deafness and took an opening in the American Asylum for the Deaf and Dumb in Hartford. From 1832 to 1837 he held a similar position in the New York Institution for the Instruction of the Deaf and Dumb.

In 1838 and for ten years thereafter he held the chair of mathematics and natural philosophy in the University of Alabama. In 1848 he was transferred to the professorship of chemistry and natural philosophy, where he remained until the election to the faculty of the University of Mississippi in 1854. His enthusiastic biographer says that in Tuscaloosa Barnard spent "some of the happiest and most fruitful years of his life.... He did more duty at the University than any one of his colleagues; his hours of leisure were spent in editing one newspaper, writing for another, contributing to a literary journal, making original scientific experiments, improving the new art of photography, and extending his mathematical investigations,—and all the while he was maturing those advanced views of college and university organization which caused him in due time to be recognized as a master of the art and science of education." [6]

He attracted public attention by a Masonic oration on Summer St. John's day, 1841. "In their love and admiration of eloquence the people of the South are thorough Greeks, and this address represented an order of eloquence which is rarely heard.... The Masonic fraternity was proud of its champion; the University was proud of its representative; men of all conditions in the State were proud of their fellow-citizen." [7] In 1844 Jefferson College, a private institution at Washington, Mississippi, conferred the honorary degree of Doctor of Laws on Barnard, the first of six such honors which came to him. In 1846 he adjudicated the boundary line between Alabama and Florida, serving as the official astronomer for both sides.[8]

In August, 1854, he was invited to go to Oxford by a friend who was applying for the chair of chemistry at the University of Mississippi. Barnard's reputation had preceded him, and the Trustees asked him to apply for the vacant chair. He promptly declined, but accepted election as professor of mathematics and natural philosophy. His friend was less fortunate, "but he bore his disappointment better than Barnard bore his new honors. The University election was a subject of interest all along the road, and when they [Barnard and his friend] had sat down to their evening meal at their first stopping-place [on the way back to Tuscaloosa], Barnard, after vainly trying to eat, rose, and left the table. The kindly landlady of the hostelry said to Johnson [Barnard's friend], 'Your friend seems to be unwell. I fear he has been unsuccessful at Oxford.' 'No, madam,' said Johnson, 'he is sick because he has succeeded'." [9]

As noted earlier, Barnard had not been in Mississippi long before President Longstreet had him undertake a study of the history of the seminary fund. He succeeded in securing the interest of Jacob Thompson in the matter. They labored together on it for several months during the winter of 1854–1855. The result was a report prepared by Barnard, adopted by the Board of Trustees, and incorporated by Governor John J. McRae in a special message to the legislature, February 6, 1856, requesting that the state acknowledge its liability for the loss to the fund in the amount of $874,324.49 and make some effort to indemnify the University.[10] Barnard also addressed a joint session of the legislature on behalf of the University.[11]

The object intended by Barnard, Thompson, and McRae was not acceptable to the legislature. But it did agree to make an appropriation to the University of a hundred thousand dollars, payable over a period of five years.[12] By the time this appropriation was achieved, Barnard had become president of the University. Waddel, who had presumably been expecting the office, stayed through the session of 1856–1857 and then resigned to become professor of ancient languages in the newly organized Presbyterian Synodical College at LaGrange, Tennessee.[13] Barnard took unconcealed delight in what he uncharitably considered Waddel's mortification and disappointment.[14]

With the assurance of an adequate income the University began a program of physical expansion, especially in the buildings devoted to the sciences. Barnard's favorite project, an astronomical observatory, was erected and the necessary equipment ordered.[15] The catalogue for the year 1857–1858 announced: "It is probable that, with the opening of the ensuing year, the electrical apparatus of the University of Mississippi will be superior to any similar collection in the United States."[16] The institution was rapidly moving to the front in the scientific world under the leadership of Barnard. In some respects its apparatus was unequalled.[17] A modern physicist states: "The presence of this high grade equipment at this early period is evidence that this institution was in reality a pioneer in the fostering of experimental science in America."[18]

There is a romantic story about a telescope ordered during the expansion. The observatory had been completed in 1859. The contract for constructing the telescope was given to Alvan Clark and Son of Cambridge, Massachusetts. At Barnard's insistence it was specified that the lens be nineteen inches in diameter, somewhat larger than the one at Harvard, and therefore, at that time the largest in the world. But before the instrument could be delivered (it was completed in June, 1861), the dogs of war were let loose and it now serves the Dearborn Observatory of Northwestern University.[19]

With nervous, irritable temperament, Barnard was restlessly active. By such energy he gained for himself nation-wide recognition and probably some reflected glory for the University. He had already in 1855 published his letters on college government. In August he read a paper before the American Association for the Advancement of Education on "Improvements Practicable in American Colleges." [20] When elected president of the University, he was, as mentioned earlier, in Albany, New York, at the opening of the Dudley Observatory, in connection with a meeting of the American Association for the Advancement of Science. In an issue of the *American Journal of Science* that same year, he published an article entitled "An Examination of the Theory Which Ascribes the Zodiacal Light to a Ring Surrounding the Earth." [21]

Two years later (1858) he was producing a prolific literature on such educational subjects as university education and the relation of university education to common schools.[22] The most notable product of his pen at this time was his open letter to the Board of Trustees setting forth his plan for making the University of Mississippi an institution worthy to stand with the best American schools.[23] As a result, the Protestant Episcopal bishop Leonidas Polk began to negotiate with him concerning the headship of the proposed University of the South.[24] Propositions from the North were also coming in.[25] Barnard's fame was established.

That same year he was invited to make an address before the alumni society of his alma mater, Yale. His subject concerned the special responsibilities and opportunities of educated men as citizens.[26] He had also succeeded the late Judge J. K. Kane, president of the American Philosophical Society, as chairman of a committee of the American Association for the Advancement of Science to inquire into the coast survey of the United States. In this capacity he prepared the report on the history, methods, and results of the survey, publishing it in November, 1858.[27]

In 1859 he contributed to the *Proceedings* of the American Association for the Advancement of Science valuable papers on the pendulum and on the means of preserving electric contacts from vitiation by sparks.[28] Yale honored him with the degree of Doctor of Laws.[29] The following year he was invited to join an expedition of American astronomers to Labrador to observe a total eclipse of the sun occurring in July. He later made a report of this trip.³⁰ The meeting of the American Association for the Advancement of Science that year, which he was unable to attend, elected him president for 1861, but because of the fortunes of war he did not function as such until 1866.³¹ The very day Mississippi seceded from the Union, January 9, 1861, he left Oxford for Washington to deliver a series of lectures at the Smithsonian Institution. The engagement was of two weeks' duration, after which he returned to the University.³²

The University itself was making substantial progress during this period. Barnard had successfully committed the Trustees to his plan for making it something more than a mere college of liberal arts, in fact making it a true university of all learning. A minor feature of the reorganization was the change in the title of the executive official from president to chancellor.³³ The library was increased, new buildings constructed, older ones enlarged, and, in recognition of the value of physical training, even a gymnasium authorized.³⁴ A growing sense of dignity was symbolized by the decision of the faculty to adopt the honorable custom of the academic procession during the commencement program.³⁵

The scheme of grading was given more regularity by providing for the ranks of excellent, good, respectable, unsatisfactory, and deficient.³⁶ In general, it is the system (indicated by appropriate letters) in use today at the University of Mississippi and most other American institutions of learning. It is significant, however, to note that instead of *respectable* and *deficient* modern schools consider the grades of C and F to be respectively *average* and *failing*. The terminology indicates a change in the temper of the times: in those old ante-bellum days a *gentleman* would certainly be *respectable*, not *average*, and only *deficient*, not *failing*.

Changes were occurring in the faculty. A few are noteworthy. Captain Edward C. Boynton, a West Pointer and veteran of the Mexican War, came to the chair of chemistry in 1856 and served until the War Between the States. He became a general officer in the

Federal army during that struggle. Of him Waddel said that though an accomplished chemist he was a "profane swearer, and under provocation gave full vent to his irritation in words unbecoming any man. . . ."[37] For the year 1860–1861 the versatile Lamar, Longstreet's son-in-law, returned to the faculty, this time in the capacity of professor of metaphysics and ethics. Alexander J. Quinche was elected professor of Latin and modern languages in 1860, resigning with the others when the University closed during the war. His greatest service came afterwards.

Burton N. Harrison, related in some way to Barnard and later to become private secretary to President Jefferson Davis with the rank of colonel in the Confederate army, was appointed tutor in 1859 and assistant professor of physics in 1860. During this interval he was the secretary of the faculty. It is therefore from his hand that many interesting details of the faculty meetings come.[38] One in particular would seem to be of some importance. An instructor with the consent of the whole faculty had disciplined a sophomore for disrespect in class, whereupon the other students had risen in revolt. Barnard succeeded in quelling the disturbance and at the meeting of the faculty on December 12, 1859, "The President[39] reported his correspondence with the rebels and their ultimate submission to the course of law." No further notice was taken of the matter except to "warn the more fractious members of the class that not only was the original movement a *combination* to resist the authority of the Faculty, and therefore *punishable by law*—but that any means which they should adopt to attain the end at first proposed, whether directly or indirectly—would still be considered a violation of the spirit of the laws provided for such cases and would be dealt with accordingly. . . ."[40] The italics are Harrison's but the language is precisely that of the Lincolnian interpretation of Southern secession.

Not technically a member of the faculty until after the war, but closely associated with it was Eugene Woldemar Hilgard. Born in the Rhenish Palatinate in 1833, he had been brought by his parents to Belleville, Illinois. Having returned to Europe for training, he had at the age of twenty received the degree of Doctor of Philosophy *summa cum laude* from Heidelberg. After spending two years in Spain, where he met his future wife, he became a chemist at the Smithsonian Institution in Washington. Later, in the year 1855, he was appointed assistant state geologist of Mississippi on Barnard's recommendation. His office being at the University, he was closely associated with Barnard, whom he assisted in learning to read scientific journals in German, Swedish, and Dutch.[41] The office was closed in 1857 and Hilgard went back to Washington, but the following year was appointed to the full position. In this capacity he labored not only in the field of geology, but also of botany, agriculture, and other related subjects. In 1860 he published the report which remains the original and definitive work on the geology of Mississippi.[42]

The progress of the University had to be financed. The first step in that direction was the unsuccessful attempt to secure recognition by the state of its obligation in regard to the seminary fund. The handsome appropriation which was a substitute for the proposed recognition was sufficient for a while. But the most significant attempt to secure adequate funds has been hitherto overlooked. At a meeting of the Trustees on July 1, 1859, "The Secretary laid before the board a communication from the President of the Faculty in regard to a memorial to Congress on the subject of a donation of land to the University." The communication was referred to a committee,[43] which at a later meeting (November 23, 1859) secured the adoption of a resolution "That a Committee of two be appointed to prepare a memorial to Congress praying a donation for an additional township of land to the University of Mississippi."[44] This committee was thereupon appointed, but that was the last heard of the matter until Chancellor Robert B. Fulton initiated his successful movement for the same purpose in 1892.[45] It is to Fulton's credit that the project was carried through to completion, but it is erroneous to state: "It seemed to have been forgotten that Mississippi was entitled to one additional township of land, at least, as had been granted to other states containing public lands, until Chancellor Robert B. Fulton, in his annual report to the Board of Trustees, 1892, called this to the attention of the Board." [46]

With all the activity and honor on the part of its chancellor, the recognition accruing to it through him, and the actual progress of the institution itself, one would assume that the University of Mississippi was making great strides in gaining the favor of its state. How fair and promising the prospect was is mentioned by several outsiders. In 1858 the commencement preacher, the illustrious Benjamin Morgan Palmer of New Orleans, wrote to the Trustees: "A brilliant future is before the University & I shall watch here progress with deep interest & fervant prayers for her prosperity and success." [47] Later, in 1869, a speaker, in his oration before the literary societies, said in part:

"Twelve years ago [1857] a stranger, passing through this portion of your State, made a chance visit to the University of Mississippi. The institution was then in the morning dawn of its usefulness and fame. Its buildings, fresh from the hands of the architect, were still bordered, close at hand, with primeval undergrowth and ancient trees. The campus and grounds, covered with a carpet newly woven in the looms of the sunbeams and the shower, lay, sheltered and quiet, like a Highland lake, in the embrace of the engirdling woods. The University, furnished with a splendid philosophical and chemical apparatus, with the nucleus of a fine library and many other educational facilities, and frequented by a large number of young men from Mississippi and the adjoining States, was, even then, the pride and intellectual glory of the State. The State itself was the ornament and the boast of the Union and of the glowing clime to which, by its geographical locality and by its social and industrial affinities, it properly belonged. That clime, known far and near, as the sunny and teeming South, abounding in hospitality, in wealth, and in capabilities of every kind, and blessed with patriarchal institutions, which civilized while they enriched beyond the dreams of avarice, was the flowing agricultural Palestine of the nation, and the cynosure, in this occidental realm, of the commercial eye of the world. The students, whom the stranger met on the campus and in the halls of the University, were preparing themselves, by fit discipline and culture, for the duties and responsibilities of citizenship and of life, in the social and political order of things that then existed." [48]

This statement, however, is a backward glance through rose-colored glasses to a time and place that either never were or died a-borning. For the promise did not materialize as one might have justifiably assumed. As a matter of fact, except for the first year of his presidency (1856–1857), the student body declined numerically under Barnard. That first year attendance had indeed reached the unprecedented height of two hundred sixty-four students. The following session it dropped to one hundred seventy-eight and the next year as low as a hundred sixty-eight. During 1859–1860 it had gone back up to two hundred sixteen, but the year afterward it was down again to one hundred ninety-six.[49]

There had been popular objection to Barnard ever since he came to the University of Mississippi as professor of mathematics. His colleague, Hilgard, invidiously intimated that the prejudice had been heightened by his ordination to the Protestant Episcopal priesthood, but the suggestion has no basis in fact.[50] However, the University was suffering from a mounting tide of criticism under Barnard's leadership. Many factors were involved, although the chancellor had the unqualified confidence of the Board of Trustees, without which his term of office would have been considerably shortened. It was the support of the Board that protected Barnard so long, in fact until after the school itself was closed by the war. On the day his resignation was accepted in late 1861, he was told by Governor John J. McRae, *ex officio* chairman of the Board of Trustees, "I shall always have one source of satisfaction in the recollection that I have voted for every measure which you have ever recommended." [51]

An attempt to answer the critics of the University was made by F. W. Keyes in an address before the alumni association, July 5, 1859.[52] In the course of his defense four major criticisms were noted and met. The first was an objection to the University as a rich man's school.[53] That, by the way, is still being said. The second was the lingering sectionalism which desired a number of public schools throughout the state instead of one university.[54] Third, there were people who did not think it advisable to have clergymen on the faculty:[55] out of a faculty of nine in the spring of 1859, three were ministers. A similar criticism had been made during the very first days of the University. The fourth criticism was directed against the fact that the University catalogue and other official publications were printed "at the North." [56] This point seems to have been the most important and with it one probably comes to the real issue underlying all the objections to the University under Barnard.

War was casting its sinister shadow upon all the events of the late eighteen-fifties. Ill-founded rumor, irresponsible gossip, nervous excitability, the sense of impending disaster were providing the tinder. Only a spark was needed to cause a holocaust. With sensitive honor passing over imperceptibly into hypocrisy, apparently insignificant occurrences could and did provoke serious convulsions. How close hypocrisy lies to honor is shown by an incident recorded in the faculty minutes of July 15, 1857. At a previous meeting a certain student had been suspended, yet at this meeting "it was moved and carried, That, in order to screen Mr. M . . . from the mortification of not appearing with his Class [at the graduation tomorrow], he be permitted to present himself with his Class, and, be presented with a blank Diploma, which he shall return after the close of the exercises." [57] How slight the occasion had to be to produce an explosion of temper can be seen in the solemn decision whereby the president was "instructed to give notice that hereafter students shall desist from throwing a reflection of the sun by means of mirrors into windows or people's faces on the campus." [58]

Of more serious proportions was what may be called the "Branham affair." It began the night of May 11, 1859, when Chancellor and Mrs. Barnard were away in Vicksburg. That night two students entered Barnard's residence on the University campus, with "shameful designs" upon one of the "defenceless female servants." [59] In the ensuing struggle one of the students, H . . . , assaulted and beat the black slave, Jane, so that for two months thereafter she showed visible bruises and for several days was unable to work. [60]

When Barnard returned, the incident was reported to him by Professor Boynton, who lived in the adjoining house, had overheard the altercation, had even seen the two students as they left, and two or three days later had learned their names through the usual student discussion of such a matter. [61] H . . . was therefore arraigned before the faculty at a meeting on May 23, 1859. Through the negligence of the secretary and the seemingly ordinary and unimportant character of the proceedings, the minutes of this meeting were not recorded: that page in the faculty book is blank except for the date.

H . . . pleaded not guilty, but failed to prove an alibi. His associate of that night refused to answer any questions. In summarizing the matter, Barnard stated that his information had first come from Boynton, that later Mrs. Barnard told him that the slave, Jane, had identified H . . . to her as the assailant, but that he himself had never spoken to the girl on the subject. [62]

After the presentation of the testimony, it was moved "That Mr. H., having been found *guilty* of the offence charged against him, be, and is hereby, suspended from the University." This motion failed to carry. It was then resolved "That, although the Faculty are morally convinced of Mr. H's guilt, yet they do not consider the evidence adduced to substantiate the charge as sufficient legally to convict him." This resolution was adopted and read publicly to the student body.⁶³ In spite of the faculty decision, Barnard did ask H . . . privately to withdraw. He did so but in the autumn applied for readmission. This also Barnard succeeded in preventing. There was some student rebellion and several men in protest transferred to Cumberland University at Lebanon, Tennessee.⁶⁴

It was not long before the story became public knowledge and was quickly seized upon by critics, especially Henry R. Branham, a physician of Oxford and son-in-law of Judge Longstreet. Branham was already hostile to Barnard. Shortly after his father-in-law had resigned, he had stated in an informal gathering of business men of the town that if he should see the University in flames he would not lift his hand to help put out the fire.⁶⁵ He now began a whispering campaign, telling everyone who would listen that Barnard was "in favor of taking negro testimony against students." ⁶⁶ The story grew as it passed from mouth to mouth. Finally, in January, 1860, it came to the attention of Barnard, who indignantly denied it. By that time the faculty was involved and divided on the issue.

In order to clarify the facts, a meeting of the faculty was held on February 2, 1860, to adopt "a true record of the proceedings of the Faculty at the regular meeting held May 23d, 1859, which proceedings had never been entered among the minutes. . . ." ⁶⁷ This was accordingly done, but since there was dissension as to details each professor was allowed to append to the minutes a note explaining the reason for his vote in regard to H. . . .

In some manner the account of the meeting leaked out and added to the gossip. The town must have been buzzing with the affair for it reached Washington, D. C., where on February 19, 1860, Jacob Thompson, President Buchanan's Secretary of the Interior and a close friend of Barnard, saw fit to write and urge him not to be "moved by these things. . . . Such trials will only prove your firmness and worth, and the mischief will fall on the heads of your adversaries." ⁶⁸ On February 29, therefore, Barnard wrote to the Board of Trustees inviting a full investigation of the charges. He asked to be removed if he was found now or at any time to have been unsound on the slavery question. But, if the injurious allegations were discovered to be false, he asked the Board's "emphatic condemnation upon an outrage . . . without a parallel in the annals of civilization." [69]

The Trustees accordingly met in Oxford, March 1 and 2, 1860, and conducted a detailed hearing of the case. Professors, students, and townspeople were called on for testimony. Dr. Branham and Chancellor Barnard secured witnesses for their sides. Under the questioning, Branham stated his objection as being based on three reasons: first, that Barnard admitted black testimony as circumstantial evidence against a student; second, that he wanted the University catalogue printed "at the North"; and third, that he had considered the offer of a position at Yale.[70] When questioned, Barnard, after recounting the incident and justifying his action, concluded by saying: "As to my sentiments on the subject of slavery . . . I am a slave holder, and, if I know myself, I am 'sound on the slavery question.' " [71]

The hearing continued until after nightfall. The following day, by a unanimous vote, the Board resoundingly vindicated Barnard in the following terms:

> *Resolved*, That the charges are, in their opinion, wholly unsustained by the evidence, and the said F. A. P. Barnard stands fully and honorably acquitted of every charge brought against him.
> *Resolved*, That after a patient hearing and investigation of all the testimony in the case, we as Trustees and as Southern men, have found our confidence in the ability and integrity of the Chancellor, and his fitness for his position, increased rather than diminished, and declare our full conviction that his labors are doing great service to the cause of education and science, and placing the reputation of the University upon an immovable basis.[72]

Because the disgruntled threatened to make an issue of the matter by an appeal to the people of the state and because the Board wished to allay any feeling that might already have arisen, the entire proceedings of this Board meeting were published as a pamphlet. Apparently nothing further was ever done, although Governor John J. Pettus expressed some dissatisfaction with Barnard and those of the faculty who supported him.[73] Anyway, there were other things now that could occupy the minds of the people.

On the campus the students were getting more and more out of hand. Cheating reached phenomenal proportions. The questions were printed in Philadelphia and some of the students had agents there who informed them when the papers were mailed and the approximate date of their arrival in Oxford. Here they were stolen from the railroad office.[74] Disorders in the chapel services became so serious that special disciplinary measures had to be invoked.[75] The fear of a black insurrection was mounting and a series of incidents in which students maltreated the college servants occurred: blacks were beaten[76] and branded,[77] and a student vigilance committee was organized in case of insurrection.[78] In late 1859 the students requested permission to form a military company.[79] The faculty, of course, did not approve all these happenings but was incapable of handling the situation.

In spite of a long-standing regulation, everyone was carrying a pistol or a dirk and violence often occurred between students. In one case a student drew his pistol and threatened another person. The faculty ruled that it was in self-defense and was to be excused on account of the "excited state of the public mind."[80] One such instance, an affair of honor, was more serious. At a ball the night of February 22, 1861 (probably given to celebrate the mustering of the University volunteers into the state troops, which had taken place during the day), a young lady of Oxford was more attentive to one of her student suitors than to the other. Sharp words ensued on the ballroom floor and the disappointed youth threatened to meet his rival after the dance. Both were armed and both had their zealous supporters.

At the end of the entertainment, the successful suitor escorted the young lady to her home, and then with his friends started to walk out to the University. The other crowd was waiting about half way. Once more sharp words flew thick and fast. Pushed together by their partisans, the disappointed one struck his rival. The latter immediately drew his pistol, shot and wounded the other, and returned to the University with his followers.

Three days later the case was tried by an Oxford court, which declared the shooting justifiable. The following day (February 26) it was tried before the faculty, the wounded man being represented by his father and the rival being accompanied by his brother and brother-in-law. By vote of the faculty the wounded student was expelled; the other one was advised to withdraw from school for a time.[81]

By now the state had dissolved its association with the Federal Union (January 9, 1861). The University was greatly excited. For ten days in January after secession, students in one dormitory defiantly flaunted the flag of the United States, while those in the other proudly hoisted the ensign of the now sovereign state of Mississippi, the "bonny blue flag."[82] The formation of the Confederacy, the approaching inauguration of Lincoln, and the threat at Pensacola, however, brought all loyalty to the defense of Southern rights. The military company, the "University Greys," was begging the Governor to have them mustered into the Confederate service.

The minutes of one of the literary societies, Phi Sigma, partially reflect the sentiment of the time. On February 22, 1861, it was "moved that two abolition books in our library be burnt. Carried."[83] On March 23, the question for regular debate was, "Ought the Southern Confederacy to establish free trade?" Little interest was exhibited in the subject, but the decision was in favor of the negative.[84] On April 27, the sum of one hundred twenty-five dollars from the society treasury was voted to the University Greys.[85]

The student military company had been organized in December,

Early views of the Lyceum, oldest building on the campus, as it appeared before (top photo) and shortly after (bottom photo) the War Between the States.

Early faculty pictures. Top photo was made shortly after the War Between the States while picture at bottom was taken around the turn of the century.

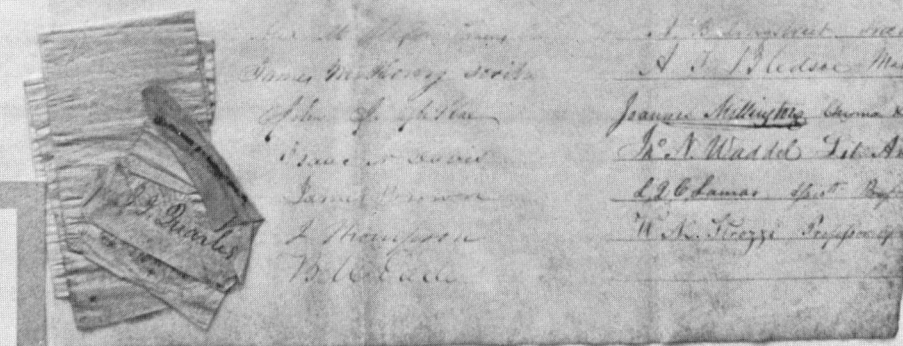

Presumably the first diploma issued by the University of Mississippi. It is dated July 17, 1851. Taken by Federal troops, it was later returned to its rightful owners. *Photograph courtesy of J. R. Cofield, Jr.*

George Frederick Holmes,
First President of the University, 1848–49.
Photograph courtesy of the *Ole Miss Alumni Review*.

Chancellor Frederick Augustus Porter Barnard who served as Chancellor from 1856 to 1861. Photograph courtesy of the *Ole Miss Alumni Review*.

Professor Lucius Quintus Cincinnatus Lamar, who served the University between the years 1850 and 1870. Later he served in Congress and became Associate Justice of the United States Supreme Court. This is reputed to be the earliest photograph of Professor Lamar.

Felix Labauve, citizen of DeSoto County, left a great portion of his estate for education of orphans of his county. One of the Trustees of the University always bears the title of "Labauve Trustee."

First gymnasium for men.

Views of the "Old Observatory" (now McCain Hall). Top photo was taken about 1859. Photo at bottom shows structure about 1897. McCain Hall is the third oldest building still standing on the campus.

1860. Its elected captain was William B. Lowry, "a tall, slender built man . . . with a classical, handsome face—courteous and refined gentleman, well-to-do and wealthy," only nineteen years of age.[86] Like others, he had come up to college with two horses, a body-servant, hunting dogs, and guns.[87] He seems to have devoted more attention to his military obligations than to his school work. For that reason, the "Lowry case" fills many pages of the faculty minutes during the early months of 1861. He was dropped from the roll of students three times because of failure to attend classes.[88] Twice he was readmitted,[89] but the third time he was unsuccessful.[90] There was a regulation requiring students expelled or suspended to leave the University within twenty-four hours and Oxford within forty-eight. Meanwhile, the officers of the Greys had been commissioned by Governor Pettus on February 7. On February 22 the company had been mustered in as part of the Mississippi state troops. Lowry therefore insisted that he had a legal right to remain with his troops. The faculty appealed to Governor Pettus to remove Lowry,[91] but the former declined to do so, stating that it was out of his power since the commission had been issued.[92]

Excitement was now at fever heat. Weapons were being furnished to the Greys. On April 4, the ladies of Oxford gave a concert to raise funds for purchasing a banner for them. Some parents, however, were apprehensive, as in all wars, and were writing to the faculty for aid in securing the release of minors from military service.[93] Many did leave the company.

But, on April 26, 1861, the company was mustered into the Confederate service. The following day a communication was received ordering them to Corinth, from which they would go on to the Virginia front. Under these orders the Greys, dressed in "grey frock coat and trousers, with red trimmings, for infantry . . . ; hat of black felt, looped up on three sides," left Oxford on May 1.[94] According to the faculty minutes of the next day, all other students had also left, except five, and they were expected to "drop off" in a few hours.[95]

About two weeks later an informal gathering of the faculty concluded the thirteenth session of the University.[96] Barnard wrote to a friend in Washington: "We are indeed inhabitants of a solitude. Our University has ceased to have visible existence. Its halls are completely deserted, and its officers are without occupation. . . ."[97]

The Board of Trustees assembled for the regular annual meeting in Oxford. On June 21, the Bachelor of Arts degree was conferred *honoris causa* on those members of the senior class who would have been graduated had the war crisis not arisen.[98] Barnard wanted the Board officially to disband the University, but the Trustees, believing that the hostilities would not be of long duration, recommended an attempt to continue and authorized the opening that autumn on September 14.[99]

Most of the faculty members stayed in the vicinity during the summer, although Barnard attended a convention of the Protestant Episcopal Church in the Confederate States in Montgomery, Alabama.[100] The Board met again in called session, September 5, and dismissed Boynton, the professor of chemistry, because of a letter he had written indicating Northern sentiments.[101] The University opened a few days later, but only four students enrolled. At a faculty meeting on September 18, 1861, the last until September 26, 1865, it was decided that the Trustees should be requested to suspend the functions of the school until peace had been achieved.[102]

Less than a fortnight later the Board assembled and acquiesced in the inevitable. The resignations of six professors (Barnard, Trotter, Lamar, Stearns, Quinche, and Harrison) were accepted. The chairs of the remaining three (Whitehorne, Moore, and Phipps) were declared vacant.[103] Professors Quinche and Harrison were designated as custodians of the buildings and other University property and were authorized to teach "such students as may apply admission." The law library was left in the care of Professor Stearns as long as he should remain in Oxford. Chancellor Barnard was requested to make a trip throughout the South to study certain military schools and investigate the possibilities for military instruction at the University.[104]

Accordingly he visited the Arsenal Academy, Columbia, South Carolina, and the Virginia Military Institute, Lexington. His report, a detailed plan, was presented to the Board in session at Jackson in late November. His conclusion, a summary of his efforts and ambitions for the University, as well as his tribulations, is well worth quoting:

"In concluding this report, and thus completing the last official communication which it will be his privilege to address to your honorable body, he cannot refrain from expressing the deep solicitude he feels for the future prosperity of an institution which, for the seven best years of his life, has absorbed all his thoughts, engrossed all his energies, and constituted the only thing on earth for which he has seemed to himself to desire to live. The ambitions which he has entertained for its growth in reputation and usefulness, for the enlargement of its scope, the expansion of the field of its operations, the elevaton of its aims, and its ultimate recognition as one among the honored agencies whose function is to be, not merely by education to diffuse knowledge among men, but by original investigation to add to the priceless mass,—these things have all been known to you, and to the few who like you have closely marked the history and watched the progress of the University. But the fond dreams of so many anxiously hopeful years have been at length rudely dissipated, and the convulsions which have shaken and are still shaking the country to its centre, have removed afar off the prospect of that distinguished preeminence in science, which seemed but recently to be opening up before the University of Mississippi. But the celebrity which the undersigned has so earnestly labored to insure to the University, though postponed, is still in store, and it will yet be realized. To another generation it may be reserved to behold the fulfillment of the brilliant destiny which awaits this noble institution; but it is a destiny which will be fulfilled—and it is this undoubting conviction which enables the undersigned, after so protracted a period of honest though possibly fruitless labor in its service—years saddened by many a wantonly inflicted and unprovoked annoyance, but illuminated also by many a bright ray of encouragement from sources worthiest of regard, and especially by many well remembered testimonials of kindness and confidence received from this honorable body—to bid it now a cheerful and hopeful farewell." [105]

On this note ended Barnard's service at the University of Mississippi. A Northern man, an ardent Unionist, temperamental and sensitive about his own importance, he had made an illustrious achievement at the University. Although frequently the center of violent controversy, he had been upheld with unbelievable loyalty by the Board of Trustees. And even now as he left, the Board, immediately before it adjourned, performed for him a gracious act, the last in its power: it conferred on him the degree of Doctor of Divinity.[106] Except for a very brief session on November 4, 1864, the Board met no more until after the war.

CHAPTER V

The Years the Cankerworm Hath Eaten

THE departure of the University Greys for the battlefront on May 1, 1861, "all in great glee," ended for the time the visible existence of the University of Mississippi. In one sense therefore the journal of the faculty is a true and revealing record; between the minutes of the meeting of September 18, 1861, and of September 26, 1865, there is simply a single blank page. That was the war.

The story of the Greys has been compiled with love and careful detail by Mrs. Maud Morrow Brown of Oxford, widow of the late Professor Calvin S. Brown of the University faculty.[1] It is sufficient here to say that at First and Second Manassas, Gaines' Mill, Sharpsburg, Gettysburg, the Wilderness, Talley's Mill, Spotsylvania Courthouse, Bethesda Church, Petersburg, and Hatcher's Run they gained "imperishable glory." At Gettysburg they reached the "high watermark of the Confederacy," forty-seven yards beyond the place reached by Pickett's men.[2] Of the few survivors none ever returned to study at the University after the war; no reunion was ever held; the sole reminder on the campus now is a stained glass window in the geology building commemorating their sacrifice "in defense of principles inherited from their fathers and strengthened by the teachings of their Alma Mater. . . ."[3]

Of more immediate interest was the scene back in Oxford. As indicated earlier, the Board of Trustees in closing the University appointed Professors Quinche and Harrison as custodians of the buildings and gave them authority to teach such students as might present themselves. These two men and their families lived in the observatory (now the chancellor's residence and headquarters of the Naval Reserve Officers Training Corps). With them also lived Dr. Hilgard and his family. Hilgard, the state geologist, was ordered by the legislature to protect the property belonging to his department.

There is some evidence that a small school was conducted for a while.[4] A report of the Board of Trustees to the legislature in 1862 referred to as many as thirty boys who were being tutored.[5] But the major portion of the time the buildings served as a hospital for wounded soldiers both Southern and Northern.[6] It apparently began on a small scale early in 1862, according to the following letter written by Private John A. Harris, 19th Louisiana Regiment, Confederate States Army, to his wife Becky. Stationed near Corinth, he and some of his comrades became ill and were hospitalized presumably at the University.

Oxford, Miss,
March 27/62

My dear Rib—

Last night while I was resting on my bed, I thought that I better write to you today, and I could not think of one thing to write. But this morning to my Surprise a friend handed me your letter of March 11. Surprise I said. It was for I had told the boys not to Send my letters down here, for fear I would not get them,—Becky—I can tell you now that I am again Stout and hearty, and will go back to camp Sunday. John Sullivan and I. Dance is quite feeble—Dont Seam to improve. This is a beautiful place, and the Sick Soldiers have enjoyed themselves very well. The Ladys come in all the time. Bring Chicken, Litebread, pies and any thing one could want. We are on the third Story, and they hardly ever get up here. But one day they came up & it looked like they were not coming into our room. I Sent out to them that they had never paid us a visit. We were Sick and they must come to See us. It was not long till they come in and Woman like come with plenty gab—Well—said they—I thought you all were Sick up here. I told them, Oh No—We were only hipoed [hypochondriac, depressed]—Was expecting a fight at Corinth and we dident want the Yankeys to kill us, So we came down here for them to take care of us—and all Such Stuff as that Which caused big laughs by the pretty cretures. The war news is Scears now and far between. No fight at Corinth yet. Nor do I believe now their ever will be a fight their. The river will Soon be down So they cant run their boats, and what Yankeys were their, I learn, have gone. They wont fight us unless they have about 5 men to our one, and they no that we have men Sufficient at Corinth to Whip ½ of Lincoln's army.

Becky I got the Braid of hair you Sent in your letter—I Shall keep it on my wrist long as I Stay in camp—I am very glad you Sent it. The Comfort you sent is in camp and I will get it when I go back.[7]

The large-scale business of hospitalization began at the University in earnest immediately after the battle of Shiloh (April 6, 7, 1862), when numbers of the Confederate wounded were sent to Oxford. All ten of the buildings on the campus were used. Most of them were supplied with cots, one was made a dispensary, another the mess hall, and still another a morgue (the "Dead House," now dismantled). The post surgeon was Dr. Thomas D. Isom, mentioned earlier as the original settler of Oxford. The women of the town served as nurses. The Confederate government sent supplies as long as possible.

Late in November news was received that General Grant was approaching Oxford and the patients were hastily evacuated to Grenada. Before Grant's troops arrived a raid was made by the Kansas Jayhawkers, who might have harmed the buildings, but they were soon brought under control by their officers before irreparable damage had been done. Burton Harrison's sister has left a graphic description of the incident: "They bore down upon the Observatory, burst in the main doors, and spread themselves all over the building, breaking up apparatus and chemicals, and then rushing into the dwelling apartments. . . . Just then they spied a large demijohn of Antimony wine, and each fellow declaring it was whiskey, . . . drank enough of the stuff to make him deadly sick. . . ."[8]

The Union army's entry into and occupation of Oxford, however, was more orderly. General A. J. ("Whiskey") Smith, in command of the van, ordered the destruction of the University buildings because they had been used for war purposes. But Hilgard made a successful plea that they be preserved on the ground that a hospital was hardly a military objective and that the Federal army could make a similar arrangement. Hilgard has stated that he "made this remonstrance by virtue of being placed by the Governor in charge of the collections of the Geological Survey. . . ." He interpreted his position as giving him "official right to stand guard over them, even during the war." [9] His suggestion was accordingly accepted and a Federal hospital was begun.

When Grant himself arrived Quinche requested his protection for the University. Grant maintained a guard about the buildings during his three weeks in Oxford. His willingness to do so is attributed to the fact that the families of Quinche and Grant had been friends in Galena, Illinois.[10] Thus the University of Mississippi did not suffer the fate of many other Southern schools or even that of the town of Oxford, the business portion of which was burned to the ground by Smith on a raid from Holly Springs, August 22, 1864. Credit for saving the University buildings must go primarily to Hilgard and Quinche, although it is possible that the former chancellor, Barnard, then in the North, may have exerted some influence in that direction.[11] Boynton is also reported to have interceded for the University, but that is hardly possible in view of his dismissal from the faculty. Hilgard definitely made his claim to the achievement when he reported to the legislature of 1863 at its meeting in Columbia.[12] After the war and the reopening of the University, the Phi Sigma literary society formally thanked both Hilgard and Quinche for preserving the property of the society during the four years of war.[13]

Grant left Oxford on Christmas day, 1862, and retreated to Memphis. General Forrest thereupon established his headquarters in Oxford, and the University of Mississippi was once more a Confederate hospital. The period was one of extreme hardship and difficulty. The wanton destruction of Oxford a little later left local supplies almost unavailable. The Confederate government was able to give only meager assistance. Hilgard tried to improvise as well as he could: he distilled alcohol from persimmons and molasses. Quinine in small quantities was smuggled out of Memphis. Many patients died during this interval for lack of proper medicines and other hospital necessities. No regular physician could be secured, but Burton Harrison's mother distinguished herself for coolness and nerve in nursing some harassing cases.

The close of the war ended the service of the University as a hospital. Approximately eighteen hundred fifty patients were cared for throughout those years. Of that number about seven hundred died and were buried in a cemetery on the campus. Because of the carelessness of some laborers in cleaning up this area, the markers were destroyed and the graves cannot now be identified. A monument erected by the Albert Sidney Johnston Chapter, United Daughters of the Confederacy, stands on the campus today to commemorate these valiant dead.

Only one meeting of the Board of Trustees was held during the war. In recognition of the critical state of the country, on December 9, 1863, the state legislature had approved an act continuing in office those who were then Trustees until their successors might be elected. A further note of crisis was expressed in the act by declaring that only three of the thirteen members of the Board would be necessary to constitute a quorum. All vacancies were to be filled by the Governor until the next session of the legislature.[14] In response to this action of the legislature and the call of the Governor the Board met in Jackson on November 4, 1864. In addition to Governor Charles Clark, only two other Trustees were present, William L. Sharkey and Alexander M. Clayton. The sole business transacted was to divide the Board into three classes, one to serve two years, the others four and six respectively.[15] Thus even during the darkest days of the declining Confederacy the corporate body known as the University of Mississippi was not forgotten.

CHAPTER VI

False Dawn

IT was the good fortune of Mississippi, as it lay prostrate before the victorious Union, to have as its Provisional Governor, appointed by President Johnson, Judge William L. Sharkey. One of his first official acts, July 1, 1865, was to summon a meeting of the Trustees of the University of Mississippi. He himself had been a Trustee ever since 1844, when the original Board was appointed and now by virtue of his office he was its president. It is indicative of high character and respect for learning that, amid defeat and chaos, he thought of the educational institution of his state.[1]

In obedience to his call, the Board met in Oxford for three days, July 31, August 1, 2, 1865, to consider the reopening of the University.[2] One of its first tasks was to examine the buildings in order to ascertain any needed repairs.[3] Although some damage had been done, the University had not suffered as many other Southern schools had. In the main, the buildings and apparatus were intact, as noted above, because of the care of Quinche and Hilgard.

The next task was the selection of a faculty. The state treasury was depleted, but the deficiency was somewhat remedied by a tax on all cotton within the state. Limited funds were set apart from this to provide for the most pressing needs of the University.[4] In consequence, four professors were designated at this meeting. John N. Waddel, D. D., who had been a member of the original Board of Trustees and later of the first faculty, was now unanimously elected to the chancellorship. General Claudius W. Sears became professor of mathematics, John J. Wheat, D. D., professor of Greek, and Alexander J. Quinche, professor of Latin. General Alexander P. Stewart was at the same time elected to the chair of physics, astronomy, and civil engineering.[5] But, when notified, he declined. Later he succeeded Waddel as chancellor. Thus the school reopened as it had opened, with only four instructors, but with two significant differences. This time there was no objection to clergymen on the faculty and the classics predominated over the natural sciences.

Waddel, son of the famed Moses Waddel, was born in Willington, South Carolina, April 2, 1812. Trained at his father's academy and Franklin College (now the University of Georgia), he moved to Alabama in 1837. Five years later he moved to Jasper county, Mississippi, where he established his Montrose Academy and as a Presbyterian minister supplied near-by churches. His fame in educational circles caused his appointment, without his knowledge, among the charter members of the Board of Trustees of the University of Mississippi, in which capacity he served until his election to the original faculty.[6]

In 1857 Waddel had gone to teach ancient languages at the new Presbyterian Synodical College, LaGrange, Tennessee, and in 1860 had been made president of that institution. When the Federal army occupied the town in December, 1862, he became a refugee. During the years from then until the end of the war, he served in turn as an agent for the Bible Society of the Confederate States, commissioner of army missions, and agent to raise funds for an orphan asylum. At the close of the war he had moved with his family from LaGrange back to Oxford.[7]

Waddel was convinced that his association with the University of Mississippi had been foreordained in the inscrutable plan of the Almighty. Back in the autumn of 1841, before he had come to Mississippi, he had been in Mobile, Alabama, on business. On one of those dreary, grey days which Mobile can have, when earth and sky and the bay all seem indistinguishable, Waddel, in a fit of loneliness, stopped in a reading-room to while away the heavy hours. At once his eyes fell by chance on the journal of the proceedings of the Mississippi legislature, in which he read about the action locating the future University near Oxford. He felt immediately that this was a case of Providential guidance: "I believe that my entering that reading-room on that occasion was under divine direction, and that my heavenly Father designed it mercifully as a means of ... comfort to me under the gloomy shadows ... then resting upon me.... Now, just there ... I was conscious of ... the possibility that I might some day be connected with that institution." [8] Much later, October 25, 1865, before the state legislature, he declared: "I have no higher ambition than to be identified with the great Educational system of Mississippi, ... I would seek no more honored resting place than one beneath its overshadowing towers...." [9]

Another post-war member of the faculty, General Sears, born in Peru, Massachusetts, November 8, 1817, was a graduate of West Point and served in the United States army until 1842. He taught mathematics at St. Thomas Hall, Holly Springs, during 1844 and 1845, and at the University of Louisiana, New Orleans, 1845–1859. From 1859 to 1861 he served St. Thomas Hall as president. During the War Between the States he rose to the rank of brigadier general in the Confederate army.[10] Having lost a leg at the battle of Nashville, he became "a familiar figure hobbling around the campus on crutches," [11] and known to the students as "Old Baldy."

Dr. Wheat came of a fine old Mississippi family, his mother having been a Millsaps. Born in Copiah county in 1826, he had done his undergraduate work at Hanover and Centre colleges. Although he became a Methodist minister, he had studied theology under the staunch Calvinists, Robert J. Breckinridge and Charles Hodge, of the Danville and Princeton seminaries respectively. An outstanding pulpit orator of great popularity, he is said to have been a "specialist on Philology and Mythology and frequently before entering upon consideration of the lesson for the day he would talk on these subjects to the delight and edification of the student body." [12] His etymological speculation was akin to that of St. Isidore of Seville, for he is reputed to have derived a slang term of the day, *skedaddle*, from the Greek *skedannumi* (put to flight) and the word *squirrel* from *skia*, meaning *shadow*, and *oura*, meaning *tail!* [13]

Quinche had served on the faculty during the session of 1860-1861, had continued to live on the campus during the war, and was yet to remain at the University for twenty-four more years—a remarkable record for a Northern man whose family had been on friendly terms with the family of General Grant.[14]

Such was the teaching staff with which the University opened the first Monday of October, 1865. The first faculty meeting of the year was held on September 26.[15] When the students began to arrive it was realized that additional instructors were needed, especially since General Stewart had declined his appointment. Therefore, at a called meeting of the Board, two others were elected, General Francis A. Shoup, to take the place declined by Stewart, and Sanford G. Burney, D. D., professor of English literature.[16] Of the six faculty members now, three were clergymen and in 1868 General Shoup was to receive orders as a priest of the Protestant Episcopal Church. Shoup was a West Pointer from Indiana who had thrown his lot with the Confederacy.[17]

Within the next few years four others were added to the faculty. In 1866 Colonel L. Q. C. Lamar was appointed to teach metaphysics and ethics as he had done the year before the war. He continued in that capacity a year and then accepted the chair of governmental science and law when the law school was resumed in 1867. The same year in which Lamar returned to the teaching staff, George Little was appointed professor of natural history and geology, the first Doctor of Philosophy employed by the University. The second one was Hilgard, the former state geologist, who in 1868 was made professor of chemistry.[18]

The most notable addition was Landon C. Garland, later the first chancellor of Vanderbilt University, elected January 21, 1867, to the chair of analytical physics and astronomy. Garland, a Virginian, had served as professor in Washington College (now Washington and Lee), as professor, vice-president, and president of Randolph-Macon, and as professor and president of the University of Alabama until its destruction during the war.[19]

The post-bellum student body was much larger than had been anticipated by the Trustees and instructors. During the session of 1865–1866 it numbered a hundred ninety-three; in 1866–1867 it was two hundred forty-four; and in 1867–1868 it was two hundred thirty-one.[20] The average age was somewhat older than before the war, there was less tendency toward frivolity, and, because of the privations of war, there was a consequent lack of preparation which had to be remedied by an increased teaching load for the faculty. From 1867 to 1870, therefore, special instruction was formally provided in the preparatory field to relieve that condition.[21]

A majority of both students and professors had been in the Confederate army. A number bore obvious marks of this experience. Many continued to wear parts of their uniforms to class. In after years a graduate of the class of 1868 said: "I suppose no body of students ever assembled at the State University that were more sober and thoughtful than those who attended the first three or four years after the war.... In such a body of teachers and students, and under such circumstances, there was bound to be a deep undertone of soberest thought." [22] The same alumnus has still further characterized the restricted life of the day when he wrote that during his period of attendance he "never left the campus, or at least its environments, a single time except once on a visit home during the Christmas holidays. And everybody else did the same thing. We had no athletics. We had fine walks around the campus and to the town of Oxford right close by. We went to church every Sunday morning and night but we belonged to the University grounds and there we were always found." [23]

The commencement of spring, 1866, was a memorable event although no one was to be graduated. The preacher was the Right Reverend R. H. Wilmer, the Protestant Episcopal bishop of Alabama,[24] who had only recently been the storm-center of two controversies. In June, 1865, he had forbidden his clergy to pray for the Federal occupying authorities. In retaliation he and the other clergymen were suspended from their duties and their churches were closed by military order. That order had not been rescinded until late December, 1865. In addition, since he had been elected and consecrated during the war, the Northern bishops had refused to recognize his orders as regular and had treated him as a schismatic until January, 1866.[25] As though to defy the conquerors, the University of Mississippi conferred the degree of Doctor of Divinity upon him at this commencement.

The school authorities had put a notice in the state newspapers informing survivors of the class of 1861 that they could receive their diplomas officially if they would return for this occasion on June 28.[26] Only one was able to respond, Captain Francis Asbury Pope, who was asked to deliver the valedictory address for his class. As befitted the circumstances, the oration was touched with pathos and emotion. At one point Pope turned and made allusion to Charles Clark, also present on the platform. Clark had been seriously crippled in battle and on returning to civilian life had been elected Governor. At the end of the war he had been ejected from office and imprisoned by the Federal troops. Thus, like President Davis, he had become in the eyes of his fellow Mississippians a martyr, a symbol of their own condition. Captain Pope's allusion and gesture loosed the pent-up emotions. "The big college hall was full of the elite of Oxford and LaFayette County. They clapped their hands until everything rang with the applause. Tears were shed all over the house. 'Twas an episode that would never be forgotten." [27]

Afterwards Chancellor Waddel delivered a laborious inaugural address on behalf of the faculty of the reopened University.[28] J. W. Clapp followed on behalf of the Trustees in a more pleasing and prophetic vein: "We have indeed lost much, but we have not lost all. There are indestructible revenues which God has given us, moral and material, the value of which cannot be estimated, and which have survived the wreck of our fortunes, and the rapine and ravages of war. We still have the same blessed sky bending over us, with its alternation of sunshine and shower,—the same generous soil around us waiting to crown again the labors of our industry with its plenteous rewards. . . . We still have our undeveloped and inexhaustible mineral resources of infinite variety and value; the unrivalled facilities for manufacturing; and now that slave labor, that insuperable barrier for the introduction of foreign labor, no longer exists, there is no conceivable reason why, with our unequalled water power and our abundance and cheapness of fuel and food, the South should not, as I believe it will, become the great manufacturing centre of the globe, and the more vigorously we apply our industry in that direction, the sooner will we become independent of oppressive export duties by establishing our market at our own doors." [29]

Straitened circumstances were a great concern in this period. The old manuscript tuition book [30] shows that many of the students, being unable to pay the annual fee of fifty dollars, were financed by various members of the faculty either by loans on easy terms or by outright gifts. The generosity of Colonel Lamar deserves high praise. The expense of textbooks was materially lessened during the session of 1865–1866 by the fact that so many had been left on the campus where they had been abandoned by the students in 1861.[31] The cost of board was moderate—about eighteen dollars a month, but even that figure seemed higher than many of the students could afford. Several of them therefore began to purchase their own supplies and prepare them at their fireplaces. Other students began to imitate this plan. When the matter came to the attention of the faculty, the unoccupied rooms in the dormitories were opened for this arrangement, "and the price of living was greatly reduced." [32]

Many things conspired to keep the "Lost Cause" before the minds of the students, and devotion to it ran high. For instance, as a part of the commencement program of 1867, an alumnus of the class of 1856, the Reverend T. D. Witherspoon of Memphis, delivered an address on "The Appeal of the South to its Educated Men." [33] He analyzed this as a threefold summons "to embalm in literature, and thus preserve in fragrant memory at least that peculiar type of civilization which has been the ornament of the South, but which is now to pass away . . .; to transmit to posterity in permanent form a fair and impartial record of the struggle which has just closed . . .;" and to prepare a peculiarly Southern series of textbooks for the youth of the South, "or we have no security for the future against a thraldom far worse than that of the bayonet." [34] Thus the legend of the Old South was already in the making.

During his imprisonment Burton Harrison wrote often to his mother and sister, who were still occupying rooms on the campus and who would continue to do so until the autumn of 1867. These letters and the ones written after his release in early January, 1866, dealing with his efforts to aid President Davis, were read to the students by Miss Harrison: ". . . the days of the past were not likely to be forgotten." [35]

The orator for the literary societies in June 1869 still further stirred the emotions by his eloquence: "At your bidding that stranger comes back to the same spot to-day, from another State and from the quiet pursuits of private life, to bear an honored part in this high festival of letters and mind. As he looks out upon the surrounding scene he finds its general features comparatively unchanged. The buildings, browner from age, the velvet campus, the flowing grounds and the partially retired, but still engirdling, woods and undergrowth, are all here. The University, having survived the perils and the ravages of war, and furnished with the same, and even greater educational resources, still dispenses the blessings of moral and intellectual culture among the people, and is going up, by sure and progressive steps, to the pinnacle of academic usefulness and renown. The same skies kindle in tropical fervor and splendor above, and the same soil teems with fertility and beauty beneath, but all else is changed. The once proud and noble State, to which the University belonged, and all men hailed as a sceptred queen in the bright sisterhood of States, lies crownless and in the dust, with the heel of the victor upon her neck and his bayonet at her throat. The South, the beautiful and abounding South, of the day of my former visit to your University [1857], has perished beneath the iron strangulation of war, and lives now only in the records of history and in the tearful memories of its sorrowing people. The young men, gathered from many broad leagues of country, to hold, by the cool streams and the still waters of peace, this annual olympia of mind, are here to qualify themselves for the career of life under social and political arrangements widely different from those of a very recent past. . . . In this stricken and sorrowing clime, we meet to-day, a portion of its disinherited people, to hold the festival of letters on the neutral territory of the Republic of mind." [36]

Earlier the Phi Sigma society had taken a collection to be contributed to the defense of President Davis. It had also tried without success to secure as its commencement orator the most famous of the "Copperheads," Clement L. Vallandigham of Ohio.[37] Another "Copperhead," however, did address the students, Daniel W. Voorhees of Indiana, the "Tall Sycamore of the Wabash." [38]

Even the Board of Trustees responded to the temper of the time with patriotic zeal. At a meeting in 1867 it offered a scholarship to the attorney William B. Reed of Philadelphia for his son, earnestly requesting that he permit the youth to be trained in the University of Mississippi, as an expression of the gratitude of the state for his voluntary services in the defense of President Davis.[39] At the same meeting it was agreed to cooperate with the legislature in regard to the free education of former Confederate soldiers at the University.[40] At the regular meeting in June free tuition was offered to the only living son of Davis. The action was to be communicated to the imprisoned chieftain to cheer him.[41] The faculty had requested the Board to confer the degree of Doctor of Laws on the former president at that time, but the Trustees deemed the proposal inexpedient.[42]

The warmest degree of fervor was probably reached in the spring of 1869, when Jacob Thompson returned, under the terms of general amnesty, to his home from long exile in Canada and Europe. He was greeted at the Oxford depot with a tremendous ovation, and Professor Lamar delivered an hour-long address of welcome.[43] At the end of the speech, as he and Thompson stepped into the waiting carriage, half a hundred students unhitched the horses and themselves drew the carriage on a triumphal journey through town to the Avent home where a brilliant reception and banquet were given in the fugitive's honor.[44]

But underneath all the privations of the period, the gloom of defeat, the romantic repining over a day that was gone, the ebullient spirit of the eternal student could not be crushed. Even so heroic an occasion as the one just related lent itself to Homeric parody. Not long afterward, about Thanksgiving time, some students were found by the chancellor in a state of intoxication. The penalty for the revellers was suspension for sixty days.[45] They were allowed to live and board in the county, but could not return to the campus until February 1, 1870. They continued their studies privately until the term of suspension expired. When that day arrived several other students secured a handcar, met their banished classmates about three miles north of Oxford, and brought them to the station. Others were awaiting their arrival. There was an enthusiastic reception. The Lamar-Thompson scene was reenacted: each of the orators for the occasion imagined himself a Lamar welcoming a Thompson to Oxford! [46]

The reopening of the University was so propitious that the Trustees were emboldened once more to ask the state to recognize its debt to the University in regard to the seminary fund and also to request an appropriation of a hundred fifty thousand dollars, payable in ten annual instalments, to make the necessary repairs and meet other pressing needs of the institution.⁴⁷ But the legislature declined to accede to the petition of the Board, although it did appropriate twenty thousand dollars for these purposes.⁴⁸ Only three days earlier, it had also chartered a lottery at Vicksburg on condition that its corporators should first pay five thousand dollars into the treasury for the use of the University.⁴⁹

"The university seemed entering on a new career of usefulness and prosperity. The perils and the desolation of the war had gone by. The empty halls and lecture rooms were again filled with eager and aspiring youths, at once the hope and the pride of the State; the professors' chairs were occupied by selections from the most honored sons of the South, and the treasury of the institution was filled with the State's ready bounty. The sky seemed cloudless as a day in June, and the memory of the pall that had recently hung over it served only to intensify the brightness of the passing hour. Yet below the horizon were the mutterings of a gathering storm." ⁵⁰

CHAPTER VII

By the Waters of Babylon

WHEN Confederate resistance ended in Mississippi, May 4, 1865, it was hoped that the orderly routine of the duly elected civil officials would be quietly resumed. But this was not to be. Governor Clark was ejected from the executive office and made a prisoner. Fortunately for the state and particularly for the University the man appointed as the Provisional Governor was William L. Sharkey, a Mississippian and for a long time a member of the Board of Trustees. He assumed the office on June 13, 1865.

A constitutional convention was held in August which abolished slavery and declared the ordinance of secession null and void. An election on October 2 resulted in the choice of Benjamin G. Humphreys as Governor and Sharkey and James L. Alcorn as Senators. Humphreys took office on October 16 and consequently was the president *ex officio* of the Trustees at the meeting in Jackson, October 23–26, when, as noted earlier, General Shoup and the Reverend Dr. Burney were elected as additional members of the faculty, and when Chancellor Waddel delivered his address on public education to the newly chosen legislature.

The mild presidential Reconstruction was not to be accepted by the vengeful Radical Republicans in the Congress. The Senate refused to seat Sharkey and Alcorn. Meanwhile the Humphreys regime continued to function. The infamous Reconstruction Acts were passed by Congress. Mississippi became a part of the Fourth Military District. By means of a redistribution of the franchise another constitutional convention was authorized.

This "Black and Tan" convention, dominated by carpetbaggers, scalawags, and blacks, met from January to May, 1868, drew up a new constitution, and called an election. At the polls in June the people of Mississippi defeated the Radical constitution and reelected Governor Humphreys. But by now the tide of Reconstruction could not be stayed. Humphreys was forced from office and General Adelbert Ames was appointed as Military Governor, holding office from June 15, 1868, to March 10, 1870.

So far there still seemed to be no interference with affairs at the University. Ames issued the warrants for its support as they came due. In fact, he was apparently not even interested in the institution. He never attended a Board meeting during his term of office and when vacancies occurred three times he appointed Trustees who were not objectionable to the people of the state. Only one of his three appointees was a Republican. All in all, Ames's policy in regard to the University was cautious and conservative.[1]

In July, 1869, however, the Radical constitution was resubmitted to the people. By a process of concession and pressure it was ratified, except for two articles. An election in November and December brought James L. Alcorn, a former Confederate general turned Republican, to the Governor's chair and sent Ames and a black, Hiram Revels, to the Senate. When the Senators were seated, the state of Mississippi was formally readmitted to the Union. Alcorn was inaugurated on March 10, 1870, and the Reconstruction was in full swing.

The heavy hand of Radicalism was now laid upon the University. On May 9 an act was passed providing for a new Board of Trustees to be appointed by the Governor. There were to be thirteen members, including the Governor, who would as heretofore be the presiding officer.[2] Alcorn appointed seven Radicals and five Conservatives. The people of the state were thoroughly alarmed and it was generally feared that pressure would soon be brought to force the admission of blacks to the institution. L. Q. C. Lamar immediately resigned his professorship of law.[3] Commencement came in the interval between the last meeting of the old Board and the first meeting of the new one. In an unprecedented action the degrees were conferred by the authority of the faculty and the executive committee of the old Board. The procedure was ratified by the new Board at its first meeting.[4]

Apprehension regarding the new trend was manifest in the enrollment during the session of 1870–1871.[5] In the early autumn of 1870, Judge Robert S. Hudson of Yazoo City had written to Waddel "requesting the views of the authorities of the Institution in relation to the admission of negroes...."[6] The chancellor at once laid the issue before the faculty. By a unanimous resolution he was requested in his reply to state that the University had been organized for whites alone, that a change in this policy could be effected only by action of the Trustees, that the Trustees had not effected such a change and apparently had no such purpose in mind, and that should such a policy be enacted all the members of the faculty then present would resign.[7] Waddel despatched the letter immediately and Judge Hudson in turn communicated it to the newspapers of the state.[8] Although it was too late to remedy the situation that year, William L. Sharkey is said to have stated that "the University was saved" by that letter.[9]

The following spring when the faculty began to negotiate for a commencement preacher, the feeling that the University was in disrepute was so widespread that three near-by Protestant Episcopal bishops in rapid succession declined the appointment, although acceptance usually carried with it the honorary degree of Doctor of Divinity.[10] Similarly the following year when Colonel J. F. H. Claiborne, the Herodotus of the state, was asked to deliver the address on the twenty-fifth anniversary of the University, he respectfully declined the invitation, pleading ill health.[11] The duty devolved upon Chancellor Waddel, who performed the task creditably and thereby presented to the public the first orderly narrative of the history of the University of Mississippi.[12] He was to elaborate the account later in his *Memorials of Academic Life*.[13]

It is interesting to observe how Waddel minimized the difficulties of the period. For instance, he reported that the Board, consisting "of an equal number of both parties," [14] "proved to be satisfactory." [15] He mentioned only two occasions "where there seemed to be appearances of a threatened storm. . . ." [16] Only once did he feel that he himself "was innocently under censure. . . ." [17] "It cannot be denied that these were troublous times for the institution. . . . But matters were managed, under divine guidance, successfully. . . ." [18]

The chancellor proved to be an able and expert tight-rope walker. Perhaps for that reason he was the best man for the place during those troublous days. A rigid censorship was imposed upon all discussions of politics on the campus. As a graduate of 1872 had described it: "Students were absolutely prohibited from mentioning politics in their speeches on anniversary, commencement, and other occasions. States' rights and secession were forbidden words." [19] All declamations had to be submitted to the scrutiny of the faculty before delivery. At least twice, daring students caused consternation by inserting unauthorized sentences in their addresses, "reflecting, in very disrespectful language, upon the party in power." [20] The Republicans present were indignant: in one case the supervising professor felt it necessary to resign; in the other Waddel was able to mollify the ruffled feelings.[21]

But repression provoked its own reaction. At the commencement of 1873 one senior gave vent to his wrath by tearing up his diploma as he received it from the hands of the venerable chancellor.[22] And as far away as Vincennes, Indiana, the editor of the *Western Sun* mused significantly: "It is a disgrace that a Mississippi boy, on his native soil, and under the roof built by the money of his ancestors, cannot pay a compliment to his own people without having a snarling set of carpet-bag curs remonstrating. This institution, which was once honored by such men as Longstreet, Bledsoe and Lamar as teachers, has certainly fallen into bad hands." [23]

There was one problem that even the diplomatic Waddel could not solve and that was the ladies! The time was a night in June, 1874; the occasion was the chancellor's reception, an annual feature of commencement week. In order to show respect and courtesy to the Trustees, he intended to introduce them to the women of Oxford who were present. He judiciously decided to consult the women first to ask if they would receive the Republican Trustees. "Every lady whom I approached declined very quietly, but very promptly." [24] The Trustees quite naturally resented the neglect and laid the entire blame on Waddel.[25] A few days later, June 26, 1874, he awoke very early in the morning and under Divine inspiration decided to tender his resignation. "This I did immediately . . . after breakfast." [26]

To be completely just, it must be noted that the Reconstruction period was not one of unrelieved evil and disorder for the University. The great accomplishment was the change from the "close college" to the university system. It began with an action of the Board, June 18, 1869, acceding to Waddel's request that he be authorized to make a tour of other schools to obtain information that would be valuable to the University of Mississippi.[27]

During the summer the chancellor visited the major Northern and Eastern universities. His recommendations, embodied in a report to the Board of Trustees, were along the lines then in effect at the University of Michigan.[28] But before this Board could act, it was replaced by the Reconstruction Board.

The latter, at its first meeting in August, 1870, had appointed a committee, headed by the Reverend James A. Lyon, D. D., to study the recommendations of the faculty on the subject and report to a later meeting.[29] At a called meeting in Jackson, October 26, Waddel's plan was accepted in its entirety.[30] Provision was made for three general departments, one of preparatory education, another of science, literature, and the arts, and the third of professional education. The first was to be effected by the establishment of a University high school. The second included six distinct courses of study: four parallel courses for undergraduates, leading respectively to the degrees of Bachelor of Arts, Bachelor of Science, Bachelor of Philosophy, and Civil Engineer; and post-graduate courses leading to the Master of Arts and Doctor of Philosophy degrees. The third general department was to be composed of two professional schools, one of law and one of medicine. The system was inaugurated as far as practicable in the autumn of 1871.

The preparatory department was immediately established and lasted until the session of 1882–1883, when a sub-freshman class was substituted in lieu of it.[31] The courses in civil engineering were discontinued in 1875 to be resumed in 1900.[32] The catalogues from 1871 to 1879 announced that the medical school would be opened as soon as the resources of the University would permit, but it was not finally opened until June, 1903.[33] The Master of Arts degree had been conferred *honoris causa* as late as 1869.

The catalogue for 1870–1871, in announcing the reorganization, offered the degree of Doctor of Philosophy, as did every succeeding catalogue through the one issued for the session of 1902–1903. The next four issues described the degree but stated that it was not then being offered. From the catalogue of 1907–1908 to the graduate school bulletin of 1948 (in which the degree of Doctor of Philosophy was offered in the field of anatomy) there was no reference to that degree in the curriculum of the University. Seventeen students had done work toward the doctorate, but only three had completed the requirements: Hubert Anthony Shands in 1893, Paul Hill Saunders in 1894, and Eugene Harper Roberts in 1895.[34] All three had also done their undergraduate work at the University of Mississippi; the first two served on the faculty for a while. Dr. Saunders later became an outstanding financier, dying in 1947. Dr. Shand's thesis, *Some Peculiarities of Speech in Mississippi*, is a creditable production and a real contribution to the world of humane learning.[35] Interestingly enough the degree has also been conferred once *honoris causa*: in 1877 the recipient was Robert Hills Loughridge, who had earned his Bachelor of Science degree in 1871 and had begun his doctoral study at the University. He was a member of the faculty, 1872–1874, and was later associated with Hilgard at the University of California.

The change from the "close college" to the university system demonstrates the unity of history even through apparent crises. It was studied and proposed while the Board of Trustees was still in the hands of the Democratic conservatives, it was put into effect by the Republican appointees, and it is still virtually in effect long after the overthrow of the carpet-bag regime. A further indication of the continuity of history may be noted in the records of the Trustees concerning a less lofty matter than the curriculum. On September 25, 1868, the old Board solemnly resolved "That the Executive Committee be authorized to have suitable privies erected in the rear of each Dormitory."[36] Two days short of a year later occurs this note: "Privys suited to the necessities of the pupils should be provided at the earliest practicable date."[37] The old Board was removed and the Radicals came to power. The same problem faced them and was dealt with in the same way. On June 26, 1873, they too, with equal dignity and dispatch, tackled the issue by resolving "That the Executive Committee be instructed to have a sufficient number of Water Closets and Privies erected by the opening of the next Session."[38] But Conservatives and Radicals both were ineffective. At long, long last—twenty years, to be exact—occurs the relieving statement that urinals were finally arranged for the convenience of the students![39]

The interest of the Radicals in black education was fulfilled in the establishment of a university for the colored people. This was done in response to a message of Governor Alcorn to the legislature.[40] In his honor it was named Alcorn University. The act incorporating the new institution provided for the appropriation of fifty thousand dollars to it for ten years. The same act made similar provision for the University of Mississippi.[41] Where the money for such a munificent expenditure was to come from was apparently no concern of the legislators then in office.

Meanwhile, on July 2, 1862, the Federal Congress had approved an act granting to each state an amount of public lands equal to thirty thousand acres for each Senator and Representative to which the state was entitled by the census of 1860. The purpose of this legislation was to provide colleges for the study of agriculture and the mechanical arts. Mississippi offered to accept the donation on October 30, 1866, but the Federal government had suspended issuance of the scrip to the Southern states. Now the Republican Governor was successful in securing the scrip, selling it, and investing the proceeds wisely. The same day that Alcorn University was chartered, May 13, 1871, the legislature assigned three-fifths of the land-scrip fund to Alcorn, the remaining two-fifths to the University of Mississippi. The latter realized ninety-five thousand dollars in state bonds bearing eight percent interest. The establishment of the Mississippi Agricultural and Mechanical College (later Mississippi State College), February 28, 1878, excluded the University from any further participation in this fund.[42]

In consequence of the grant the University was obliged to open a department of agriculture. The matter was not entirely new at the institution. Millington, of the first faculty, had from 1850 to 1853 borne the title of professor of chemistry and agriculture. In 1853–1854 J. C. Keeny was professor of chemistry, analytical chemistry, agriculture, and geology, and in 1854–1855 Lewis Harper held the dual position of state geologist and professor of geology, agriculture, and analytical chemistry.[43] Waddel reminded the Trustees of that as they planned the reorganization of 1870 [44] and asked Hilgard to secure as much information as possible regarding agricultural and mechanical colleges then in operation.

Hilgard made an investigation and filed a detailed report with the chancellor in the summer of 1871,[45] envisioning the elaborate organization needed for an adequate agricultural and mechanical institution. The Trustees, however, were exceedingly cautious.[46] Although Hilgard delivered a course of appropriate lectures during 1871–1872, the department of agriculture was not definitely begun until the next session. A small tract of land was used as a model farm under the superintendency of M. W. Philips. The opening of the mechanical college was postponed until the autumn of 1873.[47]

Hampered by lack of adequate equipment, the work languished. Hilgard left after the session of 1872–1873. The farm was continued until 1876. In 1878, as noted above, the Agricultural and Mechanical College was chartered, and thus the University was relieved of the responsibility for this field of endeavor.

In spite of the fact that from 1871 onward Mississippi students were admitted free of tuition in all divisions of the University except the law school, the attendance remained low all during the Reconstruction era. Only the presence of the preparatory students kept up the semblance of satisfactory enrollment. The following table will clarify this statement:

STUDENT ENROLLMENT

Session	Preparatory	Others	Total
1871–1872	123	138	260
1872–1873	122	180	302
1873–1874	42	166	208
1874–1875	37	100	137
1875–1876	46	85	131

As mentioned earlier, Chancellor Waddel communicated his resignation to the Board on Friday, June 26, 1874.[48] Asked to reconsider his action, he pleaded that he ought to spend the rest of his life working more specifically for his church.[49] He did consent to let the matter rest for a month. At the expiration of that interval, the Board reassembled and at Waddel's insistence accepted his resignation.[50]

Waddel had served the University of Mississippi as Trustee, professor, and chancellor successively for twenty-one years (1844–1856, 1865–1874). "His heart, his life was wrapped up in the institution." [51] He himself said: ". . . this University has my heart's affections. She was my first love. . . . One boon I ask. . . . When the touch of death shall lay me in the grave, then let me sweetly sleep beneath the shadow of her fame, and these classic groves. Content shall I be to know, and to have it known that . . . I labored for THE GLORY OF THE UNIVERSITY OF MISSISSIPPI." [52]

The day following the acceptance of Waddel's resignation a controversy which had arisen in the faculty had to be dealt with by the Board.[53] Wheat, Quinche, and Sears were involved in a disagreement as to which one was the senior professor. The significance of the quarrel lay in the fact that by law the senior professor was the vice-chancellor and would therefore be the acting chancellor until a new chancellor should be elected. The Trustees listened to their statements and then examined the record. Wheat was found to be the senior by one day and was thereupon declared acting chancellor. He served until October 19, 1874.[54]

CHAPTER VIII

The Forgotten Chancellor

A revolution was brewing that would in time remove the despot's heel from the conquered and downtrodden province of Mississippi. The first inkling of it came (1868–1871) when a ghostly army of those who died at Manassas, at Shiloh, at Chickamauga, rode once more through nights lighted by the flare of flaming crosses. Then came mob violence and bloody rioting at Meridian (March, 1871), Vicksburg (December, 1874), Clinton (September, 1875), and elsewhere.

The Trustees felt the tension as they gathered to select a successor to Chancellor Waddel. In response to their advertisement of the vacancy, only one candidate had submitted his name, Alexander P. Stewart, formerly a lieutenant general in the army of the Confederacy. His election was unanimous. The need for him was so urgent that he was notified by telegraph.[1] His reply and acceptance were equally speedy: he arrived and entered upon his duties on Monday, October 19, 1874. The University had already opened on October 7 under the direction of Acting Chancellor Wheat.[2] Stewart's inauguration took place November 10 at the Cumberland Presbyterian church in Oxford.[3] L. Q. C. Lamar, then a member of Congress, accepted the invitation to deliver the address on behalf of the Board, to which Stewart made an appropriate reply.[4]

Stewart, born in Rogersville, Tennessee, October 2, 1821, had been graduated from the United States Military Acadamy in 1842 along with James Longstreet, nephew of the former chancellor of the University of Mississippi. The following year he was detailed for duty as assistant professor of mathematics at West Point, where for two years he taught such men as George B. McClellan and Stonewall Jackson. From 1845 to 1849, from 1850 to 1854, and from 1856 until the outbreak of the war, he taught mathematics and natural philosophy at Cumberland University, Lebanon, Tennessee. During the intervening years he served on the faculty of the University of Nashville. At Cumberland he established the school of engineering and organized the college Young Men's Christian Association, reputed to be the first one in the United States. A consistent Whig in politics, he was opposed to slavery and secession, but acquiesced in the decision of his state to resist invasion. In the Confederate army he rose rapidly and made an outstanding record for himself, gaining a reputation as "Old Straight."

After the war Stewart returned to Lebanon as a surveyor until Cumberland reopened, when he resumed his place on the faculty. From 1870 until his election to the chancellorship of the University of Mississippi, he was secretary of the Mutual Life Insurance Company in St. Louis, Missouri.[5]

The election of Stewart was one of the indications which presaged the end of Radicalism in Mississippi. It had reached its zenith during the term of Governor Adelbert Ames (January 4, 1874–March 20, 1876): the lieutenant governor, secretary of state, superintendent of education and other prominent officials were blacks. But the election of late 1875 was a veritable revolution. It returned a majority of Democrats to the legislature, which convened in January, 1876, and began its task of removing the Radicals. The lieutenant governor was deposed, Ames resigned under the threat of impeachment, other officials fled, and the Reconstruction was at an end. The state could now begin its program of real rehabilitation.

One of the first acts of the new legislature, after the accession of Governor John M. Stone, was to reorganize the University. The bill, adopted April 14, 1876, raised the number of Trustees to fifteen (not including the Governor, who served in an *ex officio* capacity) and provided that five should be alumni of the institution.[6] Ten of the appointees were entirely new to the Board: the others were conservatives who had served earlier.[7]

An immediate necessity was to restore popular confidence in the University. The Trustees therefore prepared an address to the people of the state entitled "Where Shall I Send My Son?" and had it printed and distributed.[8] After viewing the situation realistically, they began with a summary of the history of the school and a statement concerning the qualifications of the faculty. The size of the University was suggested by its buildings: "They are distributed as follows: Nine Professors' residences; three Dormitories, of thirty-six rooms each, containing accommodations for two hundred and sixteen students; one Chapel, three stories in hight, with Society Halls above; one Lyceum, containing Lecture Rooms, Laboratory, Library, apparatus, collections of minerals, shells, &c., &c.: one Observatory, with one large and one smaller tower of observation for telescopes; one Preparatory Department, situated beyond the campus, very large and commodious, with ample school room for one hundred and twenty-five boys, besides affording residence for the family of the Principal and Assistant; one Gymnasium on the campus, fitted up with usual appliances for gymnastic exercises; six boarding houses."[9] Total expenses for a year were calculated on the following basis:

Board—$15 per month,	$135.00
Room,	5.00
Washing—$2 per month,	18.00
Tuition,	25.00
Books,	20.00
Wood,	18.00
Lights,	5.00
Total necessary expenses per annum,	$226.00 [10]

The naive section on "Morals and Deportment" is illuminating: "There has always been a strong religious element in the student-body. This took shape during the last session in a weekly prayer meeting, wholly gotten up and sustained among themselves without suggestion from any quarter. There was not a riotous or tumultuous gathering of any sort among the students during the last session, and there was only one expulsion of a student for improper conduct. We have been assured both by the Faculty and by the citizens of Oxford, that since the war, drinking, gambling, extravagance and dissipation of every kind has been yearly diminishing, until it is believed to have reached the minimum point. We were told by several of the students that they had never seen nor heard of a card being played for money in the University, and that they did not believe there was a boy in college who gambled. It was the remark of one of the most observant professors, that he had been more or less connected with colleges all his life, but that he had never seen one where there was so little dissipation as at the University of Mississippi. The truth is, there are no sons of rich men there, as there were before the war, and as there are still at Northern and Eastern institutions, who have gone to college simply for the sake of appearance, and who spend their time in frolicing and dissipation, alike regardless of money and the benefits of an education." [11]

The curriculum was briefly mentioned and the remarkable apparatus and equipment discussed in ample detail. Then the Trustees concluded with a fervent appeal: "We long to see the halls of our State University crowded to overflowing with eager, ambitious and studious young men. We long to see her Commencement Day a gala occasion, attracting crowds far and near to fill her campus and her Chapel; to see the distinguished men of the State seated on the rostrum listening to the youthful orators who rise with swelling hearts to make their first attempts before such hearers; to see our newspapers represented by busy reporters, each hastening to give to the public the earliest and fullest account of the Commencement Exercises; to see the audience room crowded with happy mothers and sisters and sweethearts smiling with tearful joy as the young men bid adieu to the scenes of *Alma Mater*, and step forth to meet the stern realities of active life. These are the scenes which are witnessed each year at Charlottesville and Cornell, and Yale, and Harvard, and Dartmouth. It depends upon you, fellow citizens, to say whether they shall be witnessed at *the* University of Mississippi." [12]

The effect of the address was not felt during the session of 1876–1877, but was evident the following academic year, when the enrollment rose to four hundred seventy-one, a height hitherto unachieved and not to be regained until the twentieth century.[13] Of this total, however, it must be noted that two hundred fifty-nine were students in the preparatory division. Although the number of the next session was down to three hundred nineteen, the proportion was better, since only ninety-three were preparatory boys.[14] The drop in the autumn of 1878 was probably due in part to the great epidemic of yellow fever. The opening of the University had to be delayed from September 26 to November 21 because of this.[15]

The new regime at the University was to be characterized by economy and severity. In its dying days, the Reconstruction Board had realized that the extravagant appropriations of the legislature were mere words. Even then the need for retrenchment was felt and the Board had reduced the salaries of the professors.[16] The law department had already been abandoned at the end of the school year of 1873–1874 and was not revived until January, 1877. Typical of the movement toward a reduction of the budget was the decision in 1877 to require the duties of librarian to be performed by the janitor.[17] Exactly a year later the Board proceeded to the election of the janitor-librarian.[18] This combination remained in effect until 1882, when the offices were again separated.[19]

A conscious effort was made to disabuse the public mind of the persistent idea that it was a rich man's school. The Trustees had said in their address, "The University of Mississippi is emphatically a 'Poor Man's College,'" [20] and were now trying to reinforce their statement. Tuition for students from within the state had been discontinued in 1871 but revived in 1876. Now in 1877 it was once more discontinued.[21] This partially accounts for the large enrollment during the autumn of 1877. It was also ordered that students be required to clean and scour their own rooms instead of employing servants: once a week there would be an inspection by a faculty member, "as is customary at West Point and other Military Schools." [22] Stewart's hand is clearly seen in the action.

A significant action was taken by the Board on June 30, 1881: on that day a motion was made and seconded that fraternities and secret societies be abolished at the University of Mississippi. The motion carried, but was rescinded later the same day.[23] That is the first important reference to fraternities in the manuscript minutes of the Board of Trustees, although they had been on the campus since 1850. The matter was one of increasing concern to the authorities and was to reach impressive proportions in the early decades of the twentieth century. The feeling back of the action of 1881 seems to have been threefold. First, the Board was at the moment very sensitive to the common criticism of the University as a place for wealthy men's sons only: it was making a determined effort to destroy that impression. Moreover, as will be noted below, the students of the time were rapidly losing all sense of restraint and the need for some singular disciplinary measure was imperative. Finally, the Trustees were taking seriously the assurance that life was real and earnest—the Puritan ideal was supplanting that of the Cavalier in the South.

In 1876 they "Ordered, that the Christmas Holidays be abolished & there shall be no suspension of exercises except on 25 Dec & 1st January." [24] In 1877 they resolved to memorialize the legislature to prohibit the keeping of billiard saloons and ten-pin alleys within five miles of the University.[25] In 1882, to the request that attendance at chapel be made voluntary, they gave an emphatic negative reply and insisted, with almost fanatical zeal, "That the entire Faculty should daily attend the same—except the Law Professor." [26]

The memorial to the legislature had the desired result. It was enacted into law on February 28, 1878, under penalty of a fifty-dollar fine or a thirty-day imprisonment or both.[27] At the same time there was reenacted a law, in effect since 1844 and confirmed by successive legislatures, that, under threat of similar punishment, no one "shall sell or give away vinous, spirituous or malt liquors within five miles of the University of Mississippi . . . ," except for medical or sacramental purposes.[28]

To provide still further for poorer youth to attend the University, Dr. Cowles M. Vaiden, a Trustee, began the practice in 1877 of advancing money to indigent students on their personal notes. He continued to do so until his death in 1880. The extent of his generosity is suggested by the fact that at one period there were a hundred "Vaiden Beneficiaries" enrolled at the school.[29] Of more importance, however, were the Labauve scholarships. Colonel Felix Labauve, born in France but an adopted citizen of DeSoto county, who died June 12, 1879, left a great portion of his estate to the University for the education of worthy orphans of his county.[30] As late as 1923 it was said of Labauve that he was "the only Mississippian (a foreigner by birth and a [Roman] Catholic) to make permanent provision for the education of indigent youths of the state. . . ."[31]

In addition to retrenchment and belated Puritanism, Stewart's regime as chancellor may also be characterized as one of progress, as paradoxical as that may seem. The greatest achievement of the period was undoubtedly that of securing from the state an acknowledgment of its indebtedness to the University in regard to the seminary fund—no mean accomplishment.

The disastrous loss resulting from the sale of the lands originally given by the Federal government has already been referred to above. The research done on the matter by Barnard, conveyed by Jacob Thompson to Governor McRae, and by him to the legislature, has also been noted. The state had continued to ignore its debt to the University and to make appropriations to it as to a pensioner, instead of as a creditor. The matter had been timidly broached by Waddel in the early days after the War Between the States. At Waddel's request Landon C. Garland, then professor of analytical physics and astronomy at the University of Mississippi (from 1875 to 1893 the first chancellor of Vanderbilt), made a calculation which showed the state's indebtedness to the University to be a million and a half dollars, even after deducting all appropriations.[32]

Under Stewart the issue was to be pressed to a satisfactory conclusion which would settle the principle of the matter, if not the amount. From the records of both faculty and Board it would seem that the credit for the achievement goes largely to the Trustees and more particularly to their secretary, Hampton M. Sullivan, an attorney of Oxford. But there is no doubt of Stewart's acute interest. Every summer since 1875 he had made numerous trips throughout the state speaking in behalf of the University and thus creating an atmosphere of goodwill for the school and its claims. Professor Edward Mayes of the law department was also instrumental in the consummation of this long-deferred hope: he later became the stalwart defender of the settlement.[33]

One of the first steps taken by the Board was the compilation by Sullivan of all the laws relating to the University of Mississippi.[34] The pamphlet included acts of the national Congress and of the state legislature, a memorial of the Board to the Senate and House of Representatives of Mississippi (1856), a special message of Governor McRae to the legislature (1856), and a schedule of the credit due on the seminary fund as of January 1, 1856. It was printed and distributed in late 1879 by order of the executive committee of the Board.

Early in 1880 the Board appointed a committee of four of its members—H. H. Chalmers, W. P. Harris, H. F. Simrall, and Sullivan—to memorialize the legislature and present the claims of the University.[35] An able statement of the needs and claims was prepared, concluding with an appeal to the lawmakers to provide the University with such liberal support as to cause it to be "the intellectual focus of the State, the centre of free inquiry, the crown of our educational system, the pride and glory of our people, and a seat of learning whose renown shall attract crowds from all parts of the earth, as did Cambridge, Bologna and Oxford of old." [36] On February 9 the Senate ordered the printing and distribution of two hundred fifty copies of the memorial.[37]

A joint committee on the University had been authorized to investigate the condition of the seminary fund and to report on it. The aid of C. A. Brougher, an accountant and business man of Jackson, was secured for the purpose. The result was Senate Bill 198, referred to the judiciary committee. The latter body disagreed: the majority favored passage: the minority asked for continued investigation.[38] The Senate, however, passed the bill by a vote of eighteen to twelve and sent it to the House of Representatives.[39] There the bill was passed by a vote of forty-two to forty, thirty-eight members being absent and not voting, two being paired. It became law on March 5, 1880.[40] On the same day the leased lands of the University, on which houses providing inexpensive boarding for the students had been built, were declared exempt from state, county, and municipal taxation.[41] Previously, on January 31, the same action had been taken with regard to that part of the Labauve trust fund which went into scholarships for University students.[42]

The act, so full of significance for the honor of the state and the financial stability of the University, deserves to be reproduced in full:

> AN ACT to provide for the ascertainment of the indebtedness of the State on account of the Seminary Fund, and for the payment of the interest thereon.
> WHEREAS, Under an Act of Congress providing for a grant of land for the support of a Seminary of Learning within the State of Mississippi, the Legislature of this State by enactment thereof accepted the said grant in trust, for the purpose mentioned in said Act of Congress; and
> WHEREAS, Under an Act of the Legislature of the State of Mississippi, approved March 2, 1833, the Governor of Mississippi was au-

thorized and required to appoint Commissioners to estimate the value of said lands, and have the same sold, and the proceeds returned to the treasury, for and in aid of the trust enumerated in said grant; and

WHEREAS, Under the Act entitled an Act to incorporate the University of Mississippi, approved February 24, 1844, the proceeds of the sale of the land granted by the Act of Congress aforesaid were vested, when collected, in the Board of Trustees of the said University of Mississippi, in aid of the original Act of Congress; and

WHEREAS, The State of Mississippi did collect the proceeds arising from the sale of said lands, and has never accounted for the same to the University of Mississippi; and

WHEREAS, The Joint Committee on Universities as instructed by the concurrent resolution adopted at the present session of the Legislature, have fully investigated the condition of the account of the State with said University, in respect to said fund, and have reported the sum of $544,061.23, as ascertained by the statement of said account made by C. A. Brougher, Esq., under the direction of said committee, to be the amount of the indebtedness of the State to said University on account of said Seminary Fund; now, therefore,

SECTION 1. Be it enacted by the Legislature of the State of Mississippi, That the indebtedness of the State on account of said Seminary Fund so held in trust as aforesaid, be and the same is hereby acknowledged to be the said sum of five hundred and forty-four thousand and sixty-one dollars and twenty-three cents.

SECTION 2. Be it further enacted, That said sum so ascertained to be due shall bear interest at the rate of six per centum per annum, from the first day of January, 1880, which said interest shall be payable out of the State Treasury quarterly, on the first days of January, April, July and October, in each year hereafter; and on the application of the Treasurer of said University, the Auditor of Public Accounts is hereby authorized and required to issue his warrant for the said installments of interest, in favor of the Treasurer of said University, on the Treasurer of the State.

SEC. 3. Be it further enacted, That the sum of thirty-two thousand six hundred and forty-three dollars ($32,643.00) be and the same is hereby appropriated for the year 1880, and annually thereafter, for the purpose of paying the interest due on said sum of five hundred and forty-four thousand sixty-one dollars and twenty-three cents ($544,061.23).

SEC. 4. Be it further enacted, That this act take effect and be in force from and after its passage.[43]

The faculty subsequently approved and transmitted to the Trustees a series of resolutions congratulating the Board on its successful effort and extending high praise in particular to Sullivan.[44] Chancellor Stewart himself read the resolutions before a meeting of the Board. The Trustees concurred in them and complimented its committee which had done the major portion of the work attached to the accomplishment.[45]

Sullivan further demonstrated his leadership by his efforts toward making the University coeducational. He was joined, strange as it may seem, by Judge Alexander M. Clayton, the senior Trustee both in age and in point of service on the Board. The question of state-supported education for women had been bruited as early as 1856, by Miss Sallie Eola Reneau of Grenada.[46] In that year an act was passed establishing a female college, but it was not carried into effect because of lack of endowment. Miss Reenau did not relax her efforts. She continued her propaganda and in 1872 secured an elaborate amendment to the charter of the University of Mississippi which created the "Reneau Female University of Mississippi at Oxford."[47] The chancellor of the University would be the *ex officio* president and Miss Reneau and her successors as principal of the "female department" would be *ex officio* the vice-president of the University of Mississippi. Ten months later, February 15, 1873, this legislation was repealed and thereafter Miss Reneau apparently deemed the matter hopeless.

From 1879 to 1884 Mrs. Ephraim G. (Annie Coleman) Peyton of Copiah county urged the state, through articles in the newspapers and pressure on the legislature, to make liberal provision "for the education of our daughters." In 1884 her object was fulfilled by the establishment of the Mississippi Industrial Institute and College for the Education of White Girls of Mississippi in the Arts and Sciences (now called Mississippi State College for Women) at Columbus. The school opened in the autumn of 1885.[48]

Meanwhile, despite serious opposition, Sullivan and Clayton succeeded in overcoming the objections and on June 28, 1882, the Board of the University voted to admit "females" on the same basis as men, except in the preparatory division.[49] Several attempts later to rescind the action failed and the school has remained coeducational ever since. No provision was made at this time for housing and boarding women students. The resolution admitting them stated that "no female student shall be permitted to board or lodge on the Campus, except in the homes of members of the Faculty." [50] For several years most of the girls were from the county and hence lived at home. Others lived with relatives or friends of their families. The first student body to include women had only eleven in a total enrollment of two hundred fifty-nine.[51] Six were from Lafayette county, one being the daughter of Professor Quinche. The first graduating class with women in it was that of 1885. It is worthy of note that of the honor "men" the highest ranking was Miss Sallie Vick Hill, who, singularly enough, took the Bachelor of Science degree[52] and became a member of the original faculty of the newly organized Industrial Institute and College for Women. Four years later Mayes wrote that most of the girls who came were desiring "to qualify themselves to teach." [53] It was a sedate group of young ladies who invaded these masculine precincts. In 1903 a dormitory was erected on the campus for them. Four years earlier a national sorority chartered a chapter at the University.

In addition to the admission of women to the University, the election of the first woman to the faculty also occurred during the period of Stewart's chancellorship. This was Miss Sarah McGehee Isom, daughter of the pioneer physician of Oxford referred to earlier. She was designated by the Board in the autumn of 1885 to teach elocution.[54] Her own description of her work was pretentious. It included physical training, respiration, vocal culture, articulation, orthoepy, gesture, the laws of inflection and emphasis, analysis in reading, dramatic and practical reading, artistic and oratorical recitations! [55]

Rhetoric, declamation, and speech-making had been stressed from the beginning of the University, but it was now raised to the dignity of a separate department in the curriculum. It has been said that in their love of oratory Southerners are thoroughly Greek. How true that was (it still is) may be illustrated by an account of one of the commencement occasions (that of June, 1876) during the regime of Chancellor Stewart.[56] Friday and Saturday nights were devoted to freshman declamations. On Sunday morning came the baccalaureate sermon in the University chapel. On Monday morning occurred the sophomore prize declamations with fourteen speakers. That afternoon the commencement preacher spoke again, and that night there was the annual meeting of the Phi Sigma literary society with three speakers and "miscellaneous addresses." The following day twelve students delivered speeches at the junior exhibition and that night at the annual meeting of the Hermaean literary society there were three speakers and "miscellaneous addresses." Wednesday morning was the occasion of the annual oration before the two literary societies, and the commencement preacher was also called upon for "a very few appropriate remarks." That night was devoted to the meeting of the alumni, the feature of which was an address. Thursday was commencement day. The program was as follows:

ORDER OF EXERCISES

Prayer. *Music.*

1. Greek Salutatory.   S. A. Witherspoon, Oxford, Miss.
2. Epitome   A. N. W. Smith, Erata, Miss.

Music.

3. The Frozen Dew-drop Chills the Tender Bud.
   S. L. Ledbetter, Tupelo, Miss.

4. Tyranny, the Harbinger of Civil Liberty.
>J. C. Foster, Louisville, Miss.

Music.

5. "All the World's a Stage, and all the Men and Women Merely Players."   J. F. Williamson, Sardis, Miss.
6. False Perspective.   Wm. M. Bingham, Enterprise, Miss.

Music.

7. Philosophical Oration—Thoughts Suggested by the Study of Natural Philosophy.   J. F. Rives, Jr., Hinds County, Miss.
8. The Glory of the English Race.
>S. A. Witherspoon, Oxford, Miss.

Music.

Intermission.

Music.

9. "The Suffering of Rights are Graven Deepest on the Chronicles of Nations."   R. H. Turnstall, Holly Springs, Miss.
10. Mississippi.   J. W. Kilpatrick, Corinth, Miss.

Music.

11. "Progress of the Age."   C. T. Cooper, Holly Springs, Miss.
12. Coming Events Cast their Shadows Before.
>F. E. Love, Vicksburg, Miss.

Music.

13. Determination Insures Success.
>J. W. Johnson, Pontotoc, Miss.
14. Nobility of Woman.   Jas. A. Isom, Oxford, Miss.

Music.

15. The Relation Existing Between the Thalassicola of the Radiolaria, and the Rhamphorhynchus of the Pterosauria.
>E. H. Dial, Meridian, Miss.

Music.

Awarding of Prizes and Conferring of Degrees.

Music.

16. Valedictory.   T. D. Greenwood, Okolona, Miss.

Music.

Benediction.

The only breaks in this orgy of talk were the chancellor's levee and the commencement ball. The former normally occurred on Wednesday evening but in 1876 was prevented by rain. The latter was the grand finale, the climax of the week, coming on Thursday night.

A significant change which was made during Stewart's period at the University of Mississippi marked the end of one era and the beginning of a newer phase in the history of the institution. In 1884 the Board "Resolved that hereafter all diplomas shall be in the English language," and so they have remained ever since.[57] Before this time they had, of course, been in Latin, but already the old learning which had dominated the schools of Western civilization ever since the Renaissance was in decline.

Certain changes in the policy of conferring honorary degrees were also made. The first was a decision to cease entirely from conferring the degree of Doctor of Divinity.[58] This was in accordance with a recommendation of the faculty.[59] From 1856 to 1882 twenty-five men had received the degree.[60] The number hardly indicates an abuse of the authority to confer the degree, but it was probably felt not to be entirely proper for a state-supported institution to do it. The Board was presumably right, but a touch of pathos enters the picture at this point.

Only the year before (1882) the degree had been conferred on the illustrious Methodist minister (soon to be a bishop—in 1886), the Reverend Charles B. Galloway, an alumnus of the class of 1868 and at that time a member of the Board of Trustees.[61] No degree was more justly merited, for Bishop Galloway has left his stamp on Mississippi. In the same graduation class of 1868 the first honor man had been Cornelius W. Grafton, who from 1873 to 1934 was pastor of the Presbyterian church of Union Church, a tiny village of Jefferson county, far out in the country, and who in 1916–1917 was to receive the highest honor his denomination could give, the position of Moderator of the General Assembly.[62] Galloway and Grafton were the most intimate of friends. In 1885, therefore, Galloway, unaware of the previous decision of the Board which had been passed in his absence, recommended his friend for the honorary degree of Doctor of Divinity.[63] The Board declined to reconsider its decision and Grafton had to wait ten years before receiving the degree, not from his alma mater but from the Southwestern Presbyterian University, Clarksville, Tennessee. The University of Mississippi rectified its failure thirty years later by giving him the Doctor of Laws.[64]

A similar situation, probably more embarrassing to the Trustees, occurred at the same meeting in 1885, in connection with the degree of Doctor of Laws. The Trustees had just "Resolved that it is the sense of the Board that the degree of LLD should only be conferred upon those who have made the Jurisprudence Common or Civil Law a special study." [65] Only two days earlier, at an informal meeting held without the chancellor's knowledge, the faculty had voted unanimously to petition the Board to confer that honor upon Stewart. Vice-chancellor Wheat communicated the request to the Trustees on June 24. It was too late: the Board could hardly reverse its own resolution passed only an hour or two ago.[66] Stewart was later so honored by Cumberland University and the Royal Historical Society made him a fellow.[67]

In the early days after the war the student body had been a serious group, but now the pressure of external events had been relaxed and all the old boisterous verve and lilt returned with renewed vigor. In 1880 Judge Chalmers, a Trustee mentioned earlier, wrote to the chancellor to the effect that undesirable reports were being made throughout the state concerning the immorality and intemperance at the University.[68] There had been such cases, along with drunkenness and shooting affrays.[69] Disorders had occurred at the most unlikely times and severe measures had to be adopted in the attempt to suppress them, as can be seen by reading between the lines of an action of the Board: "Resolved: That there be paid to each of the special police appointed by the sheriff to preserve order during the Commencement exercises including those at night, and including the Commencement Ball, the sum of $3.00 per day each, day and night." [70] Since hazing was reaching malicious and hazardous proportions, long resolutions were passed trying to restrain it by appealing to the sense of chivalry.[71]

Judge Chalmers's letter was discussed in the faculty meeting. The decision reached was that each member of the faculty should report all students seen off the campus or even out of their rooms during the regular study hours.[72] This action was probably effective for the moment, but not for long. The following spring a flagrantly notorious situation was discovered. Chancellor Stewart reported that he had found a lewd woman in the room of a student and was informed that several students had visited her during the day. The student in whose room she was found was immediately expelled: the case of the others was to be investigated. The faculty was mortified, but was also convinced that some of the blame lay with "corrupting influences in the town of Oxford." Hoping in a measure to check these, the chancellor was directed to inform the postmistress of Oxford about the conduct of her deputies and to threaten that if she could not correct the evil the faculty would feel constrained to lodge a complaint with the Postmaster General in Washington.[73]

And so disorders continued. One student, charged with numerous offenses, admitted only that he had voted illegally in Oxford although merely sixteen years of age! [74] The students continued to pelt stones at the trains as they passed through or stopped at the station [75] and to go to Water Valley for riotous occasions.[76] Stewart struggled against such activity valiantly but in vain. Deeply concerned for the welfare of the students, he strove by private conferences and by earnest chapel talks to bring about more restraint and discipline, but in the end the turbulence was probably one of the reasons for his decision to resign.[77]

There were not many changes in the faculty during Stewart's term of office. Landon C. Garland, professor of analytical physics and astronomy, whose coming to the University in 1867 has already been noted, left during the period. Elected first chancellor of Vanderbilt University in 1875, he arranged with his colleagues such an exchange of hours that he was able to complete his teaching in Mississippi by April 1. He then went to Europe to purchase technical apparatus for Vanderbilt before assuming the duties of his new office.[78] The following year the Board of Trustees received a claim from Garland for pay for the months of April, May, and June, 1875. The Board disallowed it.[79] But Garland did not permit the matter to rest. Early in the year 1880 he instituted a suit against the University and employed as counsel the eminent Wiley P. Harris, a former Trustee.[80] J. A. Orr, a Trustee, was retained by the Board to defend the case. The matter was satisfactorily settled out of court.

Garland's successor at the University of Mississippi was his son-in-law, Robert B. Fulton, first man of the graduates of 1869 and later to become chancellor of the University. Fulton had already come to the faculty as a tutor in 1871 and in 1872 was serving as adjunct professor in Garland's department. Edward Mayes, who would succeed Stewart and precede Fulton in presiding over the destiny of the institution, was also on the teaching staff. He was an alumnus of the class of 1868 and had finished the law school the following year. During the session of 1869–1870 he served as a tutor, but then began private practice. He was summoned in 1877 to the professorship of law, in which capacity he remained until 1892.

Stewart's days at the University of Mississippi were now drawing to a close. At the regular meeting of the Board in June, 1886, it was decided that a complete reorganization of the University should be undertaken. To achieve that end all the chairs were peremptorily declared vacant and an election of professors to fill the chairs was held. Stewart was immediately reelected, as indeed were all the other members of the faculty, although Wheat was moved from the chair of Greek to that of metaphysics.[81] But the action of the Board must have been a stinging blow to Stewart's pride. By the time the faculty heard of the action, the Board had adjourned. After giving thought to the matter, realizing the burden involved in reorganizing the curriculum, and feeling his advanced age of sixty-five, Stewart determined to resign in a dignified manner and did so at an adjourned meeting of the Trustees a month later.[82]

CHAPTER IX

The Majesty of the Law

WITH the resignation of Stewart, the Board abolished the office of chancellor and ordered the faculty to elect a chairman as the presiding officer of the University. The faculty met and by acclamation unanimously elected its law professor, Edward Mayes, to the position.[1] Dr. Wheat was still the senior professor and *ex officio* vice-chancellor, but he was now sixty years of age. Mayes was not quite forty.

Mayes was the first chief executive of the University chosen from among the alumni and also the first native Mississippian so honored.[2] Born in Hinds county, December 15, 1846, he had one year of undergraduate work at Bethany College in Virginia (now West Virginia) before the War Between the States. After serving briefly in the Confederate army he entered the University of Mississippi in the autumn of 1865. The Bachelor of Arts degree was conferred on him in 1868 and the degree of Bachelor of Laws the following year. He served one year on the faculty as a tutor in English before beginning the practice of law, first in Coffeeville, then in Oxford. In 1877 he came to the chair of law in the University and held it as long as he remained there, performing that task in addition to his function as chairman of the faculty and later as chancellor. It is of interest to note that he married a daughter of L. Q. C. Lamar and granddaughter of Judge Longstreet.[3]

At the expiration of his first year as chairman, Mayes called the attention of the faculty to the fact that the Board had fixed no definite period during which he should serve. The way was therefore open for rotation in this office. But he was again elected by a unanimous vote.[4] The following year the same disposition was made of the matter.[5]

In conformity with law and custom, Chairman Mayes made his annual report to the Board of Trustees. The report in the summer of 1889 was an elaborate one outlining a thorough reorganization of the curriculum and of the faculty. The recommendation that the office of chancellor be restored was adopted and Mayes himself was chosen to the position.[6] There had been some feeling that, as the elective chairman of the faculty, the presiding officer was the creature of the faculty, not of the Board.

The organization of the curriculum was an outstanding development. The department of science, literature, and the arts had provided three degrees, Bachelor of Arts, Bachelor of Science, and Bachelor of Philosophy. The work for the Bachelor of Arts and Bachelor of Science degrees was fairly strictly defined, but the work for the Bachelor of Philosophy degree was almost entirely elective. Under the new system the department was divided into nineteen (later twenty) "schools," each independent of the others. Seventy-five hours of satisfactory work done in any of the schools would entitle a student to a degree. If the major portion of study had been done in Latin, Greek, English, and pure mathematics, the degree would be that of Bachelor of Arts; if in zoology, mineralogy, geology, theoretical and practical chemistry, mathematics, physics, and astronomy, it would be the Bachelor of Science degree; and any courses taken, provided the necessary seventy-five hours were completed, would entitle one to the Bachelor of Philosophy degree. The scope for electives was thus widened; provision was made for advanced standing on the basis of examinations; and allowance was made for the completion of an entire course for one degree in three years.[7]

The "schools" were the usual courses in the arts and sciences, with the addition of belles-lettres (and later elocution). The English department had been giving overshadowing prominence to the study of Anglo-Saxon and the historical development of the English language to the neglect of literature. Chancellor Mayes, who had himself tutored in English literature and possessed considerable literary attainments, recommended this innovation—this study of "mere literature." He has described it thus: "It ... assumes that the student has, in the study of the five schools of ancient and modern languages [Latin, Greek, French, German, and English], acquired a certain acquaintance with their respective literatures, and embraces, so far as is possible in the time allotted [one year], a consideration of the best authors of all tongues and nationalities, without regard to the language, and with especial attention to the interrelations of national literatures to literary criticism and to the philosophy of literature." [8]

In order to stimulate attendance, Mayes canvassed the state during the summer of 1889, making addresses on the history, work, and status of the University. He spoke at twenty-three towns in all sections of the state. As a result of this effort there was an appreciable increase in enrollment.[9] Indeed Mayes's energy was almost unbounded. His vigorous activity had been demonstrated as early as 1887. In that year the catalogue had carried a statement, written by him, on "The Financial History of the University." [10] It was an analysis of the settlement of 1880, in which the state acknowledged its indebtedness to the University in regard to the seminary fund. Such a résumé of the matter was entirely appropriate for an edition of the University bulletin which was intended as one of the usual historical catalogues. But the matter was not to rest obscurely in that publication.

There had been an undercurrent of discussion in the state ever since the adjudication by the legislature of 1880. Now this catalogue came into the hands of a former Trustee (1878–1880), Senator James Z. George, who immediately took exception to Mayes's position there stated, in a series of three letters to the newspapers, entitled "An Investigation Into the Legal Obligations and Indebtedness of the State to the A. & M. College, the Industrial Female Institute, and the State University." [11] George contended that the legislature had created a debt where none existed and asserted that "as long as that act of 1880 remains on the statute book, it will be a fraud on the people of the State, as it is now a grave error and burden, though founded on an innocent mistake." [12]

Mayes met the issue in a masterly letter:

> I maintain that the Senator's argument is fallacious and misleading, and his conclusions wholly mistaken and untenable, for the following general reasons:
> FIRST.—He has overlooked facts vitally important to the proper determination of the issue presented by him.
> SECONDLY.—He has assumed, and positively announced as existent and material facts, things many of which are unsustained by proof, and some of which can be shown to have no existence except in his fancy.
> THIRDLY.—He has totally misconceived the import of the statutes of the State and of the United States, which bear on and largely control this matter; and,
> FOURTHLY.—He has invoked and applied here principles of law which have no application; overlooking or ignoring distinctions so obvious to a trained legal mind, that I should not have believed it possible to overlook or ignore them except for the fact that the undoubtedly able Senator has done so.[13]

Both the statement by George and the rebuttal by Mayes have been used extensively earlier in this history and require no further treatment. Suffice it to say that the controversy failed to disturb the settlement of 1880: it is still in effect, largely because of the impressive presentation made by Mayes. George himself was apparently convinced and later shared an important part in securing for the University an additional grant of land from the United States Congress.

Mayes took a great deal of interest also in the physical aspect of the University. It was during his term of office that a number of improvements were made: dormitories and faculty residences were renovated, brick walks were laid on the campus, a library building was erected (now the geology building), and the entire library was reclassified.[14] All this was overdue, of course, but it was the first time since the war that the University had been financially able to carry through such a program. It was indeed the first time since the days of Chancellor Barnard. When Mayes left, the University owned twenty-three buildings: six for administrative offices, lecture rooms, laboratories, library, and chapel, three dormitories, one gymnasium, one carpenter shop, and twelve residences.[15] One fraternity house had also been erected, held by a qualified fee from the University.[16] A University postoffice separate from that of the town of Oxford was also established.[17]

It was inevitable that Mayes's vigor and tireless energy would sooner or later provoke dissatisfaction just as Barnard's had. It came sooner than might have been expected. In connection with the reorganization of the curriculum, which occurred in the early summer of 1889, there had also been an upheaval in the faculty. Of the eight full professors (not counting Chairman Mayes, who was also professor of law), five were discharged. Two more resigned in accordance with their previously announced intention.

There had already been opposition among the students to some of these professors. About six months before the dismissals, the steps of the Lyceum had been painted in red with the nicknames of three professors and the words, "New blood wanted." [18] Mayes disciplined the culprits, but was probably impressed with the demonstration.

His recommendations to the Trustees and their action set in motion a heated discussion in the town of Oxford and ultimately throughout the state. Some of the oldest and most beloved professors (under whom Mayes himself had been a student) were involved. The suicide of one of these came a month or two later.[19] The result was a newspaper controversy in which Mayes's motives and actions were impugned. The chancellor was able to answer the charges successfully and to weather the storm. The Board gave him virtually unlimited authority in matters affecting the internal life of the University. The resolution is worthy of quotation:

> RESOLVED—that the Chancellor is hereby empowered in consultation with the faculty [by now hand-picked by Mayes] to determine the course of instruction in any school or department,—to prescribe what text books shall be used, and to arrange the hours of daily study, religious exercises and recitations.[20]

A progressive step taken under Mayes was the establishment of fellowships. The first one was authorized in 1887 in the department of chemistry. Four others, in mathematics, English, physics, and natural history, were set up in 1890. The fellows were to be postgraduates preparing to teach and were actively to assist in the departments to which they were assigned.[21] The first fellow of the University was John W. Provine, who served in the department of chemistry from his graduation with the Bachelor of Science degree in 1889 to 1890. He later became the president of Mississippi College, a Baptist liberal arts institution in Clinton.

A link between the days of Chancellor Mayes and the centennial year was Chancellor Emeritus Alfred Hume. According to the minutes of the Board of Trustees, Dr. Hume was elected professor of mathematics on June 23, 1890, a position he still held as the "grand old man" of the University, beloved by hundreds of former students.[22] Another eminent new member of the faculty was the late Alexander L. Bondurant, for whom the present graduate building is named. He came to the University in 1889 as assistant professor of Latin and Greek. Promoted ultimately to the office of dean of the graduate school, he was associated with the University until his death in 1937.

The University was growing up and the student body was apparently maturing with it. Because of the development of the public school system, students were coming up to the University with better preparatory training than had been previously available.[23] There remained the perennial problem of student discipline, although to a lesser degree than it had existed in earlier days. The Board took cognizance of the need for some kind of police inspection to curb gambling [24] and set expulsion as the penalty for students caught playing cards on the campus "or any other place." [25] The mayor and aldermen of Oxford received complaints that students of the University caused great disturbances at the railway depot by rushing at the trains and running through them. They even felt the necessity of passing an ordinance defining as misdemeanors loud whistling, singing, shouting, boxing, running, wrestling, and other boisterous or offensive conduct on the sidewalks. The punishment in such cases was not less than one dollar and not more than five, in addition to all costs of conviction and collection of the fine.[26] Four years later the fine was increased to not less than two or more than ten dollars! [27]

There were still occasions when firearms were brandished and used.[28] There were intermittent but troublesome quarrels between students and blacks.[29] And in at least one instance a student, in order to avoid being summoned before a grand jury, left school for eight days.[30] But, all in all, self-restraint was becoming more evident at the University. The "lilt," however, remained, as one will observe in this passage from the minutes of the faculty: "Petitions were presented from Messrs H . . . and M . . . asking for leave of absence to attend the Mardi Gras. . . . The Faculty gave them leave to go, provided they think they can stand it." [31]

One of the most valuable services performed by Mayes during his chancellorship was the preparation of his *History of Education in Mississippi*. This was completed in 1891,[32] but was not published until 1899. Somewhat more than one-third of the book is devoted to a discussion of the University of Mississippi. Thus Mayes became the second formal historian of the institution, Waddel being the first. This book was probably an outgrowth of the chapter on "Educational History," which he had written for the Goodspeed Publishing Company's *Biographical and Historical Memoirs of Mississippi*, published in 1891.[33] Just the year before, Mayes had covered himself and the University with honor by the ability and legal talent he had displayed as chairman of the committee on the bill of rights in the convention which prepared the constitution under which the government of Mississippi still functions. He is credited with the electoral law of that constitution.[34] His reputation as a leading barrister of the state was reaching national proportions.

Mayes felt that he had now come to a parting of the ways, that he had to make a choice between his profession as an attorney and his position as chancellor of the state University. The law proved the stronger urge. In a letter, dated June 23, 1891, he announced to the Trustees his intention of resigning in the near future and suggested that they begin negotiations for a new presiding official for the University. The communication was read to the regular annual meeting of the Board the following day,[35] but no action was taken. The next Board meeting on record was one in December. There are no minutes of the particular session to which the actual resignation was presented and accepted. But at the December session it was noted that Mayes had resigned and that his term of office would close at the end of the month.[36] Robert B. Fulton, a member of the faculty in the department of physics and astronomy since 1871 and by virtue of seniority the vice-chancellor, was declared acting chancellor and was to take office January 1, 1892.[37] The last faculty meeting attended by Mayes was on December 1, 1891.[38] The other December minutes record the chancellor as absent and the vice-chancellor presiding. The minutes beginning in January, 1892, mention Fulton as chancellor or vice-chancellor.

CHAPTER X

How Firm a Foundation

FULTON was the acting executive officer of the University until June 28, 1892. On that date the Board of Trustees, then in regular session in Oxford, proceeded to the election of a successor to Mayes. By a vote of five to four, Fulton was chosen chancellor over Garvin D. Shands, a former lieutenant governor of the state, who would two years later come to the faculty as professor of law and in 1897 be made dean of the law school, the first dean the University was to have.[1]

Fulton, born in Sumter county, Alabama, in 1849, entered the University of Mississippi in 1866 and received his Bachelor of Arts degree in 1869. After teaching a short while in Alabama and Louisiana, he returned to the University in 1871 as a tutor in the department of physics and astronomy. The following year he was promoted to the rank of adjunct professor and in 1875 succeeded Dr. Garland as full professor. In the shake-up which occurred in 1889, he was the only one of this rank (apart from Mayes himself) to be retained on the faculty. His twenty years of service was now rewarded by his selection for the chancellorship.[2] It was destined to be an eventful and significant period in the history of the University.

On the day after his election, Fulton made a report embodying a proposal of great consequence for the institution: he had rediscovered the fact, apparently forgotten since the days of Chancellor Barnard, that the University was entitled to a Congressional grant of at least one more township of land from the public domain.[3] He requested the Board to refer the matter to a committee with power to

108

take such steps as might seem best for the interest of the University.

The Trustees, however, failed to act. The following year Fulton repeated the results of his investigation and also stated that his correspondence with the Mississippi members of the national Senate, James Z. George and Edward Cary Walthall, had caused him to believe that Congress might be favorable to a memorial from the Board and the state legislature.[4] The Board therefore authorized the chancellor to prepare the document for their signature. After considerable negotiation and delay the matter was brought to a satisfactory, though not entirely successful, conclusion on June 9, 1894. The memorial had asked for three additional townships (that is, 69,120 acres), but only one township (23,040 acres) was granted to the University.[5]

The land thus authorized was selected from part of the public domain in Harrison and Jackson counties by the Governor in 1895.[6] The following year the legislature placed it under the control of the Board of Trustees with full power to sell the timber and lease or sell the land[7] and so it has remained ever since. Senator George played a prominent part in securing the passage of the Congressional legislation.

From the very small beginning in 1848 and the new beginning in 1865 the University had grown slowly. The time was now ripe for still further expansion and Fulton was able, in spite of opposition, to make some remarkable advances. The initial step was taken when the preparatory department was abolished at the end of the session of 1892–1893. That function had been undertaken by the University after the War Between the States because of the students who came up to the institution with insufficient training. The public school system of the state had been developed since the war and had now reached a point where the University was no longer under the necessity of providing preparatory work. The University was free now to expand in the domain of more advanced learning.

To insure a continuous stream of students adequately prepared for college, Fulton took the initiative in an arrangement by which the high schools of the state entered into an affiliation with the University. The courses offered in these schools were subject to the inspection and approval of the appropriate authorities in the University and were thus accepted at face-value for the fulfillment of entrance requirements. Over a period of time more than eighty high schools entered this scheme.

In order further to improve the quality of secondary instruction in the state, the school of education (then called pedagogy) was inaugurated during the session of 1893–1894.[8] It had already been suggested by Mayes.[9] The State Board of Education agreed to grant permanent teaching certificates to those students who successfully completed the prescribed course.[10] The noble ideals of the new venture were expressed thus:

> "1. It will furnish well-trained and thoroughly educated teachers for the higher positions in the schools of the State.
> "2. It will cultivate and foster a professional spirit among the teachers, and stimulate to higher ideals and more efficient work in all parts of educational labor.
> "3. It will tend to unify the school-system, bringing all of the secondary institutions of the State into closer touch and harmony with the University, and with each other.
> "4. It will not only promote the study of educational science, but it will render important service in bringing about a just recognition of the work and influence of the teacher." [11]

In the spring of 1899 the University began to confer an appropriate degree, that of Bachelor of Pedagogy, but by 1906 this had been changed to the ordinary Bachelor of Arts or Bachelor of Science degree, with the specification that the degree was in education. The school was characterized by progress and in 1903 was reorganized with partial autonomy under its own dean.

A related activity was the inauguration of the summer school session. In the autumn of 1892 the faculty began to make the necessary arrangements along the lines of extension work. During the academic year "institutes" were held in several of the larger towns of the state. In January, 1893, the State Superintendent of Education placed a part of the Peabody fund at the disposal of the University to be used in the training of teachers. He also agreed to combine his work with what was proposed by the University.

The result was the first summer session in June and July, 1893. A training school for those who conducted county teachers' institutes was held. Another was provided for the teachers themselves and a course in physics was offered. In the following years similar work was provided with fluctuating success, attendance varying between two hundred and five hundred students. Because of lack of funds there was no noteworthy expansion in the subjects which were offered.

New life was given to the summer session in 1900 through the philanthropy of Mrs. Fanny J. Ricks of Yazoo City, a benefactress of the University, whose name is now commemorated on a women's dormitory. Through her liberality a greatly increased schedule of studies was offered during the summers of 1900 through 1903. In the latter year she secured additional funds which still further enlarged the scope and usefulness of the work. The opportunity for study was now opened not only to teachers, but also to students desiring to advance more rapidly than the ordinary session allowed, to entering collegians who sought advanced standing in particular fields, and to graduate students.

High hopes were held for this program. The summer term was to become a rallying point for the educational forces of the state and it was believed that the results would mark an important epoch in educational advancement in Mississippi. The eventuality fully justified the hope.[12]

Still further progress was made at the University by the establishment in the autumn of 1900 of a school of engineering. It had been attempted on a minor scale twice before, in 1865–1868 under General Shoup and in 1872–1875 under General Sears. During these years only twenty students became candidates for the degree of Civil Engineer and of those only two pursued the prescribed course to the end and actually received the degree. In 1900, however, the school was based on a fairly secure foundation, although the equipment was meager and extensive work was impossible.

In 1903 the legislature appropriated money for the addition of wings to the Lyceum building. The space thus provided made the work of the engineering school easier and more efficient. The courses were expanded and included surveying, drawing, electrical engineering, analytical mechanics, descriptive geometry, and roofs and bridges. Growth was steady until 1906, when retrenchment became necessary because of lack of funds.[13]

An important development during Fulton's term of office as chancellor came with the creation of the medical department, which also took place in 1903. It had been projected as early as 1870 and a statement that such a professional school would be established at an early date occurred in the University bulletin as late as 1879. The matter then lay in abeyance until Fulton began to press it.

The inauguration of the course encountered many difficulties. The space provided was exceedingly restricted and instruction was limited to the first two years of medical work only. The problem of securing cadavers for dissection proved to be a troublesome one, which was solved only in 1906. But there was a steady increase in attendance and it was felt that the quality of the students was improving.[14] A member of the original medical faculty, Dr. P. W. Rowland, discovered the value of the deeply implanted use of oxygen in cases of lobar pneumonia and made it a part of clinical procedure.[15]

The physical development which had begun under Mayes received a renewed and spirited impetus under Fulton. Electric lights were installed at the turn of the century.[16] Telephones came into use four years later. The waterworks were improved and the use of steam heating replaced the use of the more primitive stoves and fireplaces.[17]

Vastly more important was the repairing of the old buildings and the erection of new ones.[18] The first dormitory for women was completed in 1903 and named for Mrs. Ricks, as noted earlier. The way was prepared in this way for a larger enrollment of women students. In 1904 funds were made available for the construction of an infirmary to accommodate students in case of illness. In the fifteen years of Fulton's tenure of office the student body, the teaching staff, and the annual revenues of the University had doubled.

Although the extensive building program was a necessary and progressive step, not all of it was as pleasing to the eye as it might have been. For instance, in 1903 the addition of wings to the north and south sides of the Lyceum was authorized. The construction was completed in the following year, but the chaste, classic beauty of the glorious old Greek Revival structure was marred.[19]

Among those who came to the faculty during this era two served until recently. David H. Bishop, late dean emeritus of the graduate school, received his initial appointment in 1904 as professor of English, rhetoric, and belles-lettres. The following year the name of the department was changed to English language and literature. James W. Bell, the late dean emeritus of the school of commerce and business administration, received his Bachelor of Philosophy degree from the University in 1898. After a period of teaching in the public schools of the state, he returned to the University as assistant professor of pedagogy (education) for the session of 1903–1904. Later he moved into the department of mathematics, and then into economics and political science.[20]

Two other remarkable men now deceased were also members of the faculty about the beginning of the twentieth century, Paul H. Saunders and Calvin S. Brown. Saunders, a native Mississippian who received his Bachelor of Arts degree from the University in 1890 and his Master of Arts the following year, was one of the three who have received a Doctor of Philosophy degree from this institution. It was conferred upon him at the commencement of 1894. From 1890 to 1892 he was a fellow in the department of mathematics. For three years, 1892–1895, he was assistant professor of Latin and Greek, but in 1895 he was appointed professor of Greek. He served until 1905, when he resigned to enter the business world by becoming president of a bank in Laurel. Ultimately he rose to high position as a leading capitalist and philanthropist of the state, dying in 1947.

Brown, already the possessor of the degrees of Doctor of Science and Doctor of Philosophy, came to the faculty for the academic session of 1901–1902 as acting professor of modern languages. In 1905 the department was divided and he was made professor of Romance languages. Three years later he was teaching French, German, and occasionally Italian. At intervals during his stay at the University he taught courses in the fine arts and in archeology, becoming an expert in the Indian remains of the state.[21] He was also for a while the assistant state geologist and was even offered the chair of geology, but declined it. At the time of his death in 1945 he was professor emeritus of modern languages and literature. Both Professor Saunders and Professor Brown were like medieval polymaths or representatives of the Renaissance ideal of the "universal man." They were the last of a gracious order of men.

It was during Fulton's chancellorship that history came into its own as an independent academic discipline. Until 1870 phases of it were taught incidentally by the incumbents of the classical chairs. Thereafter it had a precarious existence in varying combinations with political economy, the chancellorship, modern languages, mental and moral philosophy, logic, and rhetoric. But from 1900 onward the chair of history finally stood forth alone.

Related to the emancipation of the department of history was the organization and incorporation of the Mississippi Historical Society at the University in 1890. Many members of the faculty, regardless of their subject of specialization, participated actively in the society and contributed papers to the *Publications*. It was under the auspices of the society and the department of history that the State Department of Archives and History was ultimately established (1902)

Erected in 1889 as a library, this building later housed the law school and still later the department of geology.

An early view of the geology building showing the stained glass window.

A close-up view of the stained glass window. Window was presented by Delta Gamma Sorority.

The interior of the same building about 1900 when it was a library.

The "Old Chapel," now the "Y" building, is the second oldest building on the campus, built in 1853.

Admiral "Bull" Halsey at the centennial dedication of McCain Hall (the "Old Observatory" remodeled). *Courtesy of the Ole Miss Alumni Review.*

The beginning (above) and end of Gordon Hall (below). A dormitory well remembered by students of the 1920's. *Courtesy of the Ole Miss Alumni Review.*

Bondurant Hall. *Photograph by Louis Silver.*

The porch of Fulton Chapel looking toward the rear of the Fine Arts Center.

and that a vast output of original research in local history was promoted.²²

Meanwhile, student life was following its usual bent. One young man had torn up the picket fences on an Oxford street on Saturday night and was arrested. Tried before the faculty, he was expelled for drinking, rioting in Oxford, and "falsifying." ²³ Another youth, after a street fight, pleaded guilty in an Oxford court to the charge of assault and battery, whereupon the faculty dismissed him for those offenses as well as the additional charges of unsatisfactory academic work, non-attendance at classes, drinking, and carrying firearms.²⁴ In early 1897 some turkeys were stolen and eaten in the dormitories and the members of two fraternities were required to give written promises to suppress that type of lawlessness.²⁵ At the beginning of the new century the Trustees saw fit to charge the faculty with *absolutely* prohibiting the students from participating in any and all dancing parties in Oxford or elsewhere from the beginning of the examinations until the end of the commencement exercises.²⁶ Two students who went to town in February, 1903, were arrested and fined for intoxication and disorderly conduct. They explained to the faculty that they were subject to "cramps" and therefore drank some Jamaica ginger on two different occasions that morning (once in the dormitory, then on the walk "near the cedars"). The liquor was taken, they explained, on the advice of a physician, the father of one of the culprits, the advice having been given during the recent Christmas holidays. One of them had lost consciousness about an hour later. The faculty suspended them for a month.²⁷

In anticipation of the typical Southern mode of celebrating Christmas, the mayor and board of aldermen of Oxford in 1905 prohibited the use of fireworks, except on one's own property and except on December 23 and 24 between the hours of six and ten-thirty in the evening and on Christmas day except on sidewalks and in the vicinity of the cotton yards. The penalty was to be a fine of ten dollars.²⁸ Such a precise prohibition provoked its own violation by the American frontier spirit of the students. On the night of December 23 there was a disturbance in town created by three students who set off firecrackers on the public square and shot Roman candles at the arc light near the Baptist meeting house. They were promptly arrested and told to appear in court the following week, where they were charged with "malicious mischief." They took exception to the charge and secured its change to "disorderly conduct." The prescribed penalty of ten dollars and costs was duly imposed. They proceeded to argue the injustice of the amount and by gradual stages had it reduced to one dollar and costs. The faculty heard about the affair two and a half months later, but apparently took no action.[29]

A student development of tremendous importance began in the autumn of 1893. It was then that a regular football team was organized at the University and the playing of intercollegiate games began. The first coach was Professor Bondurant of the department of Latin, who served in that capacity as an additional duty for three years. The first game was played in Oxford against the Southwestern Baptist University (now Union University) of Jackson, Tennessee. The score was 56–0 in favor of the University of Mississippi. From then to the present athletic events have assumed increasing importance.[30] Incidentally, a further association of the classics with athletics at the University occurred in 1902 when in an economizing mood the Board of Trustees requested Dr. Saunders to take charge of the department of gymnastics in addition to his other work.[31] The following year he was relieved of this obligation.[32] It is said that Bondurant was responsible for the present school colors, red and blue. He had just come back from a period of graduate work in the East when he was made the coach. Thinking that the use of colors, as at the large Eastern schools, would add to the spirit of the sports, he began to make use of a combination of the blue of Yale and the crimson of Harvard as the colors for the University of Mississippi! [33]

Another phase of student activity was initiated by the preparation of an annual. The first one was published in 1897.[34] A contest was held to secure a suitable name for the publication. Miss Elma Coleman Meek of Oxford, then a student in the University, won the competition by proposing the name *Ole Miss*, a copyrighted designation which the annual has borne ever since. Gradually the phrase has come to be an affectionate nickname for the University, by which it is generally known throughout Mississippi and the South.[35]

Fulton himself was active in educational circles and through him the University was well on its way toward achieving a national reputation similar to that of the days of Chancellor Barnard before the War Between the States. As early as 1895 he issued the call which resulted in the establishment of the National Association of State Universities. For five successive years he was elected president of the organization.[36] At the same time the University of Mississippi became one of the six charter members of the Southern Association of Colleges and Secondary Schools (then called the Southern Educational Association). Fulton served as the second president of this accrediting organization.[37]

The latter part of Fulton's career as chancellor proved to be a trying and difficult period. Eventually it became necessary for him to resign. Several indications of trouble may be noted, small enough in themselves, but cumulative in effect. It should be remembered at the outset that he had been chosen to his office by a majority of only one vote. But his demonstrated worth and industry had probably overcome that initial handicap.

At the regular meeting of the Board of Trustees in the spring of 1900, an unprecedented action was taken. Ever since 1850 an outstanding event at the close of the academic year had been the commencement ball. The Trustees had regularly authorized the expenditure of University funds, usually a hundred dollars, to aid that purpose, even during the bleak days of the Reconstruction. Back in 1893 the Methodist and Baptist pastors of Oxford had protested the appropriation as well as the use of University buildings for dances, but the objection had been ignored.[38] Now, for the first time, the motion was defeated.³⁹ The initiative in 1900 seems to have come from within the Board, not from some outside source.

The action of the Board became known to the students as the commencement time of 1901 approached. There was an undercurrent of complaint. Consequently, in the April issue of the *University of Mississippi Magazine*, a student publication, there appeared an editorial bitterly critical of the Trustees and faculty for treating the undergraduates as children.⁴⁰ The faculty immediately dismissed the offending editor.⁴¹ A petition signed by a large number of students was presented to the faculty respectfully requesting a reconsideration of the action and the reinstatement of their associate.⁴² The reply of the faculty was an equally respectful negative.⁴³

A number of students now prepared a statement of the issue "to the people of Mississippi" and sent it to the newspapers of the state.⁴⁴ The faculty thereupon took the strong measure of giving the students three days in which to withdraw their names from the document.⁴⁵ At the expiration of the ultimatum a majority had done so. The time was extended by six and a half hours and most of the remainder acquiesced. Six recalcitrants were suspended.⁴⁶

At the meeting of the Board a month later the matter was discussed in detail and the faculty was roundly sustained in its course of action. It was then moved and carried that a vote of confidence be given Chancellor Fulton for his handling of the situation. There was one dissenting vote and the Trustee casting it was allowed to incorporate into the minutes his reason for so voting. He explained that although he personally had high regard for the chancellor, he nevertheless felt that the affair indicated that Fulton was lacking in one necessary attribute, namely, the ability to command the respect of the students.⁴⁷

Another controversy which had been brewing for a long time also reached this meeting of the Board and thus came out in the open. It was a result of the feeling that there was social ostracism of the non-fraternity men by those who belonged to the Greek-letter societies.

Action on this was delayed for a year,[48] but the issue could not wait that long. In January, 1902, there was a called meeting of the Trustees in Jackson, before which a committee of two students, one of them Lee M. Russell, later Governor of the state, appeared and made representations against the fraternities. As a result the Trustees ordered no pledging of new members by the fraternities for the rest of the session.[49]

In June of the same year the Board forbade any increase in the number of fraternities on the campus without the permission of the faculty and ordered that no pledging take place before or during the first eight weeks of the freshman year.[50] Seven months later the faculty carried the matter a step further by prohibiting membership in any "club" which had its meeting place off the campus.[51]

The issue was, of course, not settled. Some fraternities violated the one-year rule. There was intimidation of prospective pledges. Meetings were held off the campus.[52] The matter continued to plague the last days of Fulton's administration. The opposition to him became public and outspoken, reaching its culmination in 1905 and 1906.

Meanwhile, the political picture in Mississippi had undergone a subtle change. The constitution of 1890, the final act of the revolution which had overthrown the Reconstruction and insured white supremacy, had shifted the center of voting strength in the state from the older, more aristocratic, and still Whiggish southern section to the rugged, hilly region of the northeastern section. Moreover, a more popular and democratic method of choosing candidates for public office had been introduced by the law which transferred the right to nominate candidates from a party convention to a party primary election. The first man to secure the Governor's chair in this way was James K. Vardaman (1904-1908), the "Great White Chief."

The rise of the "common man" indicated a change in the political climate which would inevitably affect the University. There was a growing feeling that all state institutions should accurately reflect the democratization of the state. The University would hereafter be increasingly affected by apparently extraneous political considerations. As opportunity arose therefore the new Governor appointed his partisans to the Board of Trustees until he dominated it. Such action was not unprecedented, the most noteworthy examples being the complete shake-up in the Board at the beginning and at the overthrow of the carpet-bag regime in the state.

Early in 1905 Fulton had communicated with the philanthropist Andrew Carnegie and requested a donation to build a new library at the University. The reply was favorable, so he immediately laid the matter before the seventeen Trustees by letter. Only ten answered the chancellor's inquiry, but they approved further negotiation. As a result, Carnegie offered twenty-five thousand dollars to be met with an equal amount from the state.[53]

At the regular meeting of the Board, June 4, the matter was laid before the Trustees as a group for formal ratification. Eleven members, including Governor Vardaman, who presided, were present. But instead of approving the undertaking, they voted to reject Carnegie's offer.[54] This action constituted a major defeat for Fulton's plans. Accordingly at the next regular meeting, June 8, 1906, he presented his resignation, which was immediately accepted.[55] The following day he was elected professor of astronomy and geology, but he declined.[56] This analysis seems to be the reasonable interpretation of the documentary evidence, although Franklin L. Riley, who was at that time professor of history in the University, has stated that Fulton was forced from his position because of a student with powerful political influence.[57]

Alfred Hume, who was professor of mathematics and dean of the department of sicence, literature, and the arts, was also vice-chancellor and thus automatically became the executive officer of the University. At a called meeting of the Board two months later he was declared acting chancellor until a new chancellor should be chosen.[58] He served until July 1, 1907.

CHAPTER XI

A New Age

AN unfavorable critic has made a case for the thesis that from this point onward until quite recent times the University has, with possibly one interval of stability, been subjected to increasing political control.[1] Such an assertion is hardly true, because the University has always reflected the changes in the government of the state. The circumstances at the beginning and at the end of the Reconstruction are only the more obvious occasions. Longstreet's political activity was probably a factor in inducing the Board to accept his resignation in 1856. It was certainly a political as well as a military situation which closed the University in 1861, leaving Barnard without a job. And as for the future, it would depend on one's partisanship whether he would consider the firing and hiring of executive officers as good or bad, because all political factions have indulged in that kind of sport.

Two points should not be forgotten about any state university. First, as a university it is primarily a place of learning. As such it requires stability, security, and relative freedom to perform its task well. Too much direct political interference is not conducive to the accomplishment of its educational obligations. On the other hand, however, it is a *state* institution and hence by its very nature political. As such it is under the necessity of being responsive in some measure to changes in the political atmosphere which it breathes. It cannot be an "ivory tower" remote from the affairs of contemporary life. How these two functions of the state university are to be reconciled is no concern of a historian: he has only to record the facts so far as they are discoverable.

The University of Mississippi opened according to schedule in the autumn of 1906 with Acting Chancellor Hume presiding. At a meeting of the Board of Trustees called for November 1, Andrew Armstrong Kincannon was elected as Fulton's successor.[2] A native Mississippian, born in 1859, he entered the University of Mississippi in the autumn of 1877.[3] Although unable financially to attend continuously, he was a fair student and for the commencement of 1882 was designated as the Anniversarian of his literary society, Phi Sigma, an indication of his popularity.[4] However, he resigned the honor, left the University, and took his liberal arts degree at the Normal University, Lebanon, Ohio, where he also did graduate work.[5] Later he did some graduate study at the University of Mississippi in 1893.[6]

From 1883 to 1886 Kincannon taught in the English department at the Mississippi Agricultural and Mechanical College, Starkville. From that position he left to become superintendent of the public school system of Meridian, where he remained for ten fruitful years. He quickly took a prominent position in the educational circles of the state and was easily elected as State Superintendent of Education in 1895. Two years later he yielded to the urgent insistence of many leaders in the state and accepted the presidency of the Industrial Institute and College (now Mississippi State College for Women). Here his vigorous initiative and energetic efficiency brought him to the attention of the University Board and marked him as a likely prospect for the vacancy at the University.[7] To the surprise of all he declined to accept the position. A newspaper report said later that he refused because of insufficient salary, which at this time was only thirty-five hundred dollars.[8] Hume therefore continued as acting chancellor for the academic year.

The search for a presiding officer continued and the Trustees began to look beyond the borders of Mississippi. Finally, at a called meeting in Oxford in the late winter (March 2, 1907), James B. Aswell, State Superintendent of Education of Louisiana, was elected, his term to begin July 1, 1907.[9] The choice was apparently made on the impulse of the moment, without any preliminary consideration. A week or two later the *University of Mississippi Magazine* editorially placed a generous construction on the choice thus: "Prof. Aswell's election was wholly unexpected . . . , and is a great surprise to the whole State. . . . He comes from another State and his name cannot reasonably be dragged into State politics." [10] His acceptance seemed so certain that the catalogue containing the bulletin for 1906–1907 and announcements for the session of 1907–1908 was printed and issued in April carrying Aswell's name as chancellor-elect.[11]

But another bombshell exploded. The Board met in Jackson in May to read Aswell's letter of resignation.[12] In an angry mood, the Trustees accepted the declination, "not with thanks," as a critical reporter stated.[13] They now realized that drastic measures were necessary to secure a taker for the vacancy. The salary was raised to five thousand dollars as of January 1, 1908, a residence on the campus was to be provided for the chancellor, and his powers were enlarged so as to grant him the right to nominate the members of the faculty as well as the authority to remove them, to arrange the course of study, and so forth.[14] A newspaper account remarked: "All these extras ought to induce some good man to take the chancellorship, which now seems to be going begging." [15] Applications for the position were solicited.

When the Board assembled in Oxford next month for its regular session, the names of two applicants were officially presented and several others were informally discussed. The two who sought the place by formal application were Kincannon and the Reverend Peter G. Sears. The latter, an Episcopal clergyman, sometime principal of St. Thomas Hall, Holly Springs, a graduate of the University in the class of 1885 and a graduate student in 1895, was the son of General Claudius W. Sears, former professor of mathematics at the University. As preparation was made to vote, a communication came from

Sears withdrawing his candidacy in view of "the state of distraction and strife existing within the board of trustees, because of antagonistic political interests...." He requested that the testimonial letters supporting his application be returned to him, stating that he valued them infinitely more than a position gained by "political scramble and contention." [16] Sears's withdrawal left only the name of Kincannon for consideration. He was therefore elected, the vote standing at thirteen Trustees in favor of him, four abstaining, and one absent.[17]

A troubled era faced the University, yet withal one of great promise. The early part of Kincannon's term of office began auspiciously enough when the legislature in 1908 made the largest appropriation the University had ever received.[18] A program of great physical expansion was immediately undertaken. The infirmary was enlarged and properly equipped; a new water and sewage system was installed; the light and heating plants were extended; a new dormitory for men was erected; a new dining hall was built; a laundry building was constructed; concrete sidewalks connected most of the buildings; and much needed repairs were accomplished on the older structures. It was a veritable boom in building.[19]

Of particular significance was the erection of two new structures, the library and the Peabody building. As noted earlier, the Board had disappointed Chancellor Fulton in regard to the Carnegie library offer. Kincannon was able successfully to reopen negotiations. This time the Trustees accepted Andrew Carnegie's unconditional gift of twenty-five thousand dollars and agreed to match it with an equal amount.[20] The additional money was to come from student fees. In 1910 the Board authorized the transfer to the building fund of fifteen thousand dollars which had just been appropriated by the legislature for library equipment, since the sum was idle and could not be used until after the completion of the new library.[21] Early the following year the executive committee of the Board similarly allowed seven thousand dollars to be taken from the laundry and student cottage fund.[22] Such actions were deemed temporary and were to be replaced by the student fees.

The building was completed in the latter part of 1911. But even before it was finished, it was dedicated, May 30, 1911. In a gracious but ironic gesture Kincannon invited as the speaker for the occasion none other than the former chancellor, Robert B. Fulton, who delivered a frank though nostalgic address entitled *Opportunity*, in which he summarized the history of the negotiations for the Carnegie money.[23]

Kincannon was also active in securing the interest of the Peabody Board in aiding the development of the department of education. The agent for that foundation intimated that forty thousand dollars could be allocated for a suitable building if the University would agree to expend seventy thousand dollars annually in support and maintenance.[24] Here again the chancellor's persuasive powers obtained the desired result: the structure reached completion in 1913.[25]

Progressive steps were taken in expanding the offerings of the University by the addition of a school of pharmacy. It was created by the Board of Trustees in the summer of 1908 [26] and opened in the autumn of that year.[27] The number of students during the first years of the school was necessarily limited because of insufficient facilities and particularly lack of space.

An attempt was made to extend the medical course from two to four years. In 1908 the city of Vicksburg offered the State Charity Hospital to the University for this purpose, the property, valued at one hundred fifty thousand dollars, to revert to the city if the charity feature of the hospital should fail to be maintained. After consideration the Board of Trustees by formal resolution accepted the gift with the stipulated condition.[28] Five full professors and nine assistants were secured for the work at Vicksburg and the second half of the proposed four-year course opened in the autumn of 1909.[29] The experiment lasted only a year. Lack of sufficient funds and equipment caused the Board to discontinue this effort.[30]

From this period in the history of the University came two professors who were on the faculty until after the centennial year, Christopher Longest and William L. Kennon. The former was an alumnus, having secured his Bachelor of Arts degree in 1900. Returning to the University in 1908 as assistant professor of Latin, he soon moved into the department of Spanish and in time was promoted to the headship. He has served as director of the summer session, registrar, and director of the Alumni Loan Fund, and for one month (August, 1930) as acting chancellor. Kennon, a graduate of Millsaps College, Jackson, became assistant professor of astronomy in 1909, but was transferred to physics and astronomy two years later and remained in those fields until his death. He was a leading authority on the history of the University, especially in regard to the part played by the sciences.[31]

A portentous and forward-looking move was made by the legislature, April 14, 1910, by unifying all the boards of trustees of the state schools. At the time it was done there were four such institutions: the University of Mississippi, the Mississippi Agricultural and Mechanical College (now called Mississippi State College), the Industrial Institute and College (now Mississippi State College for Women), and Alcorn Agricultural and Mechanical College, the college for blacks. Each had its own board and for a while there was opposition to the combination for fear that each would not receive just attention. However, the action was finally accomplished, has proved itself, and has provided a pattern followed by a number of other states. The Governor and the State Superintendent of Education were continued as *ex officio* members, the Governor presiding whenever he was present. An executive secretary was employed. The new body was called the Board of Trustees of Institutions of Higher Learning in Mississippi.[32] In late 1910 a new state school, the Mississippi Normal College (later State Teachers College, still later Mississippi Southern College) was created and made subject to the Board.

The troublesome issue of the anti-fraternity agitation reached a culmination during Kincannon's term as chancellor. Reference has already been made to the rise of the problem. Now it finally came to a head. Lee M. Russell, who as a student led the fight against the fraternities, was now active in state politics and once more led the fight. The matter was discussed favorably and unfavorably in the public press and ultimately reached the floor of the state legislature. Some of the arguments used to discredit the Greek-letter societies were that they encouraged dissipation, that they led to waste of money, that they discouraged study and scholarship, that they interfered with the work of the literary societies, and that they destroyed "college spirit" by fostering cliques. But the crowning criticism was that they had been the cause of social ostracism of the non-fraternity students by the people of Oxford.[33] Whether these charges were true or not, the legislature saw fit in 1912 to prohibit secret societies in the state schools by passing a law which remained on the statute books for fourteen years.[34]

A considerable amount of difficulty was arising for the University in connection with intercollegiate athletics, particularly in regard to the eligibility of certain football players. The Southern Intercollegiate Athletic Association kept a rather close check on this matter and at one stage the University was barred from the association because a student was permitted to play after being declared ineligible.[35] At another time the University's own athletic association faced local and alumni criticism because it had to bar certain players.[36] There was acute dissension within the faculty growing out of a feeling that disproportionate emphasis was being placed on athletics.[37]

The latter portion of Kincannon's term of office was exceedingly troubled by these and other issues. One professor in resigning stated: "I charge the Chancellor with converting the University into a bureau for the distribution of political patronage in that he is largely governed by the political influence a candidate for a position in the University can wield rather than by scholarship and other requisites that go to make a successful and efficient university instructor."[38] The accusation of graft was being hurled and during the session of 1912–1913 the students painted the words, "Here it is! Graft!" in large red letters over the chancellor's seat in the chapel.[39] Legislative investigating committees, however, found no evidence of it.[40] A number of lawsuits were filed against the University on account of alleged breach of contracts and non-payment of obligations. Most of these were settled in favor of the University, but the people of the state were becoming embarrassed by the reputation the University was achieving.[41]

Political pressure on the University was especially heavy. The most serious example occurred in the autumn of 1913. Five students had been expelled for hazing freshmen. Either they or their relatives appealed to Governor Earl Brewer for redress. The latter therefore interceded for them and mentioned in a letter to Chancellor Kincannon the standing of their families. In the same communication he asked the restoration of another student similarly disciplined earlier for another offense. No choice was left to the chancellor and faculty. Kincannon asserted that he felt the sentence to be justified but that, recognizing the superior authority and presumably the superior wisdom of the Board of Trustees, he saw no alternative but to readmit the offenders.[42]

The chancellor's position was obviously precarious. Persistent rumors of his impending dismissal had begun as early as 1910 or 1911.[43] Finally, in February, 1914, he announced his resignation. The ostensible reason was that he had "simply done his work, and desires to lay down the reins." [44] But a number of years later he stated: "I resigned . . . , because I was unwilling for the School to become a political chattel.

"I accepted the Chancellorship . . . upon the distinct condition that I was to control the institution without the Board's interference. So long as the Board respected my authority as Chancellor, the institution was phenomenally prosperous. When the Board undertook to disregard my authority, I resigned. . . ." [45] He left Oxford on June 3, 1914, and the following day assumed office as superintendent of the city school system of Memphis.

CHAPTER XII

A Troubled Era

IN May, 1914, even before Kincannon left, but after he had presented his resignation, the Trustees tentatively offered the forthcoming vacancy to one of their own number, Joseph Neely Powers, the State Superintendent of Education. At the meeting on June 4, the Board confirmed its choice by authorizing its president, Governor Brewer, to cast one ballot for all to elect Powers.[1] No one else either applied or was considered for the chancellorship. Powers, born on May 15, 1869, in Havana, Alabama, had attended a number of schools for short periods of time, including one year at the Louisville Medical College, but had secured no degree. After serving many years as a teacher and school administrator, he had at the age of thirty-eight, been appointed by Governor Vardaman to the position of State Superintendent of Education to complete an unfinished term. He had then run successfully for the same office for the quadrennium of 1908–1912 and at the end of that period was reelected to serve the ensuing four years. He was, therefore, at the time of his designation as the executive official of the University of Mississippi, an *ex officio* member of the governing Board.[2]

In order to begin the task of restoring public faith in the University, the new chancellor first tackled the almost insuperable problem of banishing dissension within the faculty. The method used was not one calculated to soothe ruffled feelings: it was one of threat and intimidation. To a meeting of the faculty in the autumn of 1914, he said, "Pardon me for being so candid, perhaps so blunt, as to say with all emphasis, that if any one of you feel that you cannot deal with each other in such a spirit as to always reflect credit on the administration, that it might be well, if such there be, for them to sever their connection with the University at this time, rather than to bring trouble later." [3]

In his biennial report a year later, Powers admitted that universal favor was lacking. He then stated: "This University is thirsting for more affection from the general public.

"After a service of more than sixty-five years, we stand today, in certain quarters, without that peculiar affection to which faithful service is clearly entitled." [4] Further disapproval appeared in a letter to the chancellor from the executive secretary of the Board deploring that fact that the name of the University was declining.[5] The disaffection was probably due in part to the still rankling resentment over the expulsion of the fraternities. At any rate it appears to lie behind Powers's reference to "a time when the clouds lowered, when some members of the student body seemed to feel that we were taking away their privileges in seeking to eradicate evils that were tending to lower the moral standing of the institution...." [6]

However, in spite of ill feelings which had been engendered, the number of students increased slowly but steadily all during Powers's term, except for the war year of 1917–1918.[7] Finally, when the University opened in September, 1923, it was anticipated that nearly eight hundred students would matriculate.[8] The expectation was not fulfilled during the regular days of registration, but after a delay of a few weeks that number was reached and passed. The University and the town of Oxford were jubilant. More than two thousand people attended a festive barbecue given as a part of the "over eight hundred" celebration.[9]

The chancellor was exultant over this development (". . . this great attendance is a cause of congratulation. . . ." [10]), and began to demand enlarged facilities and appropriations, because, as he said, "We simply desire to keep up with the growth of the institution." [11] Five new dormitories were therefore constructed in 1920, one for women (Ward) and four for men (George, Deupree, LaBauve, and Odom).

Expansion brought with it a new division of the University, the school of commerce and business administration. It was organized in September, 1917, "to provide broadly trained men capable of meeting the demands of the modern business world." [12] This school has increased its offerings from sixteen courses to ninety-nine and has experienced a growth larger than that of any other division of the University, ranking immediately after the college of liberal arts in its enrollment.

The first World War had its effect on the University of Mississippi as the Spanish-American War had not. Those students who were to be graduated in 1917 were, upon enlistment in the army or navy, released from further attendance at class and were exempt from examinations. Those in good standing at the time of their withdrawal were granted their diplomas during the summer, the commencement exercises for that year being omitted. The proposed "mobilization" plans of the University were drawn up in the same month in which the United States declared war on the German government.[13]

At the opening of school that autumn the campus assumed the appearance of a military post. Regular drill was required of all men and credit toward a degree was allowed for it. Women were granted the same consideration for Red Cross work. Members of the faculty were given leave of absence for military service and the war work of the Young Men's Christian Association.[14]

The annual for 1918 was affectionately dedicated to alumni and others of the University, "who, true to the teachings of chivalric forebears for generations gone, . . . have championed the cause of honor, home and humanity. . . ." Reminiscence was inevitable for those whose school had stood the shock of an older war and so the statement concluded: "Bright be the pages which tell the deathless story of their deeds side by side with the glorious record of the University Grays! Sprung from the very womb of war, born of one mother, cradled amid the storm, in their manhood now they bear upon their brows her name, and her fair fame is forever safe in their keeping."

At the commencement of 1919 it was planned to dedicate a memorial to those students and alumni who had died in the war. The occasion was also to be the semi-centennial reunion of the class of 1869.[15] And so once more, by an ironic twist of circumstance, the former chancellor, R. B. Fulton, a member of that class, was invited to return to the University to make the chief address. But it was not to be: "While the manuscript of the ... address was being printed, a sudden illness on May 29, 1919, brought to an abrupt termination the gentle life and noble work of Robert Burwell Fulton." [16]

In January, 1920, Governor Theodore G. Bilbo's term of office ended. He was succeeded by the man who had been his lieutenant governor, Lee M. Russell. Ever since his student days the latter had been the chief agitator against the Greek-letter societies on the campus. The anti-fraternity legislation of 1912 was his achievement. Externally the law was obeyed, but there persisted a number of *sub rosa* organizations which the Trustees tried vainly to curb, one method being an enactment severely limiting the number of dances a year. The excited feelings of the students, which had gone into other channels during the war years, now broke forth in resentment against the new Governor.

On the night of October 27, 1920, in accordance with a meticulous plan guarded with remarkable secrecy, a burning effigy of Governor Russell was hanged from the flag pole in the center of the campus. The report of the incident immediately appeared in the newspapers for the next two days. On October 30 the faculty met to deal with the matter.[17] The decision was the summary expulsion of the offenders. The Board also quickly convened to investigate and found evidence of the existence of *sub rosa* fraternities.[18] Deeming them the source of the ghastly prank, the Trustees after due consideration ordered the sweeping dismissal of all those guilty of violating the antifraternity law.[19]

The University was apparently approaching another crisis in its eventful history. Public opinion in the state was becoming very bitter against its administration. The Board therefore reconsidered its drastic action a year later and reversed its decision: all those expelled at the earlier meeting were permitted to reenter.[20] It was a confession of failure and inability to enforce the prohibition against the Greek-letter societies. In time it would be necessary for the legislature to repeal the enactment.

For a while the resentment smouldered behind a façade of religion, culture, and good will. The year 1923 was ushered in with a "watch-night" service at the Presbyterian church in Oxford, in which some of the faculty took part. The theme, "The evangelization of the world for Christ in 1923," was indicative of the expansive optimism which characterized the early 1920's.[21] In this mood a group of University "evangelists," called the Flying Squadron, began to dominate the religion of the surrounding community. By March 1 they had conducted services for the Baptist and Methodist churches of Oxford and the Presbyterian church at College Hill.[22] On March 4 they were at the Oxford Presbyterian church. Twenty students and professors gave their "testimonies." On the following Sunday they went out to the town of Taylor.[23] And that autumn they were still active, but the first warm zeal was already beginning to pass away.[24]

The lyceum program, now a part of the University organization bringing visiting artists to the campus, was begun unofficially and on a small scale during this period. The first offering, presenting a vocal soloist, occurred on Saturday night, February 10, 1923.[25] A quintet followed two weeks later; two plays came in March, and a glee club in April.[26] At the beginning of the next academic year season tickets for five performances were on sale at a downtown drug store.[27]

The glee club of the University itself began to make public appearances.[28] An elaborate observance of the Mother's Day week-end was inaugurated.[29] The Young Men's Christian Association sponsored a "stunt night" for the students in the auditorium of the chapel. The departments of Latin and Greek enjoyed a banquet after the old Roman style in one of the dining halls, with a Latin address by Professor Calvin S. Brown as the main feature.[30] And the entire personnel of the second-year medical class volunteered to submit to skin graft operations in an attempt to save the life of a seven-year-old child who had been severely burned about the legs and lower part of his body.[31] But the widespread resentment against the administration of the University was growing and the ax was almost ready to fall.

The term of Governor Russell was drawing to its close. In the summer and autumn of 1923 there was a hotly contested political campaign. The successful candidate was Henry L. Whitfield, although the former Governor, Theodore G. Bilbo, had also run. Whitfield was an outstanding educator and had been president of the Mississippi State College for Women. He had been forced from the latter office by Governor Russell. His election was therefore evidence of a change in the public mind over a decade or more. The inauguration took place in January, 1924. By virtue of office he was now president of the Board of Trustees of the Institutions of Higher Learning in Mississippi.

At a meeting of the Board in the summer of 1924, the question of the chancellorship of the University inevitably arose. The Trustees were evenly divided on the subject of retaining Powers or dismissing him. The issue was solved by Governor Whitfield, who broke the tie by voting for dismissal.[32] It was then decided not to elect a chancellor immediately. Dr. Hume, the vice-chancellor, was once more declared acting chancellor for the session of 1924–1925, as he had been in 1906–1907.[33] Declining to serve thus, however, he was elected chancellor.

CHAPTER XIII

The Good Old Days

AT the close of the academic session of 1924-1925, Dr. Hume made his first report to the Board of Trustees as chancellor. This "grand old man," born in Beech Grove, Tennessee, December 1, 1866, finished seven years at Vanderbilt University in 1890 with three degrees, Bachelor of Engineering, Civil Engineer, and Doctor of Science. Coming to the University of Mississippi that autumn as professor of mathematics, he exercised a profound and lasting influence on the state as well as on the institution with which his name is inseparably linked. His administrative positions have been many: dean of the college of liberal arts, 1905-1920; vice-chancellor, 1905-1924; acting chancellor, 1906-1907; chancellor, 1924-1930 and 1932-1935; chancellor emeritus, 1935 to his death; and again acting chancellor, 1942-1943 (eighteen months) and 1946 (two months).[1]

With the educator Whitfield in the Governor's chair and the beloved "little Allie" (so Hume had long been affectionately called by the students) as executive officer of the University, there began a new era of good feeling, tranquility, progress, and public confidence in the institution. For a moment, it is true, it seemed that a belated Victorianism might prevail. In 1925 a series of rules were promulgated by the faculty for the ostensible purpose of making the University a place for study, not for recreation, amusement, and entertainment: hazing was to be dealt with severely, campus dances suspended, the use of automobiles prohibited, and no absences excused.[2]

But on March 16, 1926, a bill repealing the anti-fraternity legislation of 1912 became law. The faculty undertook to handle in a most careful fashion the reinstatement of these groups. Means were suggested whereby social ostracism of the independent students might be avoided and extravagance in expenditures curtailed.[3] The matter was so skillfully managed that fifteen thriving chapters of national social organizations for men and eight for women were on the campus, as well as twenty-three active professional and honorary Greek-letter fraternities.

Only a few days before this liberalizing legislation, Mississippi, following the lead of Tennessee, had on March 11, 1926, prohibited the teaching of the doctrine that man had either ascended or descended from a lower order of animals.[4] A storm of discussion had preceded the action and great pressure was brought to bear on the legislature to pass the bill. A timorous soul would have remained quiet. But Hume, although a loyal Presbyterian elder and a native of Tennessee, entered the lists and worked valiantly against the passage of this law, basing his objection on the ground of academic freedom. Even after the bill had passed the legislature, he wrote a letter to Governor Whitfield urging him to veto it.[5] These efforts were unavailing, but they clearly demonstrated the courageous and fearless quality of the man then at the head of the University.

Near the beginning of his term of office, Hume authorized an "alumni citizenship survey" of some importance.[6] It was done to answer some old criticisms of the University and to aid in formulating the future educational policy of the institution. Questions were asked of a number of former students, chiefly those who had attended between the years 1910 and 1920, in order to ascertain their business or profession, income, governmental service, civic, religious, and fraternal activities, and their opinion concerning the worth of their training at the University of Mississippi.

The answers to the latter section are revealing. To the inquiry, "Was the University largely responsible for your success?" three hundred thirty-nine replied affirmatively, while only eight did not think so. One man shrewdly noted: "I feel I owe a great deal to the University along lines of refinement. I could wish that my education had been more accurate." Another opinion requested was whether sufficient emphasis had been placed upon obligations to the state. There were two hundred twenty-four who replied, "Yes," one hundred nineteen who disagreed. A physician remarked, "Seldom, as I remember, was it ever mentioned," while a teacher stated, "It was forever dinged into our head. . . ." Another teacher, somewhat irrelevantly, said, "Unfortunately, the political factions in Mississippi are pretty strongly marked in University life and have been a serious menace to the proper administration of the institution."

The questionnaire next asked, "Did the University neglect your spiritual welfare?" This question provoked the expected difference of opinion: only sixty answered affirmatively, two hundred eighty-two said: "No." A typical reply was that of a physician who stated, "The most nearly perfect Christian atmosphere I have ever been in outside of home." Another asserted, ". . . it gave me the impulse to prepare for the ministry." The last query was, "Do the people of your community value and respect the University?" Two hundred eighty-three gave favorable answers, thirty dissented. One man gave high praise: "Though I am on the faculty of another State university, and one that we feel proud of, yet my undergraduate training at Ole Miss has never seemed in any way inferior to the undergraduate training of any other school I know of." One of those who dissented, an attorney in the state, took this attitude: "Many think it a second-rate college. . . . A broader social and religious view by the authorities would increase its popularity. . . . Fraternities are badly needed."

Many constructive criticisms and suggestions were offered in the replies, all obviously sincere, some representing mature and deliberate judgment, the most frequent being a desire for the removal of the University from political influences. Others stressed the need for higher scholastic requirements and larger salaries for professors. Some mentioned the value of better publicity and greater emphasis upon broader and more practical training.

This investigation seemed to set in motion something of a chain reaction, for it was quickly followed by three other studies of various phases of the life of the University. The most scientific and objective was the one by M. V. O'Shea, professor of education in the University of Wisconsin. It was proposed by Governor Whitfield, who visited O'Shea in Madison in 1925 and requested a full and thorough consideration of the entire system of public education in Mississippi, including the University.[7] On the basis of such research, recommendations for any necessary changes were to be made. With an able and adequate staff of assistants, O'Shea set to work. The Governor, deeply interested as an educator, nevertheless studiously avoided exercising any influence on the corps of investigators.[8]

The study culminated in two publications, containing results and proposals which, if carried into effect, would have effectively removed the University from the uncertainty of partisan politics. But, unfortunately, the death of Whitfield on March 17, 1927, before the completed work was published, ended a halcyon period in state affairs. The lieutenant governor, Dennis Murphree, served the remainder of the term, but already the state was plunged into a bitter campaign from which the former Governor, Theodore G. Bilbo, again emerged as victor, assuming office in January, 1928. O'Shea said of Whitfield, "anyone who knows what he achieved as governor in the betterment of economic, social, and political conditions in the state of Mississippi will understand that the state has lost one of its most public-spirited, most devoted, most unselfish, most courageous, and most far-seeing citizens." [9]

The second investigation was a thesis prepared by John C. Meadows, who in 1927 thus earned the degree of Doctor of Philosophy at the George Peabody College for Teachers. It was an attempt to identify, isolate for study, and discuss the functions of a state university, with particular reference to the University of Mississippi.[10] It was a project of thorough research and scholarship. One astounding statement reflects the effectiveness of the University through three quarters of a century: ". . . in the entire history of the University, only eight students were failures in spite of their university training." [11] The volume also devotes space to Chancellor Hume's concept of a state university. It is quoted here as an expression of the philosophy which then dominated the institution:

"The university is a place where living beings are in process of growth and development, where mental and moral forces are moulding character and shaping destinies both of individuals and states.

"The college of liberal arts is the heart of the institution and its pulse beat is felt throughout every member, imparting larger life and lasting vigor. The curriculum of the college is intended to broaden sympathies, widen horizons, deepen the foundations of character, strengthen manhood and womanhood—in a word, to furnish and equip for intelligent and contented citizenship. It seeks to develop the ability to think clearly, honestly, connectedly, logically, deeply, and through its thinkers, to handle the industrial, social, political, and religious problems which have to do with good citizenship.

"The professional schools fit men and women for lives of useful service as lawyers, doctors, engineers, teachers, pharmacists, merchants, etc. The state depends upon its professionally trained citizens to develop and conserve its natural resources." [12]

The last study of the University in this period was a literary treatment by Medford Evans. His article entitled "Oxford, Mississippi" appeared in the *Southwest Review* in the autumn of 1929.[13] Although dealing primarily with the near-by town, it was inevitable that Evans should also discuss the University. The charm of the institution and its environment was beautifully portrayed. The concluding paragraphs are interesting:

"The young life of the state comes here for its formative years. It is an attractive young life, for the most part, unsophisticated and unperverted. It grows excited at football games and in college elections, where the Eastern college man would be blasé and cynical. Ole Miss students idealize their fraternities. Here again the Easterner would yawn. . . . Mississippi students are direct in love and war. They get into fights through sheer physical exuberance; in the East one hears of student suicides from sheer world-weariness. The Mississippian falls romantically in love and runs away to get married, ruining his worldly prospects and outraging two families; the Easterner tampers with homosexuality. . . .

"The future of Mississippi lies with the young men and women who go to Oxford and the other college towns of the state every year. These young men and women are good material. Living in the rank, luxuriant swamps and forests of the state may have left many of them open to embarrassment during discussions of Nietzsche, or in the presence of a head waiter, but it has equipped them with a practical philosophy in the face of flood and disaster which is in the nature of things impossible for an undergraduate at Williams or Smith. At the University of Mississippi they acquire some of the desirable things that others get at Yale or Vassar—not all; the scholastic standards of Mississippi are not those of Yale—but neither do Ole Miss students acquire certain undesirable things. And, lest she trust her blindness to blind leadership, Mississippi, though censured from afar, will continue to work her own way, forward." [14]

Most of these statements are still true though there have been changes since then. Post-World War II students are much more sophisticated in the presence of sex, Nietzsche, and head waiters, and the scholastic standards have become increasingly higher. Yet, as Evans has said, "It is an attractive young life. . . ." May it always remain so.

The enrollment was continuing to grow throughout Hume's chancellorship. In the session of 1926–27 it passed the thousand-mark, being eleven hundred eighteen. The following year it was eleven hundred twenty, but in 1929–1930 it reached twelve hundred fifty-four.[15] Expansion of the curriculum resulted in the formation of the graduate school in 1927 as an autonomous division of the University. For buildings the legislature appropriated one hundred fifty thousand dollars for a new chapel, completed in the same year and appropriately named as a memorial to the former chancellor, Robert B. Fulton.[16] Hume was especially pleased that a chapel, more than any other building, was erected during the time he was the executive head of the institution.[17] His opinion was: "All our education should be shot through and through with the pre-eminence of moral force and spiritual power and the clear recognition of God. May the new chapel ever stand squarely, unequivocally, definitely, and positively for these principles." [18]

But an ominous note was now being struck in the affairs of the state. Governor Bilbo, in his inaugural address, January 17, 1928, urged the consolidation of the University and the Agricultural and Mechanical College and their removal to Jackson. He proposed that the buildings at the University be converted to the use of a strong teachers college.[19] The fight for and against this proposal became exceedingly bitter. The alumni of the University and of the Agricultural and Mechanical College, although otherwise intense rivals, now joined hands to defeat the purpose of the Governor. The battle in the legislature and in the public press waxed hot.

Early in February, 1928, the members of the legislature came up to Oxford to inspect the University and consider the subject of its removal or dismemberment and the future use of the existing buildings. Oxford and the University as joint hosts exerted themselves to the limit to persuade the officials not to disturb the present arrangement. A public meeting of "the friends of the University in north Mississippi" was held in the Lafayette county courthouse. The *Oxford Eagle* carried a letter by Chancellor Hume on its editorial page. And a banquet was tendered by the University.[20]

Hume had already courageously entered the fray by a public statement in December, 1927, which appeared in the leading newspapers and was now reprinted as a pamphlet and distributed by interested citizens of Oxford.[21] In the main it is a straightforward, objective defense of the present location. Only once, toward the end, does it become sentimental:

"The University of Mississippi is rich in memories and memorials, in a noble history, and in worthy traditions. . . . If its children do not come to its defense, the very stones in the memorial arches and the Confederate monument would cry out. . . . The memorial window in the old library, erected in loving memory of the University Greys, the Confederate monument near-by, and the Confederate Soldiers' Cemetery a little further removed, are as sacred as any ancient shrine, altar, or temple. Instead of moving the University away, that it might be a little easier to reach, ought not the people of Mississippi to look upon a visit here as a holy pilgrimage?"

The banquet for the legislators was marked by a number of addresses by the chancellor, the mayor of Oxford, and three alumni. The former students pleaded for appropriations instead of removal. Hume stirred the emotions by his peroration: "Gentlemen, you may move the University of Mississippi. You may move it to Jackson or anywhere else. You may uproot it from the hallowed ground on which it has stood for eighty years. You may take it from these surroundings that have become dear to the thousands who have gone from its doors. But, gentlemen, don't call it 'Ole Miss'." [22]

Sentiment prevailed and the plan of the Governor was soundly defeated. Nearly twenty years later the editor of the *Clarksdale Daily Press*, commenting on the death of Bilbo, was to say, "He did the most heroic thing I have ever known any politician in Mississippi to do. In 1928 he attempted to consolidate the State Colleges. As a member of the legislature at that time, I opposed him and, probably more than any other man, had more to do with the defeat of his program. Looking back now, I believe I was wrong and he was right. We would have under his plan built a great university without all the overlapping that the state schools now suffer. . . ." [23] Time has not yet brought in a decision and the issue is not entirely moribund. As late as January 22, 1948, a number of legislators, alumni of both the University and State College, introduced a bill to prevent the erection of a large stadium in Jackson to accommodate the football games of the schools. They detected in this project a far-seeing movement once more to attempt the consolidation and removal of the two institutions.[24]

When the Governor's plan had been destroyed, the legislature, as though to insure the permanence of the University, voted an unusually large appropriation (a million six hundred thousand dollars) for new buildings on the present site, as well as for scientific equipment and other improvements.[25] The result was the construction by 1929 of the graduate school building, the cafeteria, the gymnasium, stadium, and field house, the University high school for practice teaching, Lamar Hall for the law school, one dormitory for women and six for men, and the auxiliary steam plant.[26] It is not inconceivable that such a munificent achievement had been the ultimate intention of the Governor, who provoked it by the drastic device of suggesting removal and consolidation. Shrewd ingenuity and devious methods were certainly characteristics of "The Man" with the red neck-tie and diamond stick-pin.

By now Governor Bilbo was openly hostile to Hume's continuance as chancellor. Medford Evans had said, "The most portentous man in Oxford today is Alfred Hume. . . ."[27] He might have added in the state as well. Bilbo was publicly declaring the chancellor to be "temperamentally unfit" to hold the office. To cite Evans again, "Certainly he is temperamentally unfit to be a cat's-paw."[28] Furthermore he was adamantly opposed to the "spoils system" in Mississippi politics when it affected University personnel.[29] When Evans wrote, rumors were already afloat that as soon as the Governor had made enough appointments to control the Board of Trustees, Hume would be relieved of office. In February, 1929, the Oxford paper was referring to the political intrigue between Bilbo and the Board to oust

Hume.[30] Early the next year the student paper reported editorially: "The student body is deeply concerned over a persistent rumor that the Governor of Mississippi has formed the intention of removing Dr. Alfred Hume as Chancellor of this institution. . . ."[31]

The ax fell on June 13, 1930. On that date the Board met to consider the election of executive officials of the state schools. There were still those among the Trustees who favored Hume. Accordingly he was nominated. On the other side the former chancellor, J. N. Powers, was nominated. The vote was six for the latter as against four for the former.[32] Chancellor Hume's term of office was therefore at an end. For a brief moment between the departure of Hume and the return of Powers, Christopher Longest, professor of Spanish and director of the summer session, was acting chancellor.[33]

CHAPTER XIV

Nightmare and Restoration

THE next two years were ones which most Mississippians would like to forget. Only two of the six state schools remained untouched by the sweeping dismissals and replacements, Delta State Teachers College and Alcorn Agricultural and Mechanical College. It is instructive to note the reasons: the latter, being a black institution and having no political significance, escaped unharmed; the former, being under a separate board of trustees over which the Governor had not yet achieved control, stood fast. But with regard to the other four (the University, the Agricultural and Mechanical College, the State College for Women, and the Teachers College at Hattiesburg), the new executive officials were handed lists of faculty members and other employees, who were *personae non gratae* to the state administration and who were summarily relieved of their positions without cause and replaced by others who were acceptable.[1] In these four, one hundred seventy-nine persons were dismissed.[2] At the University the total was thirty-one removed, two demoted in rank.[3] To newspaper reporters Governor Bilbo is reputed to have said, "Boys, we have just hung up a new record."[4]

The people of the state, and indeed the nation, were shocked beyond measure. Major Frederick Sullens, editor of the *Jackson Daily News*, wrote that the faculty was not merely revised, "It was ravished. Criminally assaulted without reason, justification, or excuse."[5] The organ of the state educational association, referring to "the sordid tragedies recently enacted at our state supported colleges," remarked, "Everybody knows that two motives were uppermost, namely, to punish enemies and to reward friends." [6] Chancellor James H. Kirkland of Vanderbilt University exclaimed, "It was the most notorious and disgraceful act in the history of American Education." [7] The Southern Association of Colleges and Secondary Schools took the dramatic position that such action put the Board of Trustees "outside the category of educational bodies." [8] In Oxford it was said that "the citizens . . . regret the removal of Dr. Hume. It touches them deep in their hearts." [9]

The precarious position of the chancellor has always been recognized, but it had been a long time since the Board had reached down into the faculty and taken bold action in removals. To be sure, such procedure was not unknown. In 1886 the Board had peremptorily declared all the chairs of instruction vacant and as a result Chancellor Stewart had indignantly resigned. Again in 1889 seven of the nine full professors were relieved of their positions. But the work of 1930 was on a larger scale and moreover involved four of the state schools instead of one.

The vacancies were immediately filled. In some cases undoubtedly the new faculty members were chosen on the basis of partisan politics. The most notable instance was the new vice-chancellor, who also held the office of dean of men and head of the department of philosophy and psychology. He had been a state senator and a floor leader of the followers of Governor Bilbo. But in other cases the new professors were chosen on the basis of merit and for that reason have been continued on the faculty even after this critical period.

Meanwhile, the state was girding for the gubernatorial election of 1931. As early as the summer of 1930 candidates were announcing for the office. Most of them had in their platforms an outraged protest against the drastic procedure of Governor Bilbo and a promise that they, if elected, would remove the Board of Trustees from politics. The state was rising in revolt against the abuse of its educational institutions.

The people of the state were not alone. It was also becoming more and more apparent that the national accrediting organizations were going to interfere in "the Mississippi imbroglio." The chief of these was the Southern Association of Colleges and Secondary Schools, of which the University of Mississippi had been one of the six honored charter members in the days of Chancellor Fulton. That body met in Atlanta, December 4, 1930, and in a strongly worded resolution suspended the Mississippi institutions, the action to take effect on September 1, 1931.[10] As soon as that became known on the campus, irate students, for the second time in the history of the University, burned a Governor in effigy.[11]

Most of the other accrediting bodies rapidly followed the lead of the Southern Association and either suspended the various divisions of the University or put them on probation. No one had anticipated such widespread national action. The Board and the officials of the state schools now began a frantic effort to avert the final suspension or, failing that, to bolster the declining enrollment.[12] With all the characteristics of a candidate "stumping" the state for political office, they carried on what they euphemistically called a "campaign of information."[13] One of the Trustees proposed a much more radical solution of the problem which now faced the state. Launching a tirade against the tyranny of the Southern Association of Colleges and Secondary Schools and crying, "The doctrine of state rights is not dead," he called upon the schools of Mississippi to defy the sentence of suspension, form their own accrediting association, and summon other states to secede from the Southern Association and form a new one.[14]

All this feverish effort to escape the consequences but not the fact of politicalization of the state institutions of higher learning was of no avail. Students were going in large numbers to other schools where the work would have national recognition. For instance, during the session of 1929–1930, while Hume was still in office, a total of twelve hundred fifty-four was the enrollment. The next year uncertainty was evident but the final blow had not fallen: eleven hundred eighty-two students registered. The following session, 1931–1932, the number was down to seven hundred seventy-eight.[15]

By the summer of 1931 a new governor, Martin Sennet Conner, had been nominated in the Democratic primaries—tantamount to election in Mississippi. His stand on the school question was known to be opposed to Governor Bilbo's action. But he would not take office until January, 1932, and could not gain control of the Board of Trustees until after his inauguration. The existing regime therefore had a second academic session, 1931–1932, at its disposal.

The new Board finally appointed by Governor Conner held its first meeting on March 1, 1932, and pledged itself to "non-political, non-factional and impartial discharge of duties."[16] Three months later it unanimously reelected Dr. Hume to the office of chancellor replacing Powers, as he had once before replaced him in 1924.[17] He was also designated again the head of the department of mathematics. The restoration was to be effective on September 1, 1932.[18]

There have been many judgments passed upon this era in the history of the University. Several opinions have been indicated at the beginning of the chapter. However, one of Bilbo's opponents said later: ". . . there is no question in my mind that even though the University was discredited at that time by the Southern Association, it was Bilbo's action that finally started the University on the road to a higher standard."[19] Certainly the memory of what once happened has served to free the University from too much external supervision.

The most interesting contemporary discussion, possibly a perverse one, came from a professor at the University of Alabama. In a paper on "The Mississippi Imbroglio," Clarence Cason posed the following considerations:

"What success the Americans will have in forcing their unripe standards upon the reluctant state of Mississippi, how long the battle will last, and what its consequences may reveal are subjects for exciting conjecture. For the state of Mississippi is a bulwark of passive resistance . . . it remains a neglected outpost of the quiet splendors of the old regime. . . .

"Are there not some free spirits in America, who, momentarily dropping their masks of conformity, are able to descry a quality of hardihood in these people; a sinewy stiffness of character which, if quixotic in a measure, is still not without a kind of stark and lonely grandeur in this docile world?" [20]

The return of Hume as chancellor for the second time was a veritable restoration. Greeted with acclaim by Oxford and the University, he found the institution in dire straits. The immediate task was to secure once more the recognition of the University by the appropriate accediting bodies, in particular the Southern Association of Colleges and Secondary Schools.

An even more pressing consideration was the issue of personalities. Were all the new professors to be summarily dismissed and all those whom they had supplanted returned to their former posts? To the great credit of Chancellor Hume, no such revenge was contemplated.[21] Some of the earlier members of the faculty would be called back; some of the newer ones would be retained. Each case was to be determined individually and on its own merits. To have dealt with the matter in wholesale fashion would have been to repeat the original error in an equally unjust manner. There were some fortunate resignations, some demotions in rank, some outright dismissals. But the entire settlement—an exceedingly delicate one—was accomplished by an apparently amicable arrangement.

The local problem having been handled satisfactorily, Hume turned vigorously to the pursuit of having the institution re-accredited. As early as December, 1932, his efforts were successful in securing for the University once more membership in the Southern Association of Colleges and Secondary Schools, although with the conditional statement that, due to financial difficulties, understandable in the midst of depression, it did not meet one or more standards. A year later this qualification was removed and the University again enjoyed full status in the association it had helped to establish.[22]

Within the next two or three years the schools of the University which had been barred from or put on probation by their appropriate professional associations were restored and public confidence soon returned. Attendance began to increase immediately. In 1932–1933 it was eight hundred twenty-one; the next year, eleven hundred fifty-four; and the year following, twelve hundred ninety-seven, the last figure being the largest enrollment the school had ever had up to that time.[23]

Although the gloom of the world-wide economic depression was deepening and the University faced a disastrous lack of funds, renewed progress was evident. An important new building, the University hospital, occupied by the medical school, was completed in 1934. The department of psychology was made autonomous and the four-year curriculum in pharmacy was instituted.[24] Thus the tremendous task of reestablishing the good name of the University of Mississippi was the crowning glory of Chancellor Hume's long career at the institution.

In 1935 Hume was approaching sixty-nine years of age. He had served the University for forty-three years. Although at critical moments still in the future the University would turn to him again for guidance, it was now felt that his major achievement as an administrator had been accomplished. On January 25, 1935, therefore, he presented to the Board of Trustees his resignation as chancellor, although he retained his status as professor of mathematics and as head of that department.[25] The professorship of mathematics was the only position for which he had ever made formal application, all the others—dean, vice-chancellor, acting chancellor, chancellor, chancellor emeritus (a title he still held)—came to him without any direct or indirect solicitation on his part.[26] At the same meeting of the Board which accepted his resignation (effective June 30, 1935) and elected a new chancellor, the Trustees voted him the honorary distinction of chancellor emeritus, the first in the history of the institution.[27]

"The monument which Alfred Hume has built for himself is in the hearts and minds of his students. Like the campus negroes, who early learned to seek out 'the Doctor' when they needed a 'little loan' to tide them over a period of financial difficulty, the old grads know that they can always depend upon him to do them a good turn or to offer wise and practical advice—and a few, like the negroes, sometimes find it convenient to borrow a few dollars when they are far from home and without funds.

"And what if he does lose a few dollars now and then? His dividends for a kindly and enlightened life are of the richest: the highest praises from his colleagues, from the Board of Trustees, and from old friends and students, who always go to see him when they return to the campus; the love and veneration of all who know him well; warm letters and cards at Christmas and on birthdays from men now prominent whom he knew as freshmen and sophomores. Combining firmness with sympathy and strong moral convictions with humaneness and kindliness, Alfred Hume, worthy son of Vanderbilt, will be remembered not only as a gifted teacher and fearless administrator but also as one who exemplified in his unassuming fashion

'. . . that best portion of a good man's life,
His little, nameless, unremembered acts
Of kindness and of love'." [28]

As the student paper put it, "Chancellor Hume will never die." [29]

CHAPTER XV

The University Comes of Age

THE new chancellor was Alfred Benjamin Butts, who by the terms of his election assumed the office on July 1, 1935.[1] Although born in Durham, North Carolina, May 3, 1890, he had been brought to Mississippi at the early age of two. His undergraduate work was done at Mississippi State College, where he received the Bachelor of Science degree in 1911. Two years later the degree of Master of Science was conferred on him by the same institution. By 1915 he also had a Master of Arts degree from Columbia University and by 1920 the degree of Doctor of Philosophy from Columbia. Ten years later he secured the degree of Bachelor of Laws from Yale. From 1911 until his election to the University chancellorship, he was on the faculty of State College, going up through the ranks, finally being made vice-president in 1930. At the University he carried the title of professor of law in addition to his position as chancellor and often served on the summer faculties of such schools as Ohio State University, the University of California at Los Angeles, and the University of Hawaii.

As the Federal government began to pull the nation out of its economic illness, funds became available both from Washington and from Jackson for a reinvigoration of the University, which now experienced one of the most impressive building booms in any period of its history.[2] Between the years 1937 and 1945, a total amount of $1,260,858.39 was spent on construction. Of that sum ninety-two thousand five hundred dollars had been appropriated by the state, the remainder consisting of grants and loans from the national gov-

152

ernment and other sources.³ The major buildings were four new dormitories for men and two for women, twenty-two faculty residences and one faculty apartment, the astronomy building, the physics building, and the new observatory, but there were a number of others, such as the Rush C. Weir Student Union and the swimming pool. The Lamar bridge across the "Hilgard cut" was erected connecting the school with the town of Oxford. And recreational facilities were improved and increased.⁴ When the student union building was completed, an "open house" was held for the friends of the University. The local paper, in describing the event, mentioned that fifty-five major and minor structures were either finished or were nearing completion.⁵

The University also entered the field of publicity in order to familiarize the public with its reacquired status, good standing, and continued development. That was done chiefly through the establishment of the University News Bureau, which has grown from a part-time office to a fully equipped department of the institution.⁶ The library, long a weak spot in the entire arrangement, was expanding. A particularly generous gift was made by Mrs. Garner, widow of James W. Garner, a native Mississippian and late professor of political science at the University of Illinois. Professor Garner's library was presented to the University of Mississippi and also the amount of ten thousand dollars to purchase other books.⁷ A similar plan was put into effect by Mrs. Alexander Lee Bondurant as a memorial to her eminent husband, the late dean of the graduate school. The widow of the late Senator Byron Patton Harrison presented his office library of government documents, manuscripts, letters, telegrams, newspaper clippings, and about seventy framed pictures.⁸

On December 7, 1939, the General Education Board of the Rockefeller Foundation, New York, appropriated twenty-five thousand dollars to the University for the purchase of books and periodicals for the library. The gift was contingent upon the University's raising fifty thousand dollars from other sources for the same purpose before December 31, 1940. Through the cooperation of the Board of Trustees, the faculty and staff, and alumni and friends of the University, forty-one thousand dollars was raised during 1940. The remaining nine thousand was secured by a grant from the Carnegie Corporation of New York.[9]

Maturity and progress were the themes of the period of Chancellor Butts's administration. Even the football team felt the urge to modernity: it became the first in the nation to travel by airplane to a game when it was flown to Philadelphia to play Temple University in the autumn of 1937.[10] A Reserve Officers Training Corps unit was established in 1936. Still later a Naval Reserve Officers Training Corps unit was set up at the University.

Of even greater significance as signs of maturity and progress was Butts's formulation and operation of an excellent faculty policy. How he did it on the money he had to work with is a matter of wonder; and the fact that the faculty he accumulated were willing, with a few exceptions, to stay at the University during the days of low salary, when most of them could have left at almost any time for better pay, is a tribute to the chancellor's ability to establish a feeling of security and well-being throughout the institution.[11]

First, Butts promised that during his administration no member of the faculty or staff would be dismissed by him for political reasons, that no person would ever be recommended by him for employment for political reasons, and that no relative of his would ever be employed on the faculty or staff of the University. When he left in 1946, he was able to say that he had faithfully kept these promises.

Second, note should be made of the so-called "Ph. D. rule." Butts's own words in his final report to the Trustees are the clearest statement of this practice:

> Early in the present administration, which began eleven years ago on July 1, 1935, the rule was established that the doctor's degree would be prerequisite to the appointment or promotion of any member of the teaching faculty above the rank of assistant professor.

This rule has been rigidly followed. No exception has been made to it in any academic division or department of the University except in the School of Law, where the first bachelor's degree and the LL.B. are required for ranks above the assistant professorship, and in the Department of Accountancy, where one who is a Certified Public Accountant meets the requirement.

As a result of this policy there are now more than sixty members of the University faculty who hold the doctor's degree, as contrasted with twenty-nine in 1935. Young men on the faculty have been continuously encouraged to complete their graduate work.

The Chancellor strongly urges that this policy be continued, for the University cannot afford to do less than is done in all good universities to assure the upholding of academic standards and to maintain the quality of its work at its highest level.

Throughout the present administration every appointment and promotion has been made strictly on the basis of merit and no factor has ever been allowed to outweigh the importance of securing for each position the person who was best qualified for the duties of the position and who could be employed for the salary available.

The Chancellor also desires to emphasize to the Board of Trustees that he has never originated the appointment of any member of the faculty or staff other than deans and heads of administrative (non-academic) departments that are not part of the eight academic divisions of the University. All other members of the faculty and staff have been recommended for appointment and promotion by their department heads and deans to the Chancellor.[12]

Another keynote of this period in the history of the University was that of responsible service to the community and state. An example was the clinic for crippled children held at the University hospital early in 1942 No charge was made for the service. An outstanding pediatrician from Memphis was imported for the purpose and all parents within the outlying district were urged to bring their children for examination.[13] All in all, the University of Mississippi was struggling toward the fulfillment of the ideal expressed by Chancellor Butts in his inaugural address: "Even as Oxford and Cambridge of old, our educational institutions of today must be training schools for public service.... Universities must be free to encourage their faculties and their students to pursue new thoughts, new ideas, new tendencies, new movements, and to make as logic dictates applications of knowledge for the common good of mankind. Universities must be mindful of the economic, political, and social life of the nation." [14]

The enrollment was increasing almost beyond capacity. The problem of living quarters and housing for students became a subject of many faculty meetings.[15] During the three school years, 1935–1939, attendance passed thirteen hundred and was moving upward. By the opening of the academic session of 1939–1940 special attention was called to the matriculation of the fourteen-hundredth student, a youth from Portsmouth, New Hampshire. The town paper noted that a quarter of a century earlier an Oxford man had brought the student body up to five hundred. The University had indeed made proud progress not only in numbers but also in extent of the knowledge of its name. The fond hope was recorded that by 1949 the enrollment would reach twenty-five hundred.[16] As a matter of fact that number was reached and passed three years earlier than was anticipated. Returning prosperity, large faculty, and larger student body brought also traffic problems for the campus and the necessity of hiring special patrolmen for that purpose.[17]

In the meanwhile, events far beyond the confines of the United States began to happen which were to impinge upon the deep southern state of Mississippi and its University isolated among the hills of Lafayette county. The horizon became darker and darker. Americans began to gird themselves for the inevitable. And finally, on December 7, 1941, it happened—the United States was once more, within a brief generation, at war: "Most of us will long remember the morning of Monday, December 8, when Chancellor Butts had a radio rigged up in Fulton Chapel and students and faculty members who were not listening in elsewhere came to hear President Roosevelt's war message to Congress. There was no flag-waving, cheering,

THE UNIVERSITY COMES OF AGE   157

or braggadocio. At the end somebody in the back of the auditorium yipped 'On to Tokyo!' but nobody joined in and we all went out with little or no conversation. In a matter of weeks we were involved in questions of advising students as to which was the best of many routes into useful war-service—ERC, deferments for technical study, Selective Service—all the rest of it." [18]

Needless to say, the University felt the impact of "total war." In 1941–1942, attendance, which only the year before had been fourteen hundred seventy-three, dwindled to thirteen hundred forty-seven. The next year the downward movement continued, the size of the student body being eleven hundred eighty-eight. During 1943–1944 it reached the lowest attendance (seven hundred four) since the session of 1922–1923, although a year later the slight increase was not notable, the enrollment being only eight hundred forty-six.[19] The armed services were also making inroads into the faculty. The Trustees had adopted a liberal policy of granting leaves of absence and many professors left to perform war duties. For the period from July 1, 1942, to December 15, 1943, even the chancellor was on active duty as an officer in the Judge Advocate General's department. During the interval Dr. Hume was called to his second term as acting chancellor.[20]

As the nation girded for the critical emergency, Chancellor Butts and the mayor of Oxford made available to the War Department the facilities of the local airport and the University.[21] The Mississippi delegation in Washington was called upon to expedite the matter.[22] Early in February, 1942, it was reported that both Army and Navy were seriously considering the location.[23] There was even discussion of suspending athletics for the duration of the hostilities.[24] By springtime an elaborate Army Day observance was held on the campus with a colorful ceremonial parade of the cadets of the Reserve Officers Training Corps.[25]

In due time the University had four contracts, for medical school units of both Army and Navy, a Specialized Training and Reassignment unit, and a unit of the Army Specialized Training Program. The first trainees of any kind, a hundred sixty of them, arrived on the campus on September 26, 1942.[26] At the height of its service (1944) the University had fifty-eight men in the two medical units, eighty-nine in the Specialized Training and Reassignment unit, and four hundred seventeen in the Specialized Training Program.[27] At the same time the second semester registration showed only five hundred five civilian students, of whom three hundred sixty-five were women.[28] Thus, along with other colleges and universities throughout the nation, the campus took on the appearance of a military post.

But the spirit of the place was not broken. "A Northern Soldier" gave his impressions thus: "Ole Miss comes as a very pleasant surprise to soldiers stationed here, especially if they have come from camps elsewhere. . . .

". . . the first thing that strikes incoming soldiers, after the initial surprise of seeing the coeds here, is their great friendliness. Everyone says 'Hello.' Soldiers are so taken aback by the inversion of the procedures that they have grown accustomed to, that it takes them a great deal of time to recover. By the time they do recover, they are shipped out.

"The soldier is thus left with a very pleasant memory of Ole Miss, what he might have done while here, and is reminded that somewhere while not on furlough he was regarded as a human being. Ole Miss gets the credit for these things. . . .

"Here, at Ole Miss, dogs are friendly and gay, condescend to march with the soldiers, trotting gaily at the head of the line, go to calisthenics with them and even the messhalls. Some of the dogs even do the hated stadium run with the men. . . .

"The predominant impression left with the soldier is one of friendliness and hospitality. . . . And he approves of it wholeheartedly. Some day, he'll gather his grandchildren about him and tell them, who are eager to hear of the Battle of Tokyo, 'Now, when I was in Ole Miss . . .' Maybe he'll even root for the team."[29]

The needs of the civilian students were never sacrificed, although such a possibility would have solved many administrative problems. Underneath the tumult of war the life of the school was going on. The Religious Emphasis Week was held as usual. The Lyceum programs were continued.[30] Athletic events were resumed after having been suspended for only a year and a half, and the band still accompanied the football team on its trips.[31] The Board itself was reorganized in 1944 and removed from too close political supervision by losing its *ex officio* membership and by being given the privilege of electing its own presiding officer.

Finally, at long last, the second World War—which had taken the lives of a hundred thirty-seven sons of the University—was over. But even before the end, the faculty had begun to prepare for the onrush of returning veterans. Arrangements were made for the purchase and distribution of books and supplies under the appropriate governmental agencies. The University agreed to publish a small manual of information for those who were interested.[32] By the autumn of 1945 the returning soldier was a reality at the University of Mississippi. The attendance during that session, 1945–1946, was two thousand five, the largest enrollment in the history of the institution and two and a half times that of the preceding year.[33]

The University staggered under the impact. A rapid increase of the faculty became imperative, as well as the necessity of a vast building program to take care of the tremendous growth. It was indeed a more immediate and serious crisis for the University than the war had been. Nerves were taut. The new professors were complaining about the shortage or the inadequacy of housing. The GI's were incensed over the long cafeteria lines in which they were compelled to wait for meals. Those on waiting lists were clamoring for admission. And, as if all this upheaval were not sufficient, the term of office of Chancellor Butts was running out.[34] The Trustees were therefore faced with a difficulty of their own making, namely, the task of selecting a new executive for the University.

It was a thorough but tedious process, beginning in the early part of 1946. The qualifications of over two hundred applicants were considered. A decision was reached on June 14, when John Davis Williams, president of Marshall College, Huntington, West Virginia, was elected as Butts's successor, his term of office to begin on September 1, 1946.[35] Meanwhile, Chancellor Butts had been offered a place as a high-ranking civilian employee of the War Department and was to begin his duties in Washington on July 1. The Board granted him leave of absence from that date to August 31 and once more summoned Dr. Hume to serve as acting chancellor during the interval—his third time in that capacity.[36]

Williams was born in Newport, Kentucky, Christmas day, 1902. The Bachelor and Master of Arts degrees were conferred on him by his state university in 1926 and 1930 respectively. Columbia University granted him the Doctor of Education degree in 1940. From 1923 to 1935 he served in a number of places on the teaching and administrative staffs of secondary schools. In the latter year and until 1942 he was a member of the department of education and director of the practice school of the University of Kentucky. In 1942 he was elected president of Marshall College, where he remained until coming to the University of Mississippi.

The phenomenal expansion of the University continued. During Williams's first year the enrollment was thirty-two hundred thirteen, an increase of more than twelve hundred over the preceding year.[37] In its hundredth year the University reached thirty-four hundred fifty-eight, a far cry from the eighty students a century ago. The legislature was also generous in allocating monies to the institution. An interesting note occurs in the minutes of a meeting of the Board of Trustees in the spring of 1945: "Request that future allotments to the University be made without reference to the Seminary and Land Grant Funds, and that the Legislature be asked to make future appropriations without reference to these funds. *Approved.*" [38]

By the summer of 1947 twenty-three building projects, totaling

THE UNIVERSITY COMES OF AGE 161

over nine hundred thousand dollars, were in progress. The student publication described them as follows:

"Among the projects being built through private contractors are: construction of four new boys' dormitories, construction of temporary classrooms and the auxiliary cafeteria, construction of the faculty apartments building, renovation of the old Physics Building, renovation of Ricks Hall, and the construction and repair of heating equipment.

"Included in the projects being handled by University supervision and labor are: renovation of the Lyceum, conversion of the Armory into a recreational center, construction of a maintenance shop, construction of three greenhouses, construction of an annex building for the medical school.

"Remodeling of the Chancellor's residence, repairing and refurnishing men's and women's dormitories, repair of the storm drain on football field, construction of parking areas, grading and sodding of veterans housing area.

"Construction of sidewalks, preparation of the site and drainage for the new laundry, enclosing porch of medical school for additional classrooms, building office facilities in the power house for the superintendent of utilities.

"Installation of complete modern lighting in the library, final plans of survey for new football practice fields, and general plumbing, heating, and electrical repairs for all academic buildings."[39]

Many inadequacies remain at the University of Mississippi. Everything is not perfect. But the dawn of the new century is full of promise.

(So ended the 1948 manuscript, perhaps a proper conclusion for the occasion it commemorated, a suitable monument to a past that rapidly disappeared. Not long afterwards the mood of the times and the country changed almost beyond recognition in events that will be recounted in another volume.)

Notes

Chapter I

1. Paul H. Saunders, *Latitude and Magnetic Elements at the University of Mississippi* (Nashville, 1895), 14, 26.

2. The first stanza of the Alma Mater song of the University of Mississippi. The words were written in 1925 by Mrs. A. W. Kahle, the music by her son, W. F. Kahle. In 1937 the music was somewhat revised by Ruth McNeil.

There has been some complaint that the music is unoriginal and is the same as the so-called Cornell song, "High Above Cayuga's Waters." The criticism is without foundation. In the first place, an Alma Mater song is not supposed to be unique: it should in the very nature of the case recall older tunes that have sentimental value. For instance, the University of Pennsylvania uses the old imperial Russian anthem, which is in turn based on a popular barracks melody sung by early Russian troops. The University of Pittsburgh has adopted the music of the imperial Austrian anthem. Such cases could be multiplied. As a matter of fact, the Cornell song is not original, but is a traditional tune used by many other schools.

In the second place, however, the real basis of the University of Mississippi music is the church tune, "Autumn," written by Louis Bourgeois in 1551 for a Calvinist psalm-book of Geneva. (The hymn, "Mighty God, While Angels Bless Thee," is commonly sung to this melody today.) "Autumn" has sixty-two notes in the melody; the University of Mississippi song, sixty; and the Cornell music, fifty-two. In the Mississippi song, twenty-five notes are from the religious tune only, eighteen are the same as in both the religious tune and the Cornell song, nine are entirely original, and eight are the same as the Cornell music. There can be no doubt that the basis of the University of Mississippi Alma Mater is the church tune. It may be noted incidentally that the traditional Alma Mater music, borrowed by Cornell, is itself obviously related to the Genevan psalm tune.

3. John N. Waddel, *Historical Discourse Delivered on the Quarter-Centennial of the University of Mississippi* (Oxford, Miss., 1873), 3f.

4. N. C. Hathorn, "A Financial History of the University of Mississippi

from its Endowment in 1819 to 1900" (M.A. thesis, University of Mississippi, 1938), 1.
   5. *Ibid.*
   6. *Memorial to the Congress of the United States from the Board of Trustees of the University of Mississippi* (Nashville, 1894), 9f.
   7. *Ibid.*, 8f.
   8. *Ibid.*, 9.
   9. Hathorn, *op. cit.*, 3.
  10. *Ibid.*, 4f.
  11. *Ibid.*, 6.
  12. *Ibid.*, 7.
  13. Edward Mayes, *The State University* (Jackson, Miss., 1887), 9.
  14. *Ibid.*, 11.
  15. *Ibid.*
  16. *Ibid.*
  17. Hathorn, *op. cit.*, 10–14.
  18. Mayes, *op. cit.*, 5f.
  19. Hathorn, *op. cit.*, 14.
  20. Mayes, *op. cit.*, 11f.
  21. Manuscript Minutes of the Board of Trustees of the University of Mississippi under the date of Jan. 17, 1845. These will hereinafter be cited thus: Board Minutes, followed by the date of the meeting.
  22. Hathorn, *op. cit.*, 16.
  23. Mississippi House of Representatives, *Journal* (Regular Session, January–February, 1840), Jan. 7, 1840 (p. 17).
  24. Hathorn, *op. cit.*, 17.
  25. Edward Mayes, *History of Education in Mississippi* (Washington, 1899), 124.
  26. *Woodville Republican* (Mississippi), March 14, June 27, 1846. See also S. T. Lyle, "Conditions Relating to Sectionalism in Mississippi from 1838 to 1852" (M.A. thesis, University of Mississippi, 1932), 100–115.
  27. *Woodville Republican*, Jan. 31, 1846. See Lyle, *op. cit.*, 10.
  28. Manuscript Matriculation Book of the University of Mississippi, covering the sessions 1848–1849 through 1858–1859.
  29. *Ibid.*
  30. Mississippi *Laws* (Regular Session of Legislature, January–February, 1844), Chapter 56.
  31. Board Minutes, Jan. 17, 1845.
  32. *Ibid.*, Nov. 23, 1859; June 28, 1866.
  33. *Ibid.*, Jan. 15, 17, 1845.
  34. *Ibid.*, Jan. 15, 1846.

NOTES TO CHAPTER I

35. Manuscript Deed Book C, Lafayette County Courthouse, Oxford, Miss., 211–213.

36. J. F. H. Claiborne, *Mississippi, as Province, Territory and State* (Jackson, Miss., 1880), I, 536f.

37. J. C. Hathorn, "A Period Study of Lafayette County from 1836 to 1860 with Emphasis on Population Groups" (M.A. thesis, University of Mississippi, 1938), 35.

38. "Ole Miss' First Lady," *Ole Miss Alumni Review*, II, No. 2 (April, 1948), 15f., 23.

39. *Mississippi: A Guide to the Magnolia State*, compiled and written by the Federal Writers' Project of the Works Progress Administration (New York, 1938), 255.

40. *Ibid.*

41. *Ibid.*

42. W. B. Hamilton, "Holly Springs, Mississippi, To the Year 1878" (M.A. thesis, University of Mississippi, 1931), 200f.

43. Board Minutes, April 27, 1847.

44. *Ibid.*, Jan. 11, 1848.

45. *Ibid.*, Feb. 25, 1848.

46. *Ibid.*

47. *Ibid.*

48. *Ibid.*, July 12, 1848.

49. In the *Bulletin of the University of Mississippi* (Catalogue 1947–1948) occurred a paragraph which is a mosaic of phrases from similar statements in catalogues as early as the one of 1887. It is quoted here with each passage preceded by the date of the publication in which it first appeared:

(1912:) The University of Mississsippi is a state institution and is therefore wholly
  (1937:) non-sectarian [from 1912 to 1937 the word was *unsectarian*].
    (1912:) Religious life is fostered,
      (1946:) however, and
        (1887:) every encouragement is given to upright living and the formation of high Christian character.
          (1912:) It is believed
            (1887:) that influences are not barren of results.
    (1911:) The ministers of Oxford
      (1946:) participate
        (1911:) sympathetically and

(1946:) diligently in
      (1911:) all that concerns the welfare of the students.
   This innocuous paragraph has a background that goes back to July 12, 1848. On that date the Board of Trustees "Resolved that the evidences of Christianity be taught in the University." This motion passed over the protest of two Trustees who desired simply that for each academic session the University hire a chaplain who would open and close each day with prayer. Two days later a minister (John Newton Waddel) was elected to the faculty as professor of ancient languages.
   In protest against this definite establishment of the University of Mississippi on a Christian foundation, one Trustee, "a bold, pronounced infidel," resigned. But from that time to the present, no further objection has been registered. The formal teaching of the evidences of Christianity lasted until 1930 and there is still a course in the philosophy of the Christian religion. Three clergymen have presided over the institution during its history, Longstreet, a Methodist, Barnard, an Episcopalian, and Waddel, a Presbyterian. Many ministers have served (and continue to do so) in various capacities on the faculty. By formal action, May 18, 1944, the meetings of the Board are opened with prayer. The statement made in the catalogue of 1887, reasserted in the *Historical Catalogue 1849–1909*, that the University of Mississippi is "a Christian institution," has therefore never been successfully challenged.
   This is not to say that the University is an organ of Christian propaganda, nor that any particular variety of Christian faith is taught, nor that the beliefs and practices of other religions are hindered. As a matter of record, many adherents of other faiths come to the University, find it friendly to them, and remain loyal to their Alma Mata. But it does mean that the University of Mississippi is not, as some have called it, "a regularly organized infidel institution."
   50. Waddel, *Historical Discourse*, 9.
   51. Board Minutes, July 12, 1848.
   52. *Ibid.*, July 13, 1848.
   53. *Ibid.*
   54. *Ibid.*, July 14, 1848.
   55. *Ibid.*
   56. *Ibid.*, July 15, 1848.
   57. *Ibid.*
   58. *Ibid.*, Nov. 6, 1848.
   59. *Ibid.*, Nov. 7, 1848.
   60. *Daily Times* (Jackson, Miss.), Aug. 24, 1875. Italics mine. See A. C. Trusty, "Readings in Mississippi History: Reconstruction" (M.A. thesis, University of Mississippi, 1934), 267.
   61. Mayes, *History of Education in Mississippi*, 118.

62. Mayes, *The State University*, 2.
63. *Ibid.*, 4. Italics mine.
64. Mississippi *Laws* (Regular Session, January–March, 1846), chapter 75.
65. Mayes, *The State University*, 4.

CHAPTER II

1. Manuscript Matriculation Book of the University of Mississippi, covering the sessions 1848–1849 through 1858–1859.
2. John N. Waddel, *Memorials of Academic Life: Being an Historical Sketch of the Waddel Family, Identified Through Three Generations with the History of the Higher Education in the South and Southwest* (Richmond, 1891), 262f. Hereinafter: Waddel, *Academic Memorials* (the usual designation of this important work).
3. *Ibid.*, 263f.
4. *Ibid.*, 264f.
5. James E. Pope, "Reminiscences of Dr. George Frederick Holmes," *University of Mississippi Magazine*, XX, No. 2 (December, 1895), 3.
6. See Harvey Wish, "George Frederick Holmes and Southern Periodical Literature of the Mid-Nineteenth Century," *Journal of Southern History*, VII, No. 3 (August, 1941), 343–356. Also S. C. Mitchell, "George Frederick Holmes," *Dictionary of American Biography* (hereinafter: *DAB*), Centenary Edition (New York, 1946), IX, 164.
7. Waddel, *Academic Memorials*, 270.
8. Pope, *op. cit.*, 5.
9. *Ibid.*
10. *Ibid.*, 4.
11. *Ibid.* Mitchell, *op. cit.*, says that at his death his last word was, "England."
12. S. C. Gladden, "A History of the Department of Physics and Astronomy at the University of Mississippi 1849–1932" (a typescript in the Library of the University, 1933), 42–59. See also Edwin Mims, "Albert Taylor Bledsoe," *DAB*, II, 364f.; Waddel, *Academic Memorials*, 279–282.
13. Gladden, *op. cit.*, 26–41; Waddel, *Academic Memorials*, 251–279; T. C. Johnson, Jr., "John Millington," *DAB*, XIII, 441f.
14. Waddel, *Academic Memorials*, 278.
15. *Ibid.*, 268.
16. Gladden, *op. cit.*, 35.
17. Waddel, *Academic Memorials*, 268f.
18. Manuscript Minutes of the Board of Trustees of the University of Mississippi under the date of June 24, 1879. See also Alexander M. Clayton, *Address Delivered at the First Annual Commencement of the University of*

Mississippi (Oxford, Miss., 1849), 16f. The University possesses most of the manuscript Minutes of both literary societies.

19. Waddel, *Academic Memorials*, 267.

20. Acting President Bledsoe's address is printed with Clayton, *op. cit.*, on which see Note 18 above. The quotations are from pp. 26f.

21. Waddel, *Academic Memorials*, 270. See also his *Historical Discourse Delivered on the Quarter-Centennial of the University of Mississippi* (Oxford, Miss., 1873), 12.

22. Waddel, *Academic Memorials*, 269.

23. Manuscript Minutes of the Faculty of the University of Mississippi under the date of April 2, 1849. These will hereinafter be cited thus: Faculty Minutes, followed by the date of the meeting.

24. Faculty Minutes, April 19, 1849.

25. *Ibid.*, June 1, 1849.

26. Board Minutes, July 12, 1849.

27. Faculty Minutes, March 3, 1849, record his presence. He was not at the next meeting, according to Faculty Minutes, March 10, 1849, or thereafter.

28. Waddel, *Academic Memorials*, 271; *Historical Discourse*, 12.

29. John Donald Wade, *Augustus Baldwin Longstreet: A Study of the Development of Culture in the South* (New York, 1942), 296.

30. Bledsoe, *op. cit.*, 27.

31. Board Minutes, July 9-12, 1849.

32. Clayton, *op. cit., passim.*

Chapter III

1. Manuscript Minutes of the Board of Trustees of the University of Mississippi under the date of July 9, 1849.

2. Board Minutes, July 10, 1849. On the contrary, see Harvey Wish, "George Frederick Holmes and Southern Periodical Literature of the Mid-Nineteenth Century," *Journal of Southern History*, VII, No. 3 (August, 1941), 344: "By 1849 a disagreement between the new President and the trustees over student discipline—Holmes disliked the martinet—brought about his forced resignation."

3. Board Minutes, July 11, 1849.

4. *Ibid.*, July 12, 1849. Note especially the new regulation: "The regular exercises of each day shall begin *at sun rise* with prayer. All the Students resident in the College are required to be present, the roll will be called and absentees noted." (Italics mine)

5. *Ibid.*, July 10, 1849.

6. James E. Pope, "Reminiscences of Dr. George Frederick Holmes," *University of Mississippi Magazine*, XX, No. 2 (December, 1895), 3

7. Letter of S. C. Caldwell, Hazlehurst, Miss., to Alfred Hume, University, Miss., May 4, 1927 (in the possession of the University of Mississippi). Board Minutes, July 10, 1850, suggest a reason for Holmes' disaffection for the University:

"Mr. Clayton offered the following resolution. Resolved, that from the fact, that the salaries of the Professors of the University are paid in consideration of their services to the Institution, it is the opinion of the board, that the payment, made to the late Presdt. G. F. Holmes, is as much as was justly due to him: and that no farther allowance can be made with justice to the institution.

"Resolved, that in dissolving the connection between the sd. President and the institution, the board did not design to cast any reflection upon his character, as a man, or his reputation as a scholar.

"Resolved, that the Secretary communicate the foregoing resolution to Presdt. G. F. Holmes, which were adopted."

8. Board Minutes, Feb. 25, 1848.

9. John Donald Wade, *Augustus Baldwin Longstreet: A Study of the Development of Culture in the South* (New York, 1924), 289f.

10. *Ibid*.

11. *Ibid.*, 290.

12. Board Minutes, July 11, 1848.

13. Wade, *op. cit.*, 291; *Bulletin of the University of Mississippi* (Historical Catalogue 1849–1909), 72.

14. Board Minutes, July 14, 1848.

15. J. W. Johnson, "Biographical Sketches of Judge A. B. Longstreet and Dr. F. A. P. Barnard," *Publications of the Mississippi Historical Society*, XII (1912), 131, cites a letter by Longstreet: "Through the influence and eloquence of a Catholic member of the Board, who protested against ever putting a clergyman of any denomination at the head of the college, I was beaten by one vote."

16. Wade, *op. cit.*, 292–294.

17. *Ibid.*, 296.

18. John N. Waddel, *Memorials of Academic Life* ... (Richmond, 1891), 273. Hereinafter: Waddel, *Academic Memorials*.

19. *Ibid.*, 273; Edward Mayes, *Lucius Q. C. Lamar—His Life, Times, and Speeches 1825–1893* (Nashville, 1896), 45.

20. John N. Waddel, *Historical Discourse Delivered on the Quarter-Centennial of the University of Mississippi* (Oxford, Miss., 1873), 19.

21. *Ibid*.

22. *Ibid.*, 12.

23. *Ibid.*, 20.

24. Manuscript Matriculation Book of the University of Mississippi, covering the sessions 1848-1849 through 1858-1859.

25. Waddel, *Academic Memorials*, 276.

26. Manuscript Minutes of the Faculty of the University of Mississippi under the date of Jan. 19, 1850.

27. *Ibid.*, Jan. 24, 1850.

28. *Ibid.*, Dec. 6, 1853.

29. *Ibid.*, May 16, 1854.

30. *Ibid.*, Dec. 12, 1850.

31. Cited in Arthur Palmer Hudson (editor), *Humor of the Old Deep South* (New York, 1936), 396f. Hudson's only comment is: "The scene of the anecdote is probably the University of Mississippi. . . ." The word *probably* should be omitted.

"Old Bullet" was a nickname which the students gave Longstreet. See a feature article on C. L. Moore, of the class of 1858, in the *Blytheville Courier News* (Arkansas), March 11, 1927, in which Moore says, "We used to call him [Longstreet] Old Bullet because his head was as round as a cannon ball." See also the manuscript reminiscences of R. H. Parham, Little Rock, Ark., of the class of 1854, dated June 15, 1913 (in the possession of the University).

In the eighth stanza Longstreet is still further identified as "Judicem" (the Judge). In the ninth the initial *M* stands for Molloy who appears in the Faculty Minutes, Dec. 12, 1850. In the first stanza the change of year from 1850 to 1851 is apparently for the sake of the rhyme.

32. Board Minutes, April 9, 1852.

33. *Ibid.*, July 13, 1852. See also Johnson, *op. cit.*, 133.

34. Board Minutes, July 13, 1852.

35. *Ibid.*, June 16, 1851.

36. *Ibid.*, July 13, 1852.

37. *Ibid.*, July 14, 1852.

38. Jefferson Davis, *Address, Delivered . . . Before the Phi Sigma and Hermaean Societies, of the University of Mississippi, Oxford, July 15, 1852* (Memphis, 1852), 16. See also the brief account in *De Bow's Review*, XIV (News Series, Vol. 1), No. 1 (January, 1853), 90.

39. Cited in A. A. Madden, "Readings in Mississippi History" (M.A. thesis, University of Mississippi, 1928), 14f.

40. State of Mississippi, Governor's Letter Book, J. M. Howry to Gov. J. J. McRae, Oxford, May 1, 1854.

41. Waddel, *Academic Memorials*, 314.

42. Board Minutes, July 16, 1852; Jan. 11, 1854; July 11, 1854.

43. *Ibid.*, July 9, 1855.

44. *Ibid.*, July 11, 1855.

45. Frances Allen Cabaniss and James Allen Cabaniss, "Religion in Ante-Bellum Mississippi," *Journal of Mississippi History*, VI, No. 4 (October, 1944), 214.

46. Wade, *op. cit.*, 305–310. In regard to the development of Know-Nothingism among the Methodists of Mississippi, see N. H. James, "The Journal of Josiah Hinds April 24, 1830–July 10, 1863" (M.A. thesis, University of Mississippi, 1939), 246–252.

47. Board Minutes, July 13, 1854.

48. *Ibid.*, July 16, 1852.

49. *Ibid.*, Aug. 30, 1854.

50. John Fulton, *Memoirs of Frederick A. P. Barnard, D.D., LL.D., L.H.D., D.C.L.* (New York, 1896), 196.

51. Waddel, *Academic Memorials*, 233, 247.

52. Fulton, *op. cit.*, 198–201.

53. Board Minutes, July 11, 1855.

54. *Record of the Testimony and Proceedings, in the Matter of the Investigation, by the Trustees of the University of Mississippi, on the 1st and 2nd of March, 1860, of the Charges Made by H. R. Branham, Against the Chancellor of the University* (Jackson, Miss., 1860), 7.

55. *Ibid.*, 20.

56. *Ibid.*

57. Johnson, *op. cit.*, 144.

58. Waddel, *Academic Memorials*, 324f., 447. See also Fulton, *op. cit.*, 202.

59. Waddel, *Academic Memorials*, 349–355.

60. Fulton, *op. cit.*, 202.

61. *Annals of the American Pulpit*, IV (New York, 1857, 63–67, cited in Wade, *op. cit.*, 295. Cf. similar three-way by-play which occurred during his incumbency at Centenary College. See A. M. Shaw, "A. B. Longstreet's Brief Sojourn in Louisiana" (paper read before the South Central Modern Language Association, Norman, Okla., Oct. 30, 1948).

62. Board Minutes, July 10, 1856 (a called meeting).

63. *Ibid.*, July 14, 1856 (the regular meeting).

64. *Ibid.*, July 15, 1856.

65. *Ibid.*, July 17, 1856.

66. Wade, *op. cit.*, 2.

CHAPTER IV

1. Manuscript Minutes of the Board of Trustees of the University of Mississippi under the date of July 18, 1856.

2. Board Minutes, Aug. 19, 1856; John Fulton, *Memoirs of Frederick A. P. Barnard, D.D., LL.D., L.H.D., D.C.L.* (New York, 1896), 202

NOTES TO CHAPTER IV

3. J. W. Johnson, "Biographical Sketches of Judge A. B. Longstreet and Dr. F. A. P. Barnard," *Publications of the Mississippi Historical Society*, XII (1912), 114.

4. Fulton, *op. cit.*, 202; Johnson, *op. cit.*, 113f.

5. Johnson, *op. cit.*, 143.

6. Fulton, *op. cit.*, 87f.

7. *Ibid.*, 101f.

8. *Ibid.*, 103.

9. *Ibid.*, 194.

10. H. M. Sullivan (editor), *All the Laws and Public Resolutions in Relation to the University of Mississippi, Carefully Compiled and Chronologically Arranged* (Oxford, Miss., 1879), 33.

11. N. C. Hathorn, "A Financial History of the University of Mississippi from its Endowment in 1819 to 1900" (M.A. thesis, University of Mississippi, 1938), 38.

12. Edward Mayes, *The State University* (Jackson, Miss., 1887), 20.

13. Board Minutes, July 16, 1857; John N. Waddel, *Memorials of Academic Life . . .* (hereinafter: *Academic Memorials*) (Richmond, 1891), 330.

14. Fulton, *op. cit.*, 203.

15. *Ibid.*, 235. Some especially interesting information is given in W. L. Kennon, "A Century of Astronomy," *Ole Miss Alumni Review*, I, No. 3 (October, 1947), 7–9.

16. *Bulletin of the University of Mississippi* (Catalogue 1857–1858), 43.

17. Fulton, *op. cit.*, 231. See also *Bulletin of the University of Mississippi* (Historical Catalogue 1849–1909), 9. The latter will hereinafter be cited thus: *Historical Catalogue 1849–1909*.

18. W. L. Kennon and S. C. Gladden, "Historical Apparatus at the University of Mississippi," *American Physics Teacher* (now *American Journal of Physics*), VI, No. 1 (February, 1938), 7.

19. *Ibid.*; Fulton *op. cit.*, 244f.; S. C. Gladden, "A History of the Department of Physics and Astronomy at the University of Mississippi 1848–1932" (a typescript in the Library of the University, 1933), 7, 149–153; Edward Mayes, *History of Education in Mississippi* (Washington, 1899), 150–155; *Historical Catalogue 1849–1909*, 73; J. W. Johnson, "Biographical Sketches of Judge A. B. Longstreet and Dr. F. A. P. Barnard," *Publications of the Mississippi Historical Society*, XII (1912), 113.

20. F. A. P. Barnard, *Improvements Practicable in American Colleges* (Hartford, Conn., 1856).

21. Fulton, *op. cit.*, 446–448.

22. *Ibid.*

23. Board Minutes, July 9, 13, 14, 1858. See F. A. P. Barnard, *Letter to the*

Honorable the Board of Trustees of the University of Mississippi (Oxford, Miss., 1858).

24. Fulton, *op. cit.*, 237.
25. *Ibid.*, 240.
26. *Ibid.*, 244.
27. *Ibid.*, 242f., 447.
28. *Ibid.*, 242, n. 1; 447.
29. *Ibid.*, 244.
30. *Ibid.*, 261. During this interval William D. Moore, professor of English literature, was acting chancellor.
31. *Ibid.*, 269f.
32. Johnson, *op. cit.*, 115.
33. Board Minutes, Nov. 24, 1859.
34. *Ibid.*, Nov. 9, 1857; Fulton, *op. cit.*, 235.
35. Manuscript Minutes of the Faculty of the University of Mississippi under the date of July 10, 1857. The use of cap and gown, however, did not come until much later.
36. Faculty Minutes, March 17, 1857.
37. Waddel, *Academic Memorials*, 307.
38. Fairfax Harrison (editor) and F. B. Harrison (compiler), *Aris Sonis Focisque Being a Memoir of An American Family The Harrisons of Skimino and Particularly of Jesse Burton Harrison and Burton Norvell Harrison* (n.p., 1910), 147f.:

"During the college years [Yale, 1856–1859] Burton Harrison spent his summer vacations with his uncle in Maryland, and thus it was that he introduced into the Cary household in Baltimore the Yale songs, notably his favorite, 'Lauriger Horatius,' to the stirring air of which, thus made familiar, Miss Jennie Cary was later inspired to fit the words of [James Ryder] Randall's verses 'Maryland! My Maryland!' and so start a memorable war-song echoing down the ages."

39. This title had been changed to *chancellor* only seventeen days earlier, Nov. 24, 1859, but was probably still unfamiliar.
40. Faculty Minutes, Dec. 12, 1859.
41. Johnson, *op. cit.*, 144.
42. R. H. Loughridge, "The Life-Work of Professor Hilgard," *In Memoriam Eugene Woldemar Hilgard* (Berkeley, Cal., 1916), 21–31. Hilgard's report is entitled *Report on the Geology and Agriculture of the State of Mississippi* (Jackson, Miss., 1860).
43. Board Minutes, July 1, 1859.
44. *Ibid.*, Nov. 23, 1859.
45. *Ibid.*, June 29, 1892.
46. G. C. Hooker, "The Origin and Development of the University of Mis-

sissippi With Special Reference to Its Legislative Control" (Ph.D. Thesis, Stanford University, 1932), 24f. See also *Historical Catalogue 1849–1909*, 5.

47. Letter incorporated in Board Minutes, July 14, 1858.

48. J. W. Taylor, *An Address Delivered before the Phi Sigma and Hermaean Societies at the Commencement of the University of Mississippi on June 23, 1869* (Oxford, Miss., 1869), 3.

49. Manuscript Matriculation Book of the University of Mississippi, covering the sessions 1848–1849 through 1858–1859; Waddel, *Academic Memorials*, 299, and his *Historical Discourse Delivered on the Quarter-Centennial of the University of Mississippi* (Oxford, Miss., 1873), 13.

50. Johnson, *op. cit.*, 142.

51. *Ibid.*, 121.

52. F. W. Keyes, *An Address Delivered Before the Alumni Association of the University of Mississippi, on the 5th day of July, 1859* (Oxford, Miss., 1859).

53. *Ibid.*, 11.

54. *Ibid.*, 12f.

55. *Ibid.*, 15.

56. *Ibid.*, 19.

57. Faculty Minutes, July 15, 1857.

58. *Ibid.*, Nov. 7, 1859.

59. *Ibid.*, Feb. 2, 1860.

60. *Ibid.*

61. *Record of the Testimony and Proceedings, in the Matter of the Investigation, by the Trustees of the University of Mississippi, On the 1st and 2nd of March, 1860, of the Charges Made by H. R. Branham, Against the Chancellor of the University* (Jackson, Miss., 1860), 18. Hereinafter: *Record of the Testimony.*

62. *Ibid., passim*, especially pp. 18f., 23.

63. Faculty Minutes, Feb. 2, 1860.

64. J. L. Goodloe, "Reminiscences of the University of Mississippi," *University of Mississippi Magazine*, XXVI, No. 2 (December, 1902), 24. This article was concluded in *University of Mississippi Magazine*, XXVI, No. 3 (January, 1903), 11–15.

65. *Record of the Testimony*, 19.

66. *Ibid.*, 20.

67. Faculty Minutes, Feb. 2, 1860.

68. *Record of the Testimony*, 28.

69. *Ibid.*, 3–5.

70. *Ibid.*, 7.

71. *Ibid.*, 26f.

72. *Ibid.*, 29.

73. Cited in Charles S. Sydnor, *A Gentleman of the Old Natchez Region: Benjamin L. C. Wailes* (Durham, N. C., 1938), 232.
74. Goodloe, *op. cit.*, 13.
75. Faculty Minutes, June 23, 1860.
76. *Ibid.*, May 7, Oct. 16, Nov. 26, 1860.
77. *Ibid.*, Nov. 5, 6, 1860.
78. *Ibid.*, Oct. 16, 1860.
79. *Ibid.*, Oct. 24, 1859.
80. *Ibid.*, April 15, 1861.
81. *Ibid.*, Feb. 26, 1861. Another interesting account of this occurrence is in the contemporary diary of a student, Duncan McCollum, particularly the entries dated Feb 22, 23, 25, 26, and 27, 1861. There is a typed copy of this diary in the possession of Professor Bell I. Wiley, Emory University.
82. F. A. P. Barnard, "Autobiographical Sketch," *Publications of the Mississippi Historical Society*, XII (1912), 115.
83. Manuscript Minutes of the Phi Sigma Literary Society, covering the period from May 5, 1849, through Jan. 26, 1867. The references may be found under any specific date indicated. The library mentioned in the motion was apparently that of the society, not that of the University.
84. *Ibid.*
85. *Ibid.*
86. Maud M. Brown, *The University Greys* (Richmond, 1940), 9.
87. *Ibid.*
88. Faculty Minutes, Feb. 11, 25, March 4, 1861.
89. *Ibid.*, Feb. 18, 26, 1861.
90. *Ibid.*, March 18, 1861.
91. *Ibid.*, April 1, 8, 1861.
92. *Ibid.*, April 15, 1861.
93. *Ibid.*, April 22, 1861.
94. Brown, *op. cit.*, 9.
95. Faculty Minutes, May 2, 1861.
96. Faculty Minutes, undated note after the minutes of the meeting on May 2, 1861.
97. Fulton, *op. cit.*, 279.
98. Board Minutes, June 21, 1861. Because of the war the examination of the seniors was administered earlier than usual that year (see Faculty Minutes, April 29, 1861). Twenty-one out of the class of twenty-eight took the examination and passed, but seven were already away in the army (see Faculty Minutes, May 2, 1861). The faculty insisted upon the necessity of the examination as a prerequisite for graduation, but expressed willingness for those seven students to take it whenever they could return (see Faculty Minutes, May 2, 1861). However, the Board Minutes, June 21, 1861, record the grant-

ing of degrees to all twenty-eight. Either the Board itself overruled the faculty or Chancellor Barnard took the matter into his own hands (he was capable of this) and reported the entire twenty-eight to the Board, which then acted without question upon what it took to be the recommendations of the whole faculty.

99. Board Minutes, June 21, 1861.
100. Fulton, *op. cit.*, 283.
101. Board Minutes, Sept. 5, 1861.
102. Faculty Minutes, Sept. 18, 1861.
103. Board Minutes, Oct. 1, 1861.
104. *Ibid.*, Oct. 2, 1861.
105. F. A. P. Barnard, *Report on the Organization of Military Schools, Made to the Trustees of the University of Mississippi, November, 1861* (Jackson, Miss., 1861), 31f. C. F. Thwing, "Frederick Augustus Porter Barnard," *Dictionary of American Biography*, Centenary Edition (New York, 1946), I, 619, erroneously states, "The University, in fact, became a military school." It never did.
106. Board Minutes, Nov. 21, 1861. This degree is often neglected in treatments of Barnard.

Chapter V

1. Maud M. Brown, *The University Greys* (Richmond, 1940).
2. *Ibid.*, 45.
3. *Ibid.*, 21f
4. *Bulletin of the University of Mississippi* (Historical Catalogue 1849–1909), 29. Hereinafter: *Historical Catalogue 1849–1909.*
5. Edward Mayes, *History of Education in Mississippi* (Washington, 1899), 156.
6. Mrs. Jemmy G. Johnson, "The University War Hospital," *Publications of the Mississippi Historical Society*, XII (1912), 94–106; Willie D. Halsell, "The Oxford Hospital in 1862," *Journal of Mississippi History*, VIII, No. 1 (January, 1946), 36–44.
7. Original in the possession of Mrs. Hugh Dietrich, Washington, D. C.
8. Johnson, *op. cit.*, 99f.
9. Cited in *ibid.*, 100.
10. *Historical Catalogue 1849–1909*, 29 n. 1; 35.
11. *Ibid.*, 10, 20, 73.
12. Mayes, *op. cit.*, 157.
13. Manuscript Minutes of the Phi Sigma Literary Society, covering the period from May 5, 1849, through Jan. 26, 1867. This reference may be found under the date of October 9, 1865.

14. H. M. Sullivan (editor), *All the Laws and Public Resolutions in Relation to the University of Mississippi, Carefully Compiled and Chronologically Arranged* (Oxford, Miss., 1879), 17.

15. Manuscript Minutes of the Board of Trustees of the University of Mississippi under the date of Nov. 4, 1864.

Chapter VI

1. Edward Mayes, *History of Education in Mississippi* (Washington, 1899), 159.

2. John N. Waddel, *Memorials of Academic Life* ... (Richmond, 1891), 446, errs in the date. This book will hereinafter be referred to thus: Waddel, *Academic Memorials*.

3. Manuscript Minutes of the Board of Trustees of the University of Mississippi under the date of July 31, 1865.

4. Waddel, *Academic Memorials*, 446.

5. Board Minutes, Aug. 2, 1865.

6. W. L. Lingle, "John Newton Waddel," *Dictionary of American Biography*, Centenary Edition (New York, 1946), XIX, 229f. This is probably the place to refer to the pronunciation of the name *Waddel*. The accent should fall on the first syllable, not the last. Lingle says, "He is reputed to have said that he 'waddeled' through life thus far and could 'waddle' on to the end." The misspellings of the name in the early Board Minutes bear out the stress on the first syllable: the name appears as *Waddle* in the minutes of the meetings on Jan. 13, 14, 15, 1846, and April 26, 1847; as *Wadle*, April 27, 1847; as both *Waddle* and *Waddel*, Jan. 10, 1848; thereafter, as *Waddel*.

7. Waddel, *Academic Memorials*, 389–44. Lingle, *op. cit.*, errs in stating that Waddel became a chaplain in the Confederate army.

8. Waddel, *Academic Memorials*, 233.

9. John N. Waddel, *Address on Public Education, Delivered in the Hall of Representatives, by joint invitation of the Senate and House of Representatives* (Jackson, Miss., 1865), 15.

10. *Bulletin of the University of Mississippi* (Historical Catalogue 1849–1909), 18f. Hereinafter: *Historical Catalogue 1849–1909*.

11. C. W. Grafton, "A Sketch of the University of Mississippi Embracing the First Three Years After the Civil War" (a typescript in the possession of the University, 1927).

12. J. S. Sexton, "Dr. J. J. Wheat: An Appreciation" (a typescript in the possession of the University of Mississippi, undated).

13. *Ibid.*

14. *Historical Catalogue 1849–1909*, 28, 35.

15. Manuscript Minutes of the Faculty of the University of Mississippi under the date of Sept. 26, 1865. The meeting was opened with a prayer by Chancellor Waddel—this is the only recorded instance of such procedure in the faculty meetings.

16. Board Minutes, Oct. 25, 1865.

17. *Historical Catalogue 1849–1909*, 20f.

18. *Ibid.*, 87f., and *passim*.

19. *Ibid.*, 21–24.

20. Mayes, *op. cit.*, 182.

21. Waddel, *Academic Memorials*, 448f.

22. Cited in Allen Cabaniss, *Life and Thought of A Country Preacher: C. W. Grafton, D.D., LL.D.* (Richmond, 1942), 34f.

23. Grafton, *op. cit.*

24. Faculty Minutes, Jan. 6, 1866.

25. Walter L. Fleming, *Civil War and Reconstruction in Alabama* (New York, 1905), 327–329.

26. Cited in A. C. Trusty, "Readings in Mississippi History: Reconstruction" (M.A. thesis, University of Mississippi, 1934), 234f.

27. Grafton, *op. cit.*

28. John N. Waddel, *Inaugural Address, on the Nature and Advantages of the Course of Study in Institutions of Higher Learning* (Natchez, Miss., 1866).

29. J. W. Clapp, *Address Delivered at the University of Mississippi On Behalf of the Board of Trustees* (Memphis, 1866), 11.

30. Manuscript Tuition and Fee Book of the University of Mississippi, covering the sessions from 1865–1866 through 1872–1873.

31. Letter of George E. Critz, Coleman, Texas, to H. M. Faser, University, Miss., March 14, 1927 (in the possession of the University of Mississippi).

32. Grafton, *op. cit.*; Cabaniss, *op. cit.*, 37.

33. T. D. Witherspoon, *The Appeal of the South to its Educated Men. An Address Before the Alumni Association of the University of Mississippi* (Memphis, 1867).

34. *Ibid.*, 5, 9, 15. Note, however, the realistic attitude expressed on pp. 7f.: "But as beautiful as the South has been, with the sunlight of more than an earthly glory resting upon it, we may not close our eyes to the fact, that the day of its beautiful civilization has passed away. . . . A stern realism is to take the place of that idealism which once threw its charm over the Southern mind and heart. The sturdy warfare to be waged with penury and adversity, must bear us too far in the direction of homely enterprise and practical endeavor, to leave much opportunity for the exercise of that chivalrous spirit of devotion to sentiment, which once made us knight-errants of gallantry and prowess under all their forms. In the competition of labor with labor, in the strife of

tongue with tongue, society must assume altogether a different phase, and those distinctive qualities which once constituted the crown of its glory must be numbered with the things that were."

35. Grafton, *op. cit.*; James E. Walmesley, "Some Unpublished Letters of Burton N. Harrison," *Publications of the Mississippi Historical Society*, VIII (1904), 81-85. It is of interest to recall that Miss Anna Porter Harrison (later Mrs. George W. Sulser) was the composer of the music of the song, "In the Gloaming."

36. J. W. Taylor, *An Address Delivered before the Phi Sigma and Hermaean Societies at the Commencement of the University of Mississippi on June 23, 1869* (Oxford, Miss., 1869), 3f.

37. Manuscript Minutes of the Phi Sigma Literary Society, covering the period from May 5, 1849, through Jan. 26, 1867. This reference is found under the date of Feb. 2, 1867.

38. Grafton, *op. cit.* Voorhees is usually described as the "Tall Sachem of the Sycamores."

39. Board Minutes, Jan. 22, 1867.

40. *Ibid.*, Jan. 24, 1867.

41. *Ibid.*, June 26, 1867.

42. Faculty Minutes, June 19, 1867.

43. *Weekly Delta* (Friar's Point, Miss.), May 12, 1869, quoted in P. L. Rainwater (editor), "Letters to and from Jacob Thompson," *Journal of Southern History*, VI, No. 1 (February, 1940), 110f. This and the references in Notes 44, 45, and 46 below establish an approximate date, the springtime of 1869, of Thompson's return from exile to Oxford, Miss. See the general statement by C. S. Sydnor, "Jacob Thompson," *Dictionary of American Biography*, XVIII, 460: "Certainly not earlier than the summer of 1868 he [Thompson] returned to Oxford. Soon after this he settled permanently in Memphis."

44. Letter of S. C. Caldwell, Hazlehurst, Miss., to Chancellor Alfred Hume, University, Miss., May 4, 1927 (in the possession of the University of Mississippi).

45. Faculty Minutes, Nov. 22, 1869.

46. Grafton, *op. cit.*

47. Board Minutes, Oct. 20, 1866.

48. H. M. Sullivan (editor), *All the Laws and Public Resolutions in Relation to the University of Mississippi, Carefully Compiled and Chronologically Arranged* (Oxford, Miss., 1879), 18.

49. *Ibid.*

50. Mayes, *op. cit.*, 162.

Chapter VII

1. Edward Mayes, *History of Education in Mississippi* (Washington, 1899), 162; John N. Waddel, *Memorials of Academic Life. . . .* (Richmond, 1891), 473. The latter will be hereinafter cited thus: Waddel, *Academic Memorials*.

2. H. M. Sullivan (editor), *All the Laws and Public Resolutions in Relation to the University of Mississippi, Carefully Compiled and Chronologically Arranged* (Oxford, Miss., 1879), 18f.

3. Mayes, *op. cit.*, 164.

4. Manuscript Minutes of the Board of Trustees of the University of Mississippi under the date of Aug. 15, 1870.

5. See figures in Mayes, *op. cit.*, 182.

6. Manuscript Minutes of the Faculuty of the University of Mississippi under the date of Sept. 29, 1870.

7. *Ibid.*

8. Waddel, *Academic Memorials*, 466–468.

9. *Ibid.*, 469.

10. Faculty Minutes, April 18, 25, May 9, 1871.

11. Board Minutes, June 22, 1872, Feb. 4, 1873.

12. John N. Waddel, *Historical Discourse Delivered on the Quarter-Centennial of the University of Mississippi* (Oxford, Miss., 1873).

13. Waddel, *Academic Memorials*, 246–308, 445–487, 494–496.

14. *Ibid.*, 472.

15. *Ibid.*, 470.

16. *Ibid.*, 473.

17. *Ibid.*

18. *Ibid.*, 474f.

19. Letter of S. C. Caldwell, Hazlehurst, Miss., to Chancellor Alfred Hume, University, Miss., May 4, 1927 (in the possession of the University of Mississippi).

20. Waddel, *Academic Memorials*, 473.

21. *Ibid.*, 473f.

22. Letter of D. C. M. Bingham, Pontotoc, Miss. to Chancellor Alfred Hume, University, Miss., March 30, 1928 (in the possession of the University of Mississippi).

23. Cited in A. C. Trusty, "Readings in Mississippi History: Reconstruction" (M.A. thesis, University of Mississippi, 1934), 258.

24. Waddel, *Academc Memorials*, 495.

25. *Ibid.*

26. *Ibid.*, 494f.

27. Board Minutes, June 18, 1869.

28. John N. Waddel, *Report of a Tour of Observation among the Various Colleges and Universities of the United States; Undertaken by order of the Board of Trustees of the University of Mississippi, during the summer of 1869* (n.p., n.d.)

29. Board Minutes, Aug. 15–17, 1870.

30. *Ibid.*, Oct. 26, 1870.

31. Mayes, *op. cit.*, 166; *Bulletin of the University of Mississippi* (Historical Catalogue 1849–1909), 11. The latter will hereinafter be cited thus: *Historical Catalogue 1849–1909*.

32. *Historical Catalogue 1849–1909*, 63.

33. *Ibid.*, 67f.

34. *Ibid.*, 235, 239, 242.

35. H. A. Shands, *Some Peculiarities of Speech in Mississippi* (Boston, 1893).

36. Board Minutes, Sept. 25, 1868.

37. *Ibid.*, Sept. 23, 1869.

38. *Ibid.*, June 26, 1873.

39. *Ibid.*, June 12, 1893.

40. James L. Alcorn, *Special Message on the Subject of the Establishment of a University for the Colored People, Etc.* (Jackson, Miss., 1871).

41. Sullivan, *op. cit.*, 20.

42. *Ibid.*, 17f.; Mayes, *op. cit.*, 168; Waddel, *Historical Discourse*, 36.

43. *Historical Catalogue 1849–1909*, 38, 87.

44. Board Minutes, Oct. 26, 1870.

45. Eugene W. Hilgard, *Report on the Organization of the Department of Agriculture and the Mechanic Arts* (n.p., n.d.)

46. Board Minutes, Aug. 30, 1871.

47. *Ibid.*, June 20–27, 1872; Mayes, *op. cit.*, 169.

48. Board Minutes, June 26, 1874.

49. Waddel, *Academic Memorials*, 496.

50. Board Minutes, July 27, 1874.

51. Caldwell, Letter.

52. Waddel, *Historical Discourse*, 40.

53. Board Minutes, July 28, 1874.

54. *Ibid.*; Faculty Minutes, Oct. 19, 1874.

Chapter VIII

1. Manuscript Minutes of the Board of Trustees of the University of Mississippi under the date of Oct. 7, 1874. Barnard had been similarly notified.

2. Manuscript Minutes of the Faculty of the University of Mississippi under the dates of Oct. 7, 19, 1874.

3. *Ibid.*, Nov. 10, 1874. Edward Mayes, *History of Education in Mississippi* (Washington, 1899), 175, erroneously places the inauguration in December.

4. Faculty Minutes, Nov. 10, 1874.

5. Marshall Wingfield, "Old Straight: A Sketch of the Life and Campaigns of Lieutenant General Alexander P. Stewart, C. S. A.," *Tennessee Historical Quarterly*, III, No. 2 (June, 1944), 99–113.

6. H. M. Sullivan (editor), *All the Laws and Public Resolutions in Relation to the University of Mississippi, Carefully Compiled and Chronologically Arranged* (Oxford, Miss., 1879), 24f.

7. *Bulletin of the University of Mississippi* (Historical Catalogue 1849–1909), 82. Hereinafter cited thus: *Historical Catalogue 1849–1909*.

8. *Where Shall I Send My Son? An Address To the People of Mississippi, By the Trustees of the State University* (n.p., 1876).

9. *Ibid.*, 10.

10. *Ibid.*, 11.

11. *Ibid.*, 13.

12. *Ibid.*, 22.

13. *Historical Catalogue 1849–1909*, 338.

14. *Ibid.*

15. Board Minutes, Nov. 20, 1878.

16. *Ibid.*, June 18, 1875. It would be going too far afield to attempt a detailed discussion of salaries at the University of Mississippi, but a sampling of what was paid to the chancellor throughout the years may serve as a relative standard of judgment. That salary was $2,000 in 1848; $2,500 in 1854; $2,500 in 1865; $2,750 in 1873; $3,000 in 1876; $3,500 in 1900; $4,800 in 1930; $8,500 in 1946; and $10,000 in 1947.

17. Board Minutes, June 28, 1877.

18. *Ibid.*, June 28, 1878.

19. *Ibid.*, June 29, 1882.

20. *Where Shall I Send My Son?*, 11.

21. Board Minutes, Jan. 26, 1877.

22. *Ibid.*, June 30, 1881.

23. *Ibid.*

24. *Ibid.*, June 29, 1876. The issue of the Christmas holidays was an old one faced by the Trustees and faculty since the earliest days of the University, but always unsuccessfully, because the students simply refused to be Puritans. In 1854 they had gained their point by composing a little doggerel song and singing it to a popular minstrel tune. (From a letter of C. L. Moore, Blytheville, Ark., to R. H. Thompson, Jackson, Miss., March 30, 1927—in the possession of the University.)

25. Board Minutes, June 28, 1877.

26. *Ibid.*, June 29, 1882.

27. Sullivan, *op. cit.*, 26.
28. *Ibid.*, 25.
29. N. C. Hathorn, "A Financial History of the University of Mississippi from its Endowment in 1819 to 1900" (M.A. thesis, University of Mississippi, 1938), 91.
30. Paul H. Saunders, "Colonel Felix Labauve," *Publications of the Mississippi Historical Society*, VII (1903), 131–140; Lucille W. Banks, "Romantic Career of Felix Labauve Furnishes Beautiful Chapter in History of Mississippi," *Commercial Appeal* (Memphis), July 22, 1923, 13f.
31. Banks, *op. cit.*, 14.
32. John N. Waddel, *Historical Discourse Delivered on the Quarter-Centennial of the University of Mississippi* (Oxford, Miss., 1873), 27.
33. Edward Mayes, *The State University* (Jackson, Miss., 1887), *passim*.
34. Sullivan, *op. cit.*, *passim*.
35. Board Minutes, Jan. 12, 1880.
36. Mississippi Senate, *Journal* (Regular Session, January–March, 1880), Feb. 6, 1880 (p. 264).
37. *Ibid.*, Feb. 9, 1880 (p. 281).
38. *Ibid.*, Feb. 23, 1880 (p. 389).
39. *Ibid.*, Feb. 25, 1880 (p. 438).
40. Mississippi *Laws* (Regular Session of Legislature, January–March, 1880), Chapter 48.
41. *Ibid.*, Chapter 55.
42. *Ibid.*, Chapter 50.
43. *Bulletin of the University of Mississippi* (Historical and Current Catalogue 1887), 168f. Hereinafter cited thus: *Historical Catalogue 1887*.
44. Faculty Minutes, June 23, 1880.
45. Board Minutes, June 23, 1880.
46. Mayes, *History of Education in Mississippi*, 245f.
47. Sullivan, *op. cit.*, 20–22.
48. Mayes, *History of Education in Mississippi*, 246–252.
49. Board Minutes, June 28, 1882.
50. *Ibid.*
51. *Historical Catalogue 1887*, 87f.
52. *Ibid.*, 92.
53. Mayes, *History of Education in Mississippi*, 178.
54. Board Minutes, Sept. 2, 1885. See "Ole Miss' First Lady," *Ole Miss Alumni Review*, II, No. 2 (April, 1948), 15f., 23.
55. *Historical Catalogue 1887*, 140.
56. "Commencement Exercises of the University of Mississippi," *University of Mississippi Magazine*, I, No. 7 (June, 1876), 236–242.
57. Board Minutes, June 25, 1884.

58. *Ibid.*, June 28, 1883.
59. Faculty Minutes, June 27, 1883.
60. *Historical Catalogue 1849–1909*, 96–99.
61. Board Minutes, June 27, 1882.
62. Allen Cabaniss, *Life and Thought of A Country Preacher: C. W. Grafton, D.D., LL.D.* (Richmond, 1942), *passim.*
63. Board Minutes, June 24, 1885.
64. Cabaniss, *op. cit.*, 56, 62.
65. Board Minutes, June 24, 1885.
66. *Ibid.*
67. Wingfield, *op. cit.*, 121.
68. Faculty Minutes, Oct. 8, 1880.
69. *Ibid.*, Dec. 4, 1877; May 28, 1878; March 13, April 15, 1879.
70. Board Minutes, June 24, 1878.
71. *Ibid.*, June 27, 1878. Some of the forms of hazing were called "kangarooing" and "bumping the seniors."
72. Faculty Minutes, Oct. 12, 1880.
73. *Ibid.*, June 10, 14, 1881. The relation between the disciplinary matter and the postmistress of Oxford is not clear, but the references occur together in the same minutes.
74. *Ibid.*, Feb. 23, 1882.
75. *Ibid.*, May 9, 1882.
76. *Ibid.*, Nov. 23, 1883.
77. *Historical Catalogue 1849–1909*, 75.
78. *Ibid.*, 21f., 24.
79. Board Minutes, June 28, 1876.
80. *Ibid.*, Jan. 13, 1880.
81. *Ibid.*, June 24, 1886.
82. *Ibid.*, July 27, 1886.

Chapter IX

1. Manuscript Minutes of the Faculty of the University of Mississippi under the date of July 29, 1886.
2. *Bulletin of the University of Mississippi* (Historical Catalogue 1849–1909), 75. Hereinafter cited thus: *Historical Catalogue 1849–1909*.
3. Edward Mayes, *History of Education in Mississippi* (Washington, 1899), 212.
4. Faculty Minutes, July 1, 1887.
5. *Ibid.*, June 29, 1888.

NOTES TO CHAPTER IX

6. Manuscript Minutes of the Board of Trustees of the University of Mississippi under the date of Aug. 6, 1889.
7. *Ibid.*; Mayes, *op. cit.*, 178-181.
8. Mayes, *op. cit.*, 179; *Historical Catalogue 1849-1909*, 46f.
9. Mayes, *op. cit.*, 181.
10. *Bulletin of the University of Mississippi* (Historical and Current Catalogue 1887), 158-171.
11. These articles were reprinted as a pamphlet—J. Z. George, *The State University: An Investigation Into "the Legal Obligations of the State to the A. & M. College, the Industrial Female Institute, and the State University"* (Jackson, Miss., 1887).
12. *Ibid.*, 18.
13. Edward Mayes, *The State University* (Jackson, Miss., 1887), 1.
14. *Historical Catalogue 1849-1909*, 75f.
15. Mayes, *History of Education in Mississippi*, 201.
16. *Ibid.*
17. Faculty Minutes, Jan. 4, 1887.
18. *Clarion-Ledger* (Jackson, Miss.), Sept. 5, 1889.
19. Professor Quinche was the victim of this tragedy.
20. Board Minutes, June 27, 1889.
21. Mayes, *History of Education in Mississippi*, 181f.
22. Board Minutes, June 23, 1890.
23. Mayes, *History of Education in Mississippi*, 278-290.
24. Board Minutes, June 23, 1891.
25. *Ibid.*, June 25, 1891.
26. Manuscript Minutes of the Mayor and Board of Aldermen, Oxford, Miss., under the date of Aug. 8, 1888.
27. *Ibid.*, July 6, 1892.
28. Faculty Minutes, April 21, 1890.
29. *Ibid.*
30. *Ibid.*, Dec. 6, 1887.
31. *Ibid.*, Feb. 7, 1888.
32. Mayes, *History of Education in Mississippi*, 182.
33. *Biographical and Historical Memoirs of Mississippi* (Chicago: The Goodspeed Publishing Co., 1891), II, 300-347.
34. *Historical Catalogue 1849-1909*, 76.
35. Board Minutes, June 24, 1891.
36. *Ibid.*, Dec. 3, 1891.
37. *Ibid.*
38. Faculty Minutes, Dec. 1, 1891.

Chapter X

1. Manuscript Minutes of the Board of Trustees of the University of Mississippi under the date of June 28, 1892.
2. *Bulletin of the University of Mississippi* (Historical Catalogue 1849–1909), 76–78. Hereinafter cited thus: *Historical Catalogue 1849–1909*.
3. Board Minutes, June 29, 1892.
4. *Ibid.*, June 12, 1893.
5. *Memorial to the Congress of the United States from the Board of Trustees of the University of Mississippi* (Nashville, 1894), *passim*; Annie Berry, "University Land Grants," *University of Mississippi Magazine*, XXVII, No. 5 (February, 1904), 27–31.
6. N. C. Hathorn, "A Financial History of the University of Mississippi from its Endowment in 1819 to 1900" (M.A. thesis, University of Mississippi, 1938), 60.
7. *Ibid.*, 60f.
8. Board Minutes, June 15, 1893.
9. *Historical Catalogue 1849–1909*, 66.
10. D. T. Measells, Jr., "History of the Expansion of the University of Mississippi 1848–1947" (M.A. thesis, University of Mississippi, 1947), 94f.
11. *Bulletin of the University of Mississippi* (Catalogue 1893–1894), 198.
12. Measells, *op. cit.*, 29f.
13. *Ibid.*, 84–88; *Historical Catalogue 1849–1909*, 63–65.
14. Measells, *op. cit.*, 88–90.
15. *Ole Miss Alumni News*, XI, No. 2 (March, 1944), 8.
16. Board Minutes, July 17, 1900.
17. *Ibid.*, June 17, 1902.
18. Manuscript Minutes of the Faculty of the University of Mississippi under the date of Feb. 13, 1903.
19. On all this construction, see Measells, *op. cit.*, 103f., 110f.
20. *Ole Miss Alumni Review*, I, No. 2 (July, 1947), 9, 27.
21. His notable contribution to this subject was his *Archeology of Mississippi* (University, Miss., 1926).
22. *Historical Catalogue 1849–1909*, 48–57.
23. Faculty Minutes, Dec. 18, 1894.
24. *Ibid.*, May 21, 1895.
25. *Ibid.*, March 1, 1897.
26. Board Minutes, June 6, 1900.
27. Faculty Minutes, Feb. 18, 1903.
28. Manuscript Minutes of the Mayor and Board of Aldermen, Oxford, Miss., under the date of Dec. 18, 1905.
29. Faculty Minutes, March 5, 1906. Lest I give a misleading notion of stu-

dent life during this period, let me hasten to add that the year 1904 saw a University of Mississippi student, Ebb J. Ford, among the first Americans to receive a Rhodes Scholarship. Since his day thirteen others have been so honored. They are listed here chronologically, each one's name followed by the year of his appointment: R. C. Beckett, 1907, T. T. McCarley, 1908, L. E. Farley, 1910, John W. Kyle, 1913, T. F. Mayo, 1914, W. L. Finger, 1916, Bryan England, 1918, L. M. Jiggits, 1919, W. H. Drane Lester, 1922, E. Wilson Lyon, 1925, Myres S. McDougal, 1927, Calvin S. Brown, Jr., 1930, and J. Hector Currie, 1938.

30. W. A. Henry, Jr., "History of the Football Team," *University of Mississippi Magazine*, XXVI, No. 6 (April, 1903), 32-40. The article, "Football in Rebtown," *Ole Miss Alumni Review*, II, No. 2 (October, 1948), 50-64, 78, is an excellent recent history of the team. It lists as members of the first team (1893) the following: W. C. Collier, G. M. Jones, R. H. Bourdeaux, L. P. Brady, B. P. Smith, J. R. Tipton, E. R. Russel, A. H. Roudebush (captain), W. H. Cook, R. V. Booth, J. K. Cowan, Claude Sill, W. B. Blake, Eric Scales, T. C. Kimbrough, and W. L. Foxworth. A member of the team in 1898 to achieve fame was Hugh L. White, Governor of Mississippi from 1936 to 1940.

31. Board Minutes, June 17, 1902.

32. *Ibid.*, June 2, 1903.

33. *Mississippian* (student publication, University of Mississippi), Jan. 16, 1937.

34. *Ibid.*, Oct. 10, 1936.

35. Board Minutes, June 1, 1903; dedicatory page of the 1945 *Ole Miss* (student yearbook); Alfred Hume, "The University of Mississippi," *Southern Association Quarterly*, V, No. 3 (August, 1941), 359-369, especially p. 361.

36. Alfred Hume, "Robert Burwell Fulton: Chancellor of the University of Mississippi, 1892-1906," *Southern Association Quarterly*, III, No. 4 (November, 1939), 537-539.

37. *Ibid.*, 537, note.

38. Board Minutes, June 13, 1893.

39. *Ibid.*, June 5, 1900.

40. *University of Mississippi Magazine*, XXIV, No. 7 (April, 1901).

41. Faculty Minutes, May 2, 1901.

42. *Ibid.*, May 8, 1901.

43. *Ibid.*, May 9, 1901.

44. *Ibid.*, May 14, 1901; *Daily Clarion-Ledger* (Jackson, Miss.), May 16, 1901.

45. Faculty Minutes, May 15, 1901.

46. *Ibid.*, May 18, 1901.

47. Board Minutes, June 5, 1901.

48. *Ibid.*

49. *Ibid.*, Jan. 4, 1902. Because University of Mississippi students have had to fight for their fraternities, they idealize them. See J. H. Napier, III, "Campus History Shows Extinct Greek Groups," *Mississippian*, Feb. 20, 1948, and Tom Bourdeaux, "The 'Greeks' At Ole Miss," *Ole Miss Alumni Review*, II, No. 2 (October, 1948), 46–49. The proliferation of honorary and professional groups may be noted in any issue of the University bulletin.

50. Board Minutes, June 17, 1902.

51. Faculty Minutes, Feb. 24, 1903.

52. E.g., see *ibid.*, May 2, 1905. A legislative investigating committee even took cognizance of the issue and published a report of fifty-seven pages concerning it, *Testimony Introduced Before Investigating Committee on Colleges and Universities, at Oxford, Miss.* (Jackson, Miss., 1904).

53. R. B. Fulton, *Opportunity: An Address delivered at the Dedication of the New Library, University of Mississippi, Tuesday evening, May 30th, 1911* (Woodstock, Vt., 1911), 9.

54. Board Minutes, June 4, 1905.

55. *Ibid.*, June 8, 1906.

56. *Ibid.*, June 9, 1906.

57. F. L. Riley and Dumas Malone, "Robert Burwell Fulton," *Dictionary of American Biography*, Centenary Edition (New York, 1946), VII, 72.

58. Board Minutes, Aug. 23, 1906.

Chapter XI

1. G. C. Hooker, "The Origin and Development of the University of Mississippi With Special Reference to Its Legislative Control" (Ph.D. thesis, Stanford University, 1932), 339.

2. Manuscript Minutes of the Board of Trustees of the University of Mississippi under the date of Nov. 1, 1906.

3. *Bulletin of the University of Mississippi* (Historical Catalogue 1849–1909), 178. Hereinafter cited thus: *Historical Catalogue 1849–1909*.

4. *Ibid.*, 336.

5. *Ibid.*, 79.

6. *Ibid.*, 327.

7. *Ibid.*, 79f.; "Chancellor A. A. Kincannon," *University of Mississippi Magazine*, XXXI, No. 1 (October, 1907), 3–6.

8. *Daily Clarion-Ledger* (Jackson, Miss.), May 19, 1907.

9. Board Minutes, March 2, 1907.

10. *University of Mississippi Magazine*, XXX, No. 6 (March, 1907), 256.

11. *Bulletin of the University of Mississippi* (Catalogue 1906–1907), 8.

12. Board Minutes, May 18, 1907.

13. *Daily Clarion-Ledger*, May 19, 1907.

NOTES TO CHAPTER XI

14. Board Minutes, May 18, 1907.
15. *Daily Clarion-Ledger,* May 19, 1907.
16. *Ibid.,* June 5, 1907.
17. Board Minutes, June 4, 1907.
18. *Historical Catalogue 1849–1909,* 80.
19. *Ibid.; Biennial Report of the Chancellor of the University of Mississippi, December 1, 1909, to July 1, 1911,* xvi–xviii.
20. Board Minutes, Jan. 28, 1909.
21. *Ibid.,* May 30, 1910; *Biennial Report,* xvii.
22. *Biennial Report,* xvii.
23. R. B. Fulton, *Opportunity: An Address delivered at the Dedication of the New Library, University of Mississippi, Tuesday evening, May 30th, 1911* (Woodstock, Vt., 1911), *passim.*
24. *Biennial Report,* xiv.
25. *Mississippian* (student publication, University of Mississippi), Nov. 11, 1911; Nov. 2, 1912.
26. Board Minutes, June 1, 1908.
27. *Biennial Report,* xivf.
28. Board Minutes, March 28, 1908.
29. *Historical Catalogue 1849–1909,* 80f.
30. Board Minutes, July 10, 1910.
31. *Ole Miss Alumni Review,* I, No. 2 (July, 1947), 27. Others mentioned in this citation are as follows:

"Dr. John Nesbit Swan, head of the Department of Chemistry at the time of his death in June, 1936; began teaching at the University as acting professor of chemistry in 1912–13....

"Dr. Alfred W. Milden, dean emeritus of the College of Liberal Arts and professor of modern languages and literature at the time of his death in February, 1944; began teaching at the University in 1910–11.

"Judge T. C. Kimbrough, dean of the School of Law at the time of his death in December, 1945; began teaching at the University in 1920–21.

"Dr. P. W. Rowland, professor of pharmacology at the time of his death in October, 1943; began teaching at the University in 1903.

"Professor Oliver A. Shaw, Dean Emeritus of the School of Education at the time of his death in April, 1945; came to the University as Dean of the School of Education in 1920."

To this list should be added the name of the long-time professor of philosophy, Dr. Winn David Hedleston. He was connected with the University from 1908 until the shake-up in 1930. He died in 1936. See E. C. Scott (compiler), *Ministerial Directory of the Presbyterian Church, U. S. 1861–1941* (Austin, Texas, 1942).

32. Board Minutes, Sept. 23, Nov. 4, 1910.

33. *Shall Fraternities Live?* (n.p., 1910), 4–11.
34. Hooker, *op. cit.*, 212.
35. *Mississippian*, Jan. 21, 1914.
36. *Ibid.*, Oct. 19, 1912.
37. Manuscript Minutes of the Faculty of the University of Mississippi, session of 1912–1913, *passim*; L. Deister, *Chancellor A. A. Kincannon and the University of Mississippi* (n.p., 1913).
38. Deister, *op. cit.*
39. *Ibid.*
40. *Oxford Eagle* (supplement), March 28, 1912. See also *Report of the Joint Legislative Investigating Committee Elected Under Senate Concurrent Resolution Number Seven* (Jackson, Miss., 1913), 80.
41. *Report of the Joint Legislative Investigating Committee*, 91.
42. Faculty Minutes, Nov. 3, 1913.
43. *Mississippian*, Jan. 20, 1912.
44. *Ibid.*, Feb. 18, 1914.
45. Letter of A. A. Kincannon to G. C. Hooker, July 31, 1931, quoted in Hooker, *op. cit.*, 215.

Chapter XII

1. Manuscript Minutes of the Board of Trustees of the Institutions of Higher Learning in Mississippi under the date of June 4, 1914.
2. G. C. Hooker, "The Origin and Development of the University of Mississippi With Special Reference to Its Legislative Control" (Ph.D. thesis, Stanford University, 1932), 215.
3. Manuscript Minutes of the Faculty of the University of Mississippi under the date of Sept. 16, 1914. Hooker, *op. cit.*, 218, n. 1, says: ". . . this was the first time in the history of the University that the Chancellor had threatened to use such tactics [i.e., intimidation] with the faculty." Hooker is not entirely accurate: something similar had occurred earlier under Mayes.
4. *Biennial Report of the Chancellor and of the Secretary of the University of Mississippi to the Legislature of the State and to the Board of Trustees of the University and Colleges* (Memphis, 1915), 4.
5. Faculty Minutes, Sept. 22, 1914.
6. *Biennial Report*, 11.
7. D. T. Measells, "History of the Expansion of the University of Mississippi 1848–1947" (M.A. thesis, University of Mississippi, 1947), 117.
8. *Oxford Eagle*, Sept. 20, 1923.
9. *Ibid.*, Nov. 22, 1923.
10. *Biennial Report*, 11.

11. *Ibid.*, 12.
12. *Bulletin of the University of Mississippi* (School of Commerce and Administration, 1929), 4.
13. Faculty Minutes, April 29, 1917.
14. Alfred Hume, "The University of Mississippi in the World War" (a typescript in Chancellor Hume's possession).
15. Faculty Minutes, Feb. 13, 1918.
16. R. B. Fulton, *Address Before the Alumni of the University of Mississippi at the Unveiling of the Memorial to Those Who Made the Supreme Sacrifice in the Great War, and at the Semi-Centennial of the Class of 1869* (New York, 1919), note on the cover.
17. Faculty Minutes, Oct. 30, 1920.
18. Board Minutes, Nov. 2, 1920.
19. *Ibid.*, Nov. 15, 1920.
20. *Ibid.*, Sept. 3, 1921.
21. *Oxford Eagle*, Jan. 4, 1923.
22. *Ibid.*, March 1, 1923.
23. *Ibid.*, March 8, 1923.
24. *Ibid.*, Sept. 27, 1923.
25. *Ibid.*, Feb. 8, 1923.
26. *Ibid.*, Feb. 22, March 1, April 19, 1923.
27. *Ibid.*, Nov. 22, 1923.
28. *Ibid.*, April 19, 1923.
29. *Ibid.*
30. *Ibid.*, March 29, 1923.
31. *Ibid.*
32. Board Minutes, July 15, 1924.
33. *Ibid.*

Chapter XIII

1. W. Alton Bryant, "Alfred Hume: Distinguished Alumnus," *Vanderbilt Alumnus*, XXXIII, No. 8 (September, 1948), 13f. Dr. Bryant is a nephew-in-law of Chancellor Hume.
2. *Oxford Eagle*, Aug. 27, 1925; manuscript Minutes of the Faculty of the University of Mississippi under the date of May 25, 1925; Alfred Hume, "Chancellor's Report," June 6, 1930 (a mimeographed report in Chancellor Hume's possession).
3. *Biennial Report of the University of Mississippi to the State and to the Board of Trustees of the University and Colleges* (n.p., 1927), 14–16.
4. G. C. Hooker, "The Origin and Development of the University of Mis-

sissippi With Special Reference to Its Legislative Control" (Ph.D. thesis, Stanford University, 1932), 260.

5. *Mississippian* (student publication, University of Mississippi), March 12, 1926.

6. *Bulletin of the University of Mississippi* (Alumni Citizenship Survey, 1926).

7. M. V. O'Shea, *A State Educational System at Work* (Washington, 1927), iii.

8. *Ibid.*, iv.

9. *Ibid.*, vi. The other book is M. V. O'Shea, *Public Education in Mississippi: Report of A Study of the Public Educational System* (Jackson, Miss., 1927).

10. John C. Meadows, *The Function of a State University* (Nashville, 1927).

11. *Ibid.*, 96.

12. *Ibid.*, 104f.

13. Medford Evans, "Oxford, Mississippi," *Southwest Review*, XV, No. 1 (Autumn, 1929), 46–63.

14. *Ibid.*, 63.

15. D. T. Measells, "History of the Expansion of the University of Mississippi 1848–1947" (M.A. thesis, University of Mississippi, 1947), 117.

16. *Biennial Report*, 22f.

17. *Ibid.*, 22.

18. *Ibid.*, 23.

19. Mississippi House of Representatives, *Journal* (Regular Session, January–April, 1928), Jan. 17, 1928 (pp. 109–173).

20. *Oxford Eagle*, Feb. 2, 1928.

21. *Chancellor Hume Strongly Opposes the Removal of the University of Mississippi* (Oxford, Miss., 1928).

22. *Oxford Eagle*, Feb. 9, 1928.

23. Cited in *Jackson Daily News* (Mississippi), Aug. 28, 1947.

24. *Commercial Appeal* (Memphis), Jan. 23, 1948.

25. Bryant, *op. cit.*

26. *Bulletin of the University of Mississippi* (Catalogue 1946–1947), 39f.

27. Evans, *op. cit.*, 58.

28. *Ibid.*, 59.

29. Bryant, *op. cit.*

30. *Oxford Eagle*, Feb. 28, 1929.

31. *Mississippian*, April 19, 1930.

32. Board Minutes, June 13, 1930.

33. *Ole Miss Alumni Review*, I, No. 2 (July, 1947), 27. See also diplomas

delivered at the August commencement, 1930, signed by Dr. Longest as acting chancellor.

Chapter XIV

1. Manuscript Minutes of the Board of Trustees of Institutions of Higher Learning in Mississippi under the dates of June 27, 28, 1930.
2. Clarence Cason, "The Mississippi Imbroglio," *Virginia Quarterly Review*, VII, No. 2 (April, 1931), 238
3. *Mississippi Educational Advance*, XXII, No. 2 (November, 1930), 41.
4. Cason, *op. cit.*, 238.
5. *Jackson Daily News* (Mississippi), June 29, 1930.
6. *Mississippi Educational Advance*, XXII, No. 1 (October, 1930), 9.
7. *Daily Clarion-Ledger* (Jackson, Miss.), Dec. 7, 1930.
8. *Mississippi Educational Advance*, XXII, No. 4 (January, 1931), 103.
9. *Oxford Eagle*, June 19, 1930.
10. *Mississippi Educational Advance*, XXII, No. 4 (January, 1931), 103.
11. *Times-Picayune* (New Orleans), Dec. 8, 1930; *Commercial Appeal* (Memphis), Dec. 8, 1930.
12. Board Minutes, June 18, 1930.
13. *Oxford Eagle*, March 26, 1931.
14. *Jackson Daily News*, Feb. 14, 1931.
15. D. T. Measells, "History of the Expansion of the University of Mississippi 1848-1947" (M.A. thesis, University of Mississippi, 1947), 117.
16. *Oxford Eagle*, March 3, 1932.
17. Board Minutes, June 2, 1932.
18. *Oxford Eagle*, June 9, 1932.
19. Editorial from the *Clarksdale Daily Press*, cited in the *Jackson Daily News*, Aug. 28, 1947.
20. Cason, *op. cit.*, 229f.
21. Board Minutes, June 10, 11, 1932.
22. *Ole Miss Alumni News*, XI, No. 2 (March, 1944), 2.
23. Measells, *op. cit.*, 117.
24. *Ole Miss Alumni News*, XI, No. 2 (March, 1944), 2.
25. Board Minutes, Jan. 25, 1935.
26. W. Alton Bryant, "Alfred Hume: Distinguished Alumnus," *Vanderbilt Alumnus*, XXXIII, No. 8 (September, 1948), 13f.
27. Board Minutes, Jan. 25, 1935.
28. Bryant, *op. cit.*
29. *Mississippian* (student publication, University of Mississippi), April 27, 1935.

Chapter XV

1. Manuscript Minutes of the Board of Trustees of Institutions of Higher Learning in Mississippi under the date of Jan. 25, 1935; *Mississippian* (student publication, University of Mississippi), Feb. 2, 1935.
2. D. T. Measells, "History of the Expansion of the University of Mississippi 1848–1947" (M.A. thesis, University of Mississippi, 1947), 112.
3. *Bulletin of the University of Mississippi* (Catalogue 1938–1939), 20.
4. *Bulletin of the University of Mississippi* (Catalogue 1946–1947), 39f.
5. *Oxford Eagle*, Oct. 12, 1939.
6. Manuscript Minutes of the Faculty of the University of Mississippi under the date of Sept. 14, 1935.
7. *Ibid.*, Feb. 20, 1939.
8. *Ole Miss Alumni News*, XI, No. 2 (March, 1944), 6.
9. Board Minutes, Jan. 25, 1941 (Chancellor's Report).
10. *Oxford Eagle*, Oct. 2, 1937.
11. As indicated in frequent public statements made by Chancellor J. D. Williams.
12. Board Minutes, June 7, 1946 (Chancellor's Report).
13. *Oxford Eagle*, Jan. 8, 1937.
14. *Bulletin of the University of Mississippi* (Inauguration of Alfred Benjamin Butts as Chancellor, 1936), 17f.
15. E. g., see Faculty Minutes, April 6, 1937.
16. *Oxford Eagle*, Oct. 26, 1939.
17. *Ibid.*, April 24, 1941.
18. As related to me by a faculty member who was present on that occasion.
19. Measells, *op. cit.*, 118.
20. *Oxford Eagle*, June 18, 1942.
21. Faculty Minutes, Jan. 7, 1942.
22. *Oxford Eagle*, Jan. 15, 1942.
23. *Ibid.*, Feb. 5, 1942.
24. *Ibid.*, Feb. 19, 1942.
25. *Ibid.*, April 2, 1942.
26. *Ibid.*, Sept. 3, 1942.
27. *Ole Miss Alumni News*, XI, No. 2 (March, 1944), 3. A grand total of all military and naval personnel stationed at the University of Mississippi during the war is not available. It is estimated at several thousand.
28. *Ibid.*
29. *Ibid.*, 6.
30. E.g., see *Oxford Eagle*, Feb. 19, April 16, 1942.
31. Faculty Minutes, Oct. 6, 1942.

32. *Ibid.*, Aug. 25, 1944.
33. Measells, *op. cit.*, 118.
34. There had been a difficult situation, and many factors were involved. The resignation was not voluntary, but it must be remembered that it was then customary for the chancellor to be elected for only a year at a time. Technically, therefore, my statement—that Butts's term of office was "running out"—is correct.
35. Board Minutes, June 14, 1946.
36. *Mississippian*, June 21, 1946.
37. Measells, *op. cit.*, 118.
38. Board Minutes, June 14, 1945.
39. *Mississippian*, July 24, 1947.

Bibliographical Note

The primary sources for a centennial history of the University of Mississippi are the minutes of the Board of Trustees and of the faculty. The University possesses five manuscript books containing the Board Minutes from the first meeting, January 15, 1845, to May 29, 1922. (In the autumn of 1910 the trustees of all the state schools were united in one Board of Trustees of Institutions of Higher Learning in Mississippi.) From 1922 onward, the records are in the office of the Executive Secretary of the Board, Jackson, Mississippi. The University receives typewritten or mimeographed copies of relevant portions of the minutes.

Some of the earlier minutes were published, notably the *Record of the Testimony and Proceedings, in the Matter of the Investigation, by the Trustees of the University of Mississippi, on the 1st and 2nd of March, 1860, of the Charges Made by H. R. Branham, Against the Chancellor of the University* (Jackson, Miss., 1860). Most of the minutes of the Reconstruction Board appear only in printed form, not in manuscript at all. They are as follows: the meetings on June 22-24, 27, 28, August 30, 1871, in *Minutes of the Board of Trustees of the University of Mississippi with an Appendix Containing Documents in Reference to the Organization of the College of Agriculture and the Mechanic Arts in Connection with the University* (Oxford, Miss., 1871); the meetings on June 20-22, 24-27, 1872, in *Minutes of the Annual Meeting of the Board of Trustees of the University of Mississippi* (Columbus, Miss., 1872); the meetings on February 4-6, June 23-27, 1873, in *Minutes of a Called Meeting of the Board of Trustees of the University of Mississippi* (Oxford, Miss., 1873); and the meetings on June 22-27, July 27, October 5-7, 1874, in *Minutes of the Annual Meeting of the Board of Trustees of the University of Mississippi* (Oxford, Miss., 1874). The minutes from January 15, 1845, to November 21, 1861, have been typed and annotated as a thesis: Florence E. Campbell, "Journal of the Minutes of the Board of Trustees of the University of Mississippi 1845-1860" (M.A. thesis, University of Mississippi, 1939).

The Board minutes are of utmost importance, not only for what they record, but also how they are recorded. Generally speaking, they fall into three stages of development. During the first phase the mintues are verbose, stilted, and legalistic. The Board apparently sat as a court and all its procedure was conducted in parliamentary fashion. Then came a period, from the Reconstruction to the First World War, when the Board was conducted in the manner of a political convention or caucus: the minutes faithfully reflect the change of attitude. The later minutes are briefer and less revealing, indicating that the Trustees now transact their business after the style of a board of directors of a corporation.

The complete minutes of the faculty are also in the possession of the University. There are five journals, dating from the first meeting of the faculty, November 13, 1848, to the present. In the more recent period the minutes have been typed and pasted in the record-book.

The faculty minutes are a fascinating study. They are, in the nature of the case, much more voluminous and much more lively than the Board minutes, for they deal directly with the intimate details of campus life. They, too, fall generally into a threefold classification. In the earlier days the faculty, like the Trustees, sat as a judicial body and the minutes are written in the wordy language of a court. The minutes of the middle period almost suggest the meeting of a military staff. And since the first World War, they are similar to the minutes of a committee or conference.

Other manuscripts of importance are the minutes of the Phi Sigma and Hermaean literary societies, the matriculation books, and the tuition and fee books. Since 1894 a careful file of the chancellor's correspondence has been kept and there are a few letters earlier than that date. The University also has access to some reminiscences written by alumni now dead. Of these sketches of varying length and unequal value, the most useful as well as the most extensive are the memoirs of Ephraim N. Lowe, former state geologist and member of the faculty. Others were prepared by C. W. Grafton, J. S. Sexton, G. E. Critz, D. C. M. Bingham, C. L. Moore, R. H. Parham, and S. C. Caldwell.

Invaluable as sources of information have been the University catalogues. Those in the Library of the University begin with the session of 1852–1853 and continue to the present, except for the three academic years of 1855–1856, 1856–1857, and 1858–1859, and of course the war period 1861–1865. Especially important is the *Historical Catalogue 1849–1909*, ably edited by Chancellor Emeritus Alfred Hume (then vice-chancellor). Other printed records are the student yearbook or annual, *Ole Miss* (first issued in 1897), the commencement programs, the official journals of the Mississippi Senate and House of Representatives, and the *Laws* of the state. A convenient compilation of the last is H. M. Sullivan (editor), *All the Laws and Public Resolutions in Relation to the University of Mississippi, Carefully Compiled and Chronologically Arranged* (Oxford, Miss., 1879).

Newspapers have been consulted. The Oxford *Eagle* has, of course, been of prime importance. Very useful also were the Memphis *Commercial Appeal* and the Jackson *Daily Clarion-Ledger* and *Daily News*. But special attention should be directed to the student publications, which serve in the dual capacity of being both primary and secondary sources. The earliest of these was the *University of Mississippi Magazine*, a monthly journal or review, which was begun in 1875. In 1907 a more popular weekly paper, the *Varsity Voice*, was undertaken. However, both were suspended in 1911 and combined in the *Mississippian*, a weekly newspaper which is still in existence.

Several theses written for the degree of Master of Arts have dealt with the University, the town of Oxford, or Lafayette county. Two which were directed by the author have aided him immeasurably: D. T. Measells, "History of the Expansion of the University of Mississippi 1848–1947" (M.A. thesis, University of Mississippi, 1947), and Frances R. Huff, "The Relationship of Oxford and the University of Mississippi 1848–1947" (M.A. thesis, University of Mississippi, 1947). A useful thesis, although not entirely reliable, is one by Grover C. Hooker, "The Origin and Development of the University of Mississippi With Special Reference to Its Legislative Control" (Ph.D. thesis, Stanford University, 1932). Of inestimable value has been a typescript by Professor S. C. Gladden, "A History of the Department of Physics and Astronomy at the University of Mississippi" (1933).

As indicated elsewhere, the present volume is the third history of the University. The first was Chancellor John Newton Waddel's *Historical Discourse Delivered on the Quarter-Centennial of the University of Mississippi* (Oxford, Miss., 1873). The material was later incorporated in his *Memorials of Academic Life: Being an Historical Sketch of the Waddel Family, Identified Through Three Generations with the History of Higher Education in the South and Southwest* (Richmond, 1891), usually referred to as *Academic Memorials*. The other is Chapter IX, "The University of Mississippi," in Chancellor Edward Mayes's *History of Education in Mississippi* (Washington, 1899). Two books which have been helpful are John Fulton, *Memoirs of Frederick A. P. Barnard, D.D., LL.D., L.H.D., D.C.L.* (New York, 1896), and Maud M. Brown, *The University Greys* (Richmond, 1940). Many pamphlets and articles have been used, but these are sufficiently indicated in the appropriate Notes.

Index

Academic procession, adopted for commencement, 40
Agriculture Department, 78, 79
Alcorn, Governor James L., 71; appointees on Board of Trustees, 72; requests black university, 77
Alcorn Agricultural and Mechanical College, 77, 78
Alma Mater (song), 3, 162
"Alumni citizenship survey," 136–138
Ames, Adelbert, military governor, 72; attitude toward University, 72, 82
Annual, *see* Ole Miss
Astronomy, *see* Observatory
Aswell, James B., 122, 123
Athletics, during World War II, 157, 158

Barnard, Frederick Augustus Porter, president and chancellor, 31, 32; investigates seminary fund, 32, 37; reputation grows, 32; sketch, 35–37; varied activities, 38–40; plans for University, 39, 40, 41; criticism of, 44, 45, 48, 49; in "Branham affair," 47, 48; final report, 53, 54; resignation, 54, 58, 121
Bell, James W., sketch, 113
Bilbo, Governor Theodore G., 132, 134, 138; proposes removal to Jackson, 141; hostility toward Hume, 143, 144; burned in effigy by students, 147; benefits to University, 148
Bishop, David H., 113
"Black and Tan" convention (1868), 71, 72
Bledsoe, Albert Taylor, 11; sketch, 15, 16, 19, 20; becomes acting president, 19, 20; resignation, 31
Bondurant, Alexander Lee, 105; first football coach, 116; suggests school colors, 116

Bondurant, Mrs. Alexander Lee, 153
Boynton, Edward C., 40, 41, 46; dismissed, 52; part in preserving University buildings, 58
Brandon, Governor Gerard C., 6
Branham, Henry R., 32, 33, 47, 48
"Branham affair," 46–49
Brewer, Governor Earl, 128, 129
Brougher, C. A., 89, 90
Brown, Governor Albert G., 7
Brown, Calvin S., sketch, 113, 114, 134
Brown, James, trustee, horse's tail cut off, 26, 27
Brown, Maud Morrow, 55
Buildings, early, 13, 14, 31; under Barnard, 40; after Reconstruction, 83; first women's dormitory, 92; under Mayes, 103, 104; under Fulton, 112, 113; under Kincannon, 124, 125, 130, 131; under Hume, 141, 143, 150; under Butts, 152, 153, 154; under Williams, 160, 161
Burney, Sanford G., 63, 71
Butts, Alfred Benjamin, chancellor, sketch, 152; development of University, 152–156; faculty policy, 154, 155; idea of a university, 155, 156; service during World War II, 160; termination of service, 159, 160, 194

Carnegie, Andrew, grant refused, 120; gift for library accepted, 124, 125
Carnegie Corporation of New York, 154
Cason, Clarence, quoted, 148, 149
Cemetery, Confederate, on campus, 59, 142
Certificates, teaching, 110
Chairman of the faculty (title), adopted, 100
Chalmers, H. H., trustee, 88, 96, 97

INDEX

Chancellor, authority, 105, 123; creature of the Board, 101
Chancellor (title), adopted, 40; abolished, 100, 101; restored, 101
Chancellor emeritus, first, *see* Hume, Alfred
Chisholm, John, of Alabama, 9
Clapp, J. W., trustee, 65, 66
Clark, Governor Charles, 59, 65, 71
Clayton, Alexander M., trustee, 8, 20, 59; efforts for coeducation, 91, 92
Clergymen, on faculty, 23, 30, 32, 45, 61, 62, 165
Coeducation in state, early efforts for, 91, 92
Commencement, first, 20; no graduates (1866) 64–66; (1867) 67; speakers refuse (1871) 73; Republican trustees rebuffed, 75; social affairs, 75; program (1876) 93–95; order during, 97; (1919) 132
Commencement ball abolished, 117, 118
Commerce and Business Administration, School of, 131
Confederate Cemetery, on campus, 59, 142
Confederate monument, on campus, 59, 142
Conner, Governor Martin Sennet, 148
Constitutional convention (1865) 71; (1868) 72; (1869) 72
Craig, John J., 9
Curriculum, early, 10, 29; under Waddel, 75–77; under Mayes, 101, 102, 104; Hume's concept of, 139

Davis, Jefferson, 27, 68, 69
"Dead House," 57
Dean, first, 108
Degrees, offered, 76, 101, 110, 113; conferred by faculty, 73
Degrees, Ph.D., offered, 76, 77, 113
Degrees, honorary, conferred on class of 1861, 52, 65; proposed for Jefferson Davis, 69; policy for conferring, 95, 96; impossible for Stewart, 96; conferred on various recipients, 31, 34, 54, 65, 77, 95, 96
Department of Archives and History (state), 114
de Soto, Hernando, 3

Diplomas, in English language, 95
Discipline, faculty, of and by, 27, 30, 86, 118, 129, 130
Discipline, student, 18–20, 27, 41, 45, 46, 47, 49, 50, 51, 69, 86, 87, 97, 98, 104, 106, 115, 116, 118, 128, 132, 133, 135
Dogs, on campus, 158
Dormitories, *see* Buildings

Education survey, public, 138
Education, School of, 110
Electric lights, 112
Elocution, as subject, 92, 93
Engineering, civil, 76
Engineering, School of, 111, 112
English language and literature, Department of, 101, 102, 113
Enrollment, early sessions, 24; under Barnard, 44; during War Between the States, 52; after, 64; during Reconstruction, 79; after, 85; under Fulton, 113; in 1923, 130; under Hume, 140, 141; in early 1930's, 147, 148; after reaccrediting, 150; under Butts, 156; during World War II, 157, 158; after 159, 160
Equipment, laboratory, 38
Evans, Medford, quoted, 139, 140
Evolution, 136
Examinations, senior (1861), 174, 175
Expenses, in 1870's, 83

Faculty, first, 10, 11, 14–17; in "Branham affair," 47; resignations (1861), 52; after War Between the States, 60–64; on admissions of blacks, 73; first woman on, 92, 93; under Stewart, 98, 99; resign in reorganization (1886), 98, 99; under Mayes, 104, 105; under Fulton, 113; dismissed in part by Bilbo, 145, 146; reconstitution by Hume, 149; policy of Butts, 154, 155. See also, Clergymen; Discipline, faculty
"Father of the University of Mississippi," 8
Fellowships, 105
Firearms, 11, 49, 106, 115
Fireworks, 25, 116
"Flying Squadron," 133
Football, first team, 116, 186; 127, 154
Forrest, Nathan Bedford, 58

INDEX 203

Fraternities, banned and restored (1881), 86; house erected, 104; opposition to, 118, 119, 126; banned at state schools, 127, 130; reinstated, 136. *See also* Sororities
Freemasonry, 8, 9, 36
Fulton, Robert Burwell, chancellor, 42, 43, 98; acting chancellor, 107; sketch, 108; growth of University under, 111–113; activities, 117; as administrator, 118, 120; resignation, 120; address at library dedication, 125; death, 132; chapel named for, 141; 147

Galloway, Charles B., trustee, 95, 96
Garland, Landon C., 63, 64, 88; suit against the University, 98
Garner, James W., 153
Garner, Mrs. James W., 153
General Education Board, grant for library development, 153, 154
George, James Z., 102, 103, 109
Gholson, William Y., trustee, 8
Glee club, 134
Grading scheme, under Barnard, 40
Graduate School, 141
Grafton, Cornelius W., 95, 96
Grant, U. S., occupies Oxford, 58, 63
Greek letter organizations, *See* Fraternities; Sororities

Harper, Lewis, 35, 78
Harris, John A., 56
Harris, Wiley P., trustee, 88, 98
Harrison, Anna Porter, 57, 178
Harrison, Burton N., 41, 52, 55, 56, 67, 172
Harrison, Byron Patton, 153
Hawkes, Francis L., trustee, 8
Hazing, 97, 128, 135
Hedleston, Winn David, 188
Hermaean literary society, 18, 28, 93, 196
Hilgard, Eugene Woldemar, 35, 41, 42, 43, 56; protects University buildings, 58, 60, 63; 78, 79
"Hilgard Cut," 153
Hill, Sallie Vick, 92
History, Department of, 114
Holidays and vacations, 86, 181
Holmes, George Frederick, president, 10, 11; sketch, 14, 15; leaves University, 19; resignation, 21, 22, 167, 168
Hospital, 113, 124, 150
Howry, James M., trustee, 8
Hudson, Robert S., 73
Hume, Alfred, chancellor, chancellor emeritus, 105; acting chancellor, 120, 122; chancellor, 134; sketch, 135; on academic freedom, 136; "alumni citizenship survey," 136–138; concept of a state university, 139, 141; on removal of University, 141, 142; criticized and removed by Bilbo, 143, 144; reelected, 148; administrative difficulties, 149; resignation, 150; tribute to, 151; acting chancellor, 158, 160
Humphreys, Governor Benjamin G., 71, 72

"Institutes," 110, 111
Isom, Sarah McGehee, 92, 93
Isom, Thomas Dudley, 9, 57

Jefferson College, 4, 36

Kahle, Mrs. A. W., 162
Kahle, W. F., 162
Kansas Jayhawkers, 57
Keeny, J. C., 78
Kennon, William Lee, 126
Keyes, F. W., 45
Kimbrough, T. C., 188
Kincannon, Andrew Armstrong, chancellor, sketch, 122; elected, 123, 124; criticism of, 127, 128; resignation, 128
Kirkland, James H., quoted, 146

Labauve, Felix, 87
Labauve scholarships, 87, 89
Lafayette County, 9
Lamar, Lucius Quintus Cincinnatus, 31, 35, 41, 52, 63, 66, 69, 73, 81
Lamar Bridge, 153
Lamar Hall, 143
Land grants, 3–6, 42, 43, 78, 108, 109, 160. *See also* Seminary funds
Law, School of, 31, 63, 76, 85
Lea, Pryor, trustee, 8
Leake, Governor Walter, 4
Library, first location, 13; Thompson's gift to, 21; under Barnard, 40; librarian-janitor, 85; erected, 103, 104; gifts

of Bondurant, Garner, Harrison collections, 153; new buildings, 124, 125
Literary societies, 18, 27, 28, 196. *See also* Hermaean literary society, Phi Sigma
Little, George, 63
Longest, Christopher, offices held, 126; acting chancellor, 144
Longstreet, Augustus Baldwin, president, 21; sketch, 22–24; administrative problems, 24–33; personal activities, 29–31; pastoral activity, 32; resignation, 33, 34, 121; nicknamed "Old Bullet," 169
Lottery, chartered on behalf of University, 70
Loughridge, Robert Hill, 77
Lowry, William B., captain of University Greys, 50, 51
Lyceum Building, 9; described, 13, 92; additions, 112
Lyceum programs, 133, 159
Lynch, Governor Charles, 6
Lyon, James A., 75

McCaughan, John J., trustee, 8
McNeil, Ruth, 162
McNutt, Governor Alexander G., 5, 6
McRae, Governor John J., 37, 44, 45, 87, 88
Martin, John D., 9
Martin, Sarah, 9
Mayes, Edward, chairman of the faculty, chancellor, 12, 88, 92, 98; sketch, 100, 102; reply to George, 103; administrative problems, 104; historian of the University, xi, 106; activities, 106, 107; resignation, 107
Meadows, John C., 138, 139
Medicine, School of, 76, 112; 4-year course begun and discontinued, 125; 149
Meek, Elma Coleman, names annual *Ole Miss*, 117, 186
Milden, Alfred W., 188
Military company, formed, 49; becomes University Greys, *q. v.*, 51
Millington, John, 11; sketch, 16, 17; 31; 78
Mississippi, readmitted to Union, 72
Mississippi Agricultural and Mechanical College, *see* Mississippi State College
Mississippi Historical Society, 114

Mississippi Industrial Institute and College for the Education of White Girls of Mississippi in the Arts and Sciences, *see* Mississippi State College for Women
Mississippi Railroad Company, 5
Mississippi State College, 78, 79, 141
Mississippi State College for Women, 91, 92
Mississippi, University of, site, 3; selection of site, 6, 7; location, 9; seal, 7; founding act, 7; charter amended, 91; coeducation permitted, 92; reorganization, 98, 99; as state institution, 12, 121, 139, 164, 165; Christian character, 164, 165; influence on former students, 136–138; Early campus described, 13, 14, 28, 43, 44; as wartime hospital, 56–59; buildings spared, 57, 58, 59; First session, 10, 11, 17–20; criticism (1859), 45; at time of secession, 50–54; war sessions, 51, 52; during War Between the States, 55–59; after, 67, 68, 69; during Reconstruction, 72–80; criticism (1881), 86; during World War I, 131; during World War II, 156–159; problems after World War II, 159, 160; Barnard's plan, 39, 40; under Barnard, 43–45; under Waddel, 75–80; under Kincannon, 124, 125; Land grants or seminary funds, 3–5, 37, 42, 69, 87–91, 102, 103, 108, 109, 160; financial support, 12, 37, 42, 43, 69, 70, 77, 78, 85, 87–91, 102, 103, 113, 124, 141, 143, 152, 160; Political influence at, 121, 127, 128, 141, 143, 144, 145–148; suspended by accrediting bodies, 147; reaccredited, 149, 150; Publicity, 83–85, 102, 147, 153
Moore, W. D., 57
Murphree, Dennis, lieutenant governor, 138

National Association of State Universities, 117
Naval Reserve Officers Training Corps, 154
Nichols, William, architect, 8

Observatory, 38, 83
"Old Baldy," *see* Sears, Claudius Wistar

INDEX

"Old Bullet," *see* Longstreet, A. B.
"Old Bullet" et Pueri, 25, 26
"Old Straight," *see* Stewart, A. P.
Ole Miss (annual), 117, 131; origin of name, 186
"Ole Miss" (nickname), 117
Oratory, student, 93–95
Orr, J. A., trustee, 98
O'Shea, M. V., 138
Oxford (town), 8, 9, 58
"Oxford, Mississippi" (article), 139, 140

Palmer, Benjamin Morgan, 43
Peabody Building, 124
Peabody fund, 111
Pegues, Alexander H., trustee, 8
Pettus, Governor John J., 49, 51
Peyton, Mrs. Ephraim G. (Annie Coleman), 91
"Ph. D. rule" for faculty, 154, 155
Pharmacy, School of, 125, 150
Phi Sigma, literary society, 18, 28, 50, 58, 68, 93, 122, 196
Philips, M. W., 79
Phipps, Jordan M., 31, 52
Planters' Bank, 5
Poindexter, Governor George, 4
Political interference at University, 121, 128, 141–144, 145–150
Politics (state), 30, 31, 72–75, 82, 83, 119, 120, 134, 138, 146–148
Pope, Francis Asbury, 65
Powers, Joseph Neely, chancellor, sketch, 129; 134, 144
Preparatory department, 75, 76, 83, 109
President, title of administrative officer, abolished, 40
Privies, 77
Professional schools, under Waddel, 76
Provine, John W., 105
Psychology, Department of, 150

Quinche, Alexander James, 41, 52; custodian of University property, 53, 55, 56, 60; friendship for U. S. Grant, 58, 63; 80; 184
Quitman, Governor John A., trustee, 6, 7, 8

Reconstruction, 71–75
Reconstruction Acts, 71
Reed, William B., 68

Religious Emphasis Week, 159
Reneau, Sallie Eola, 91
"Reneau Female University of Mississippi," 91
Reserve Officers Training Corps, 154
Revels, Hiram, 72
Rhodes scholars from University, 186
Ricks, Mrs. Fanny J., 111, 113
Ricks Hall, 111, 113, 161
Riley, Franklin L., 120
Roberts, Eugene Harper, 76
Rowland, P. W., 112, 188
Runnels, Governor Hiram G., 6
Russell, Governor Lee M., 119, 127; student resentment of, 132, 134

St. Thomas Hall, 17, 62, 123
Salaries, 85, 109, 122, 123, 168, 181
Saunders, Paul Hill, 76; sketch, 113, 114; 116
Scholarships, 68; Labauve, 87, 89
School colors, 116
Sears, Claudius Wistar, 60; sketch, 62; 80, 111, 123
Sears, Peter G., 123, 124
Sectionalism, 45, 67–69, 147
Seminary funds (or grants), 3–6, 37, 42, 43, 69, 70, 87–91, 102, 103, 108, 109, 160
Shands, Garvin D., 108
Shands, Hubert Anthony, 76
Sharkey, Governor William L., trustee, 8, 59, 60, 71, 73
Shaw, Oliver A., 188
Shoup, Francis A., 63, 71, 111
Simrall, H. F., trustee, 88, 89
Smith, A. J. ("Whiskey"), 58, 59
Sororities, 92. *See also* Fraternities
Southern Association of Colleges and Secondary Schools, University charter member, 117; 146; suspends state institutions, 147; 166; readmits University, 149, 150
Southern Educational Association, *see* Southern Association of Colleges and Secondary Schools
Southern Intercollegiate Athletic Association, 127
Steam heating, 112
Stearns, William F., 9, 31; given custody of law library, 52; resignation, 52

Stewart, Alexander P., chancellor, 11, 12, 61, 63; sketch, 81, 82; administration characterized, 87; seminary funds, 87, 91; 96; as disciplinarian, 97, 98; resignation, 99, 146
Stockard, James, 8
Stockard, Sarah, 8
Stone, Governor John M., 82
Student body, first, 7, 13, 19
Student discipline, *see* Discipline, student
Student life, 18, 19, 24-29, 49-51, 64; cost of living after War Between the States, 66; censorship, 74, 84, 86, 96-98, 106; 115-117, 132-134, 139, 140, 181
Student losses, War Between the States, 55; World War II, 159
Student misconduct, 24, 25, 49, 50, 69, 74, 104, 106, 115, 116. *See also* Discipline, student
Student pranks, 24-27, 46, 69
Student regulations, 86, 167. *See also* Discipline, student
Student Union Building, 153
"Stunt night," 134
Sullens, Frederick, quoted, 145, 146
Sullivan, Hampton M., trustee, 89, 90, 91
Summer sessions, early, 111
Swan, John Nesbit, 188

Telephones, 112
Telescope, *see* Observatory
Thompson, Jacob, trustee, 8, 11, 21, 23, 32, 37, 47, 69, 87, 178
Trotter, J. F., 52
Trustees, Board of, University (before 1910), 7, 8; first meeting, 8; original educational program, 9, 10; early powers, 11; purchase Millington's apparatus, 17; first commencement, 20; 22, 23; 26, 27; discipline faculty, 30; memorial to Congress, 42, 109; 44; "Branham affair," 47-49; during War Between the States, 52, 53, 54, 59; (1865) 60, 61; (1870's) 71-77; reorganized, 82, 83; abolish and restore fraternities, 86; change title of executive officer, 40, 100, 101; 104, 105; abolish commencement ball, 117, 118; suspend organization of fraternities, 119; refuse Carnegie library grant, 120; partisanship on, 120; interference by, 146; abolished (1910), 126
Trustees, Board of, Institutions of Higher Learning (after 1910), organized, 126; dismiss students, 132, 133; political control, 143, 144; non-political, 148; reorganized (1944), 159
Tuition, 68; discontinued and restored, 85, 86

University (post office), established (1889), 104
University Greys, officers commissioned, 50, 51; mustered into state troops, 51; into Confederate service, 51; furnished weapons, 51, banner, 51; actions during War Between the States, 55; memorials, 55, 142
University News Bureau, 153
University of Mississippi Magazine, 118, 123

Vaiden, Cowles M., trustee, 87
Vallandigham, Clement L., 68
Vardaman, Governor James K., 119
Ventress, J. Alexander, trustee, 8
Voorhees, Daniel W., 68

Waddel, John Newton, trustee, chancellor, 8, 11, 17, 18, 19, 23, 24; pastoral activity, 30, 32; "premonition," 32, 62; resignation as professor, 37, 38; elected chancellor, 60; sketch, 61, 62; inaugural, 65; 71, 73, 74; resignation, 75, 79, 80; 87; historian of the University, xi, 74, 106; pronunciation of name, 176
Walthall, Edward Cary, 109
War service units, World War II, 157, 158
Waterworks, 112
Weir, Rush C., Student Union Building, 153
Wheat, John J., 60; sketch, 62, 63; acting chancellor, 80, 81; 96, 99, 100
"Where Shall I Send My Son?" 83
Whitehorne, Henry, 52
Whitfield, Governor Henry L., 134, 136, 138
Wilkinson, Edward C., trustee, 8
Williams, John Davis, chancellor, sketch, 160

Willing, R. P., 28, 29
Wilmer, R. H., 65
Winans, William, 30, 31
Witherspoon, T. D., 67, 177

Women students, 91, 92

Yellow fever, 85 (1878)
Young Men's Christian Association, 134

DAVIDSON COLLEGE
LIBRARY

...out for **two weeks**. Books
Books on regular order to be renewed.
must be presented at...

A fine is charged...
...gulations at the discretion of

Special books ar...
brary staff.

*The Country
of the Blue*

Other Books by Charles Edward Eaton

Poetry

The Bright Plain
The Shadow of the Swimmer
The Greenhouse in the Garden
Countermoves
On the Edge of the Knife
The Man in the Green Chair
Colophon of the Rover
The Thing King
The Work of the Wrench
New and Selected Poems, 1942–1987
A Guest on Mild Evenings

Short Stories

Write Me from Rio
The Girl from Ipanema
The Case of the Missing Photographs
New and Selected Stories, 1959–1989

Novel

A Lady of Pleasure

Critical Biography

Karl Knaths: Five Decades of Painting

The Country of the Blue

Charles Edward Eaton

Cornwall Books
New York • London • Toronto

© 1994 by Rosemont Publishing and Printing Corporation

All rights reserved. Authorization to photocopy items for internal or personal use, or the internal or personal use of specific clients, is granted by the copyright owner, provided that a base fee of $10.00, plus eight cents per page, per copy is paid directly to the Copyright Clearance Center, 222 Rosewood Drive, Danvers, Massachusetts 01923. [0-8453-4850-7/94 $10.00+8¢ pp, pc.]

Cornwall Books
440 Forsgate Drive
Cranbury, NJ 08512

Cornwall Books
25 Sicilian Avenue
London WC1A 2QH, England

Cornwall Books
P.O. Box 338, Port Credit
Mississauga, Ontario
Canada L5G 4L8

The paper used in this publication meets the requirements of the American National Standard for Permanence of Paper for Printed Library Materials Z39.48-1984.

Library of Congress Cataloging-in-Publication Data

Eaton, Charles Edward
    The country of the blue / Charles Edward Eaton.
      p.   cm.
    ISBN 0-8453-4850-7 (alk. paper)
    1. Water—Poetry. I. Title.
    PS3509.A818C64 1994
    811'.54—dc20   94-13790
                                                                           CIP

PRINTED IN THE UNITED STATES OF AMERICA

To Isabel

He had merely waked up one morning again in the country of the blue, and had stayed there with a good conscience and a great idea until he died.

—Henry James, *The Next Time*

Contents

Acknowledgments	11
I. Summer of the Sea	
Cahoon's Hollow, Looking Down	17
The Javelin	17
Trade Winds	19
A Tin of Sardines	20
Palmy Days	21
Blue Landscape	23
Horses by the Sea	24
Long Hours in the Sun	25
The Clutch	26
A Charmed Life	27
Private Eye	28
Touch and Go	29
II. The Boat People	
The Riverboat	33
Periscope	34
The Torpedo	35
The Reef	37
The Iceberg	38
The Love Boat	39
Screwdriver	40
Outrigger	41
Argonaut	42
The Pier	44
The Winged Eye	45

III. A Retrospective of Swimmers

The Trellis	49
In Cold Blood	50
The Sun Says Grace	51
Water Snakes	52
Vulcan at Sunrise	53
Quicksand	54
Up Close and Personal	55
The Spool	56
The Turn-On	57
Sunbather in Autumn	58
The Hinge	59
The Afterworld	60

IV. Inland Waters

River Job	65
The Aquarium	66
The Aquamarine	66
The Swamp	67
Wall Fountain	68
White Lake	69
Claws	70
The Blue Window	71
Whirlpool	72
The Crane	73
The Towline	74
The Swan at Sunset	75
The House on the Hill	76

V. Blue Book

Water Wings	81
The Recovery	82
Picasso's Egg	83
Loose Ends	84
The Wisteria Sailor	86
The Fling	86
Islands Beyond A	88
Dipstick	89

Body Blow	90
The Vise	90
The Art of Quotation	91
Blue Blazes	92
The Book Club	94

VI. The Cove

Land's End	97
The Man with the Blue Spine	98
The Vigneron	99
Squeeze Play	99
The Child of Life	100
Message from Metamorphosis	101
The Goblet	102
Wild Oats	103
Blue Dancers	104
The Pond	105
The Truss	106
The Premise	107
Last Word	108
The Cove	109

Acknowledgments

Permission to reprint from the following sources is hereby acknowledged.

Agni Review: "The Vigneron"
Amelia: "The Sun Says Grace" and "The Fling"
Ariel (Canada): "The Winged Eye"
Blue Unicorn: "The Torpedo," "The Iceberg," and "The Man with the Blue Spine"
Cat's Ear: "Blue Landscape" and "The Swamp"
Centennial Review: "The Truss"
Chariton Review: "Touch and Go," "The Riverboat," "Quicksand," "The Vise," and "Blue Blazes"
Chronicles: "The Trellis," "Long Hours in the Sun," "Dipstick," and "The Afterworld"
Commonweal: "The Pond"
Connecticut Poetry Review: "The Javelin"
Crab Creek Review: "The Reef"
Cream City Review: "Screwdriver"
Creeping Bent: "The Towline"
Crosscurrents: "The Crane"
Epoch: "Cahoon's Hollow, Looking Down"
Folio: "Loose Ends" and "Outrigger"
Forum (University of Houston): "Wall Fountain"
Four Quarters: "The Premise"
Hawaii Review: "The Love Boat" and "Blue Dancers"
Hellas: "The Swan at Sunset"
Hollins Critic: "Claws" and "Last Word"
Images: "The Pier"

International Poetry Review: "Islands Beyond A"
Laurel Review: "Up Close and Personal" and "The Hinge"
Lullwater Review (Emory University): "The House on the Hill" and "Wild Oats"
Midwest Quarterly: "The Art of Quotation"
Mississippi Valley Review: "Land's End"
Modern Poetry Studies: "River Job"
Nexus: "Water Snakes" and "The Recovery"
Paintbrush: "Trade Winds," "Palmy Days," "The Spool," and "The Turn-On"
Pembroke Magazine: "Picasso's Egg," "Message from Metamorphosis," and "The Goblet"
Poem: "A Tin of Sardines," "Vulcan at Sunrise," "White Lake," and "The Wisteria Sailor"
St. Andrews Review: "Private Eye"
Salmagundi: "Water Wings" and "The Cove"
Skylark (Purdue University): "Sunbather in Autumn"
The Smith: "In Cold Blood," "The Book Club," and "The Child of Life"
Sonora Review: "Periscope"
South Carolina Review: "The Aquarium" and "Squeeze Play"
Southern Poetry Review: "The Clutch"
Webster Review: "A Charmed Life"
West Branch: "The Aquamarine"
West Hills Review: "Whirlpool"
Wisconsin Review: "Argonaut"

*The Country
of the Blue*

I. Summer of the Sea

CAHOON'S HOLLOW, LOOKING DOWN

Melville admired a whale because he went five miles
 downstairs,
Perhaps, beneath that pressure, feeling more alive—
Man, perforce, must make a much more shallow dive:
Beautiful swimmer with his lodestone of despairs.

But, summer of the sea, you do not need discount the grace
Of swimmers, nor against their courage cavil,
When they must circumscribe and kiss the navel
Of the water in some blue, impassioned, minuscule embrace.

Forget the metaphor, forget the whale, remember when,
Smelling of salt, perhaps indeed remiss,
The swimmer must unfinger the seductive kiss,
Spread out, like joined antitheses, his dual, two-vaned fan.

While heart hammers secret, battered images against the
 ground,
It seems, great plunger, you incited him
To such dissatisfaction with his natural rhythm
That he looks fallen there from stairs whose final step he
 found.

THE JAVELIN

After what seemed a cosmic orgasm,
The shuddering sky, the frenzied birds,

He woke up by the atoll's blue lagoon
As if pinned there like an afterimage,
Something not supposed to go in the glow—
The flamingos had flown, the sky was calm,
But something like a javelin held him
In place, stuck with this strange everafter.

One eye opened, a fanlight on the world:
A very ordinary man subdued,
The warm print of a woman by his side—
Two eyes, and his whole destiny came back:
This morning feeling of being impaled,
Trussed, in bed, though he was fully naked.
Something, someone, wanted his heart left there,
And so it was, like the only keepsake.

Sometimes the imprint will cost just this much,
The imagination so overspent,
The woman, birds, hiding on the island,
And just this rich compensatory scene
As if one were at least well laid out for love—
I suspect you know these mornings after,
The absurd dreams with the main point plunged in:
One always lives in a hail of happenstance.

I put it to you now much more simply—
Even the swizzle stick in the strong drink
Lends its lissome weight, stalls on an ice cube.
Her dropped earring has a light lethal point,
The lore of the whetstone in manic birds—
But you will learn to move each day, transfixed,
While the javelin wavers in the air
As if it still knows the qualms of winning.

TRADE WINDS

After the love affair, when the blisters
Had peeled from the mind, the palm oil applied
To the skin aroused with sexual friction,
The trade winds came in to soothe and bless you.

The lover was there, of course, beside you.
You still fingered each other's nerves a bit,
Fondled the relaxed fruits of the body,
Embrocated the listener with love words.

It was good to feel that the hand knew
The picked-over places of passion,
That it lay, idle as an octopus,
As if, many-armed, we dream of mansions.

You might drink a sip of that cool water,
I take another whiff of your perfume.
We feel like a stack of several people,
This way, that way, the luscious bones and flesh.

Invited—whatever I admire in you,
Admitted—wherever you have wished to roam.
Our lifted knees could make tents for Arabs,
The rugs, shoes at the entrance, blowing sand,

As if any country could be conjured—
In the corners of the rooms the rolled-up maps.
How long does it live, the afterimage,
How does one keep the skeleton from the feast?

Turn this way, that way, legs now masts aloft—
A schooner pulls its anchor from my chest;
Your lips taste again of fruited islands,
There is an apple where an absence was.

I know that we must lapse, the commonplace
Will air the sheets, brush off the husks and rinds—
Come back in less than a year and you find
That transience leaves no pips, no cobwebs.

Therefore some would set up in the plaza
At once the pillory of our well-being,
The head and legs stuck out like meat for birds,
No pizzicato, no sails, no trade winds.

And you and I in dreams must mop that face,
Let it loll back and forth in the hand's musk
As if one spiced and spiced a meated skull,
The gap of desire having no drop cloth.

Where are the pins and needles, where the lyre?—
Pick me a place that you have felt the stocks:
We have come back to the room to render
Unto caesuras winds that make us sail.

A TIN OF SARDINES

Had he been too long at sea, found the catch too thin,
And knew, having slept on that blue corpulence over and over
    and come up hungry,
That he must carry about his person little fishes in a tin?

He liked to pull it out, put it on his desk in sunlight
As if he brought a scattered essence of the sea together,
In spite of all those soft, fat, blue days had made it somewhat
    right.

Perhaps one must be merciless a bit, too much taken with a
    sense of doom,

To shrink the nets, collapse leviathans one could not catch,
And let all fishing expeditions end in this quiet room.

Still, a light, almost like radium, is emanating from the can,
A bit of brilliant ore from the sea laid there like loot
To say that fishers, in their way, are miners to a man.

One turns the key upon compaction of more devastating scenes—
Ah, Sardinian, it is as though you curled your iron, contemptuous lip
And showed sardonic précis of the passion of sardines.

In such emphasis the world is pressed together and cannot turn—
You are glad to have food upon the table, keep winding back the lip,
But wonder if voluptuous containment leaves too much radium burn.

PALMY DAYS

Even the lover left in the lurch spreads
His hand like a frond, wanting and asking.
Stranded on the island with that rich palm,
He remembers the feel of her ripe breasts.

Now is the time to make a brilliant life
Of being underestimated, judged
As a castoff from the sensuous sea,
A man dumped back on his own desire.

What does one do in this situation?—
Go back to the six, seven, fantasies

A day?—the one gloriously fulfilled:
The coming in together on surf boards,

The huge white horn of a curling wave,
The sprawled plenty on the beach, lip and breast,
Under the very tree you now implore,
This idol with sealed fountain at the top.

It is time to be theatrical, trash
The bloodstream with extreme pictures, milk oil,
Palm-sugar from the tree, and remember
How your bodies were like a pair of tongs

That could pick up compressed desire, squander
It in cubes, one lump, or two, through the long
Afterswoon of love, the diminished thump,
The sea combing through a finished thing.

I will not leave a mist of metaphors,
The foghorn moaning, calling to failure—
That clear day is a diamond in the brain.
We lay on its table, hiding facets,

The undersides of what we would not see,
This keeping troubles to ourselves, this lie
Of riches, that the sea was not too bland,
That no hammer could split the perfect stone.

Still, by the tree, among brilliant splinters,
I must be the pointillist with the paste
And you the undine of the underside:
Here is the taste of your soul from my lips.

On this mosaic of broken diamonds,
It is so hot it burns our tender feet—
I have some little shade in my spread hand:
The slashing tree spikes sunlight everywhere.

BLUE LANDSCAPE

In that blue landscape the sky is full of rooks:
The saturated blue and those excited cries—
You will not find the likes of this in ordinary books.

The color seems to blow like smoke, the lead bird swerves—
If I were dressed in denim, a life of Riley sort of man,
I would not like to come upon the secret of my nerves.

This is certainly not the place for luscious life, love, mating—
The full-blown has been altogether swept away,
And on its stem we feel the brain quietly pulsating.

The rooks are casing crops from their perch on hay:
You must be a sorry and sardonic sight to them,
Having wandered here from absinthe and the blue café.

It is exactly just the time to hoot and clap your hands:
I am Apollo rising in the sunlight with ambrosial locks
And not the latest member of earth's lost tribes and
   wandering bands.

This is an exercise—practice it on Riley's time, the luxe, the
　　luscious living—
The world is mediocre, limp, without something like this force,
A god in this blue field to rout the rooks of your misgiving.

HORSES BY THE SEA

He could feel the metal between his teeth
Just before a kiss and it went too far—
Not like a bit that would pull him up short—
A light taste of steel on his tongue and then
The abandon of the horse in the head,
The lather, the full sweat, the cruppered tail.
The tongue having hurdled the curb will learn
The rich dissolution of its liquids.
They may not fully know what love can be,
Those without this fitting in the mouth,
As if subtleties weighted with sorcery
Should rise and rise to the top of the throat
To become a barrier just in the nick
Of time when the land falls off to the sea.
You have seen the lovers sauntering down there
Through wild flowers as if earth were meadow
And the huge, dangerous height behind them,
That breather, that light pause, before the plunge—
Most of us want to crack the universe
Open with love, the deep, plangent orgasm.
But some still like a staff to the music
Where the notes can read the signs of the road,
Not a stockade but a snaffle on the way.
It may be you like heavy metal rock,
But even at its strongest, sensual best,
Somewhere down the road a dead, beaten animal.
And yet our own reveries rear up at us

As we try to silver the taste of steel—
That last, blinding view of our own lovers
Leaping on the backs of horses by the sea,
The notes falling out of the staff, the huge
Music of it all, the rich, full sunset
Hiding behind the crossbars of the clouds.

LONG HOURS IN THE SUN

Do you remember, all those years ago, long hours in the sun,
To the beach, and back again, always moving free of
  shadow?—
Few words were even thought, and spoken—for long hours—
  not one.

You did not think a single minute on how life aborts—
The fruit was ripening, the sea was full, the trees were
  shimmering:
You came out from the only shell you wore—espadrilles and
  shorts.

The succubus was in your room, here the sumptuous lay *sub
  verbo*—
I wonder if we do not all count upon these underlying plots:
You want the shade, the well—I want the endless summer and
  the glow.

But this we share—the inexpressible to live at ease—the
  surd—
I lie, subaltern, unsuborned, disarmed, unprocessed for a
  while,
And do not want to point at you or you the gun of any word.

How is it then that things are still so fat and fulsome for the
   knife?—
When you go home and see the faces, books, the boudoir sotte
   voce,
The sentence lashes, rips for any lucid oil, a drop of sublife.

Those lovely hours in the sun, the sentence slashed and
   milked to drouth—
I think I parse a pattern in the powers of life: Sun dogs bark
Subalterns home to open faces, books, closed lips, prim
   mouth.

THE CLUTCH

If you measure your life with calipers,
The mouth of the lover may seem too thick—
It is the brush of the lips that matters,
It is the subtle engagement that counts.

Just how wide is the sea for your sources
If you think of yourself as a piston?
Go easy—push in a foot like a clutch
As if you kept a blue machine idling.

Let the touched lover see how gold and tooled
You are all over, levers at her breast,
The thrilling rub of chassis everywhere,
This interlocking sense of pause and push.

Later, in the driver's seat and bowling
Along the sea, alerted to your thrust,
You have established your intuitions,
No caroming, no crashing off the road.

I parked this image once and let it purr,
My feet still blue in my socks, lips tingling,
Did what I could at last to calibrate
The relaxed ease of a perfect motion.

One could almost doze in this hazed hiatus,
All things still, yet powerful and throbbing,
The girl drawn close and the sleek hood shining,
The sea at the pleasure of your pedal.

One sighs as one sights the fork in the road,
Dreams of calm evening and the driftwood fire.
Is it the time, place, for disengagement,
Will the motor of the world forgive us?

I watch it all through sand-stung windshield,
Longing for singed meat and burnt marshmallows,
The red ball of the sun a beckoning—
I hear the sea murmuring for my foot.

A CHARMED LIFE

So any mountain was his Sugar Loaf,
The sea his aphrodisiac which filled
His mind and heart only with blue stories—
This—while the silver tongs picked one small cube
For his morning coffee, the sea view culled
By the window to one strait, blue page,
The sectioned orange, diminished flotilla—
Unless one is enamored of paradox
One can never lead a charmed life, the ship
Moving in the mouth, the tongue turning the spray.
Just so, the sirens move along the veins
As the story in the window leaches,

The fingers spread out like mountain climbers,
A support group for the final assault—
It is always in the moment, the furrow
Of the future, the keel of the orange
Goes easy, launching in the avid throat;
The unruptured eye and the fineness of the fins—
There is no end of time in any vein.
One lifted finger, and the mountain soars,
The sleek savages clamor toward your tongue,
The tongs have long since loosed their measured grasp—
Of course, we discount these peaks of ecstasy,
This ravishment along the river's reach,
For something in the long run breaks the spell.
The fingers fade on the blue slope, the girls
Languish on some vague, secret rock,
The hull of the orange punctured of all juice.
Where do we go from here? I only say,
This revery at the breakfast table
Still roves and reams the impassioned detour
As if one latches on to hills, high spots—
Pips on the breast one will never spit out,
The seamless sighting of the open sea.

PRIVATE EYE

Those palms, that blue sea, which beckon through the snow:
The haunting music, those brown voluptuous girls, the fruited
    air—
How can one pierce the snowstorm with such a cameo?

Blue and green and blue again may not suffice
For those who see it every day—they plunge
A hole in it to see this land of filigree and ice.

Imagination says to an imagination: Let the others starve—
Grass skirts, dazzling beaches versus diamonded igloo:
The Sun God and The Snow Man—Everybody wants to carve!

Here in the whirling blizzard one does what one has to do—
Occlude, conclude, one has the only aperture there is:
An island lei-ed with flowers intaglioed on blue.

You rush, of course, and find the wind is steady with its brake,
The blue eye turns as heavy as a paperweight—
How could there be another cataract in every single flake?

Someone—someone stronger?—is pushing holes into the
   sky—
Why is one so much in a world one does not really want
Unless the islands are focussing their lapidary eye?

TOUCH AND GO

Some day, no doubt, they may ask you: Why this?
Why that? But then you will be well beyond
Hatred and heartbreak, tugged, untuggable.
They may find you grooming the glistening sea,
Pinch it as they do luxurious stuff
But learn that it leaves, and leaves no indigo.
They may place you underneath the fabulous tree
Earringed with cherries, the woman, her cat,
How you set them there in content boudoir.
They could see your lovers fresh from the yolk
With a clear golden glaze brushed over them
As if the sun cracked an egg on the beach—
More homely, they could watch you by the fire
Teaching the clinkers to talk in a red
And bluish garden, the sinuous, muttered thing,

Or stand by the fat little boy pissing
In the fountain a solution of sources.

Why go on and on when they mean to come in,
Poke the oval, make it bleed, wipe a word
That is still damp in the blotting paper,
Lift up the necklace you put on the breast
To look for the torsion of blue and green—
Why not? What else?—the laying on of hands.
Just that the jogged sea has such savoir-faire
And remembers the fine comb in its locks.
Just that the pink cheeks, pink tongue of the cat
Chime and the wind keeps tinkling the earrings.
Ah, those lovers! How each day the sun holds
Up the handsome egg—the two, the tondo!—
I will indeed circle round and round you
Only to see what you have made of things,
Brushed also everywhere with circumspection,
The bruise bounding back from the stomach punch;
A glancing blow moves on, shooting the stars:
The reeling axis when wantons collide,
The head-on thing, the headlands enantlered.

Therefore, one cannot mind the merest touch—
The cheeks of one world against another,
The sea like a cool compress, the grasses
That sweep the skin, their lashes filled with dew.
We turn and, in time, are touched all over,
Not that we count on music of the spheres,
Or a light of love like a ruby rubbed—
Alive to shoulders listing in dark hallways:
Some must, some magic, in a sliding pause.

II. The Boat People

THE RIVER BOAT

He loved the river boat because it was
Lazy, gentle, responded to the tides—
The different rouge of morning and sunset
As though the girl at his side tinted it.

Out for sexual adventure, they made
The river indulge them, the papyrus,
The exotic birds, the boat's slow paddle
Echoed by the shore's beast-drawn waterwheel.

Their little portable cranked out love songs
As if lovers poured through a turnstile—
One could have them naked or fully clothed:
Nothing too coarse or too fine for the needle.

The aimlessness of it all was perfect—
It gave coitus the force of a peg.
If the universe moves too forcefully,
Even a glancing kiss rips off its skin.

All that they wanted was to be buoyed
Unobtrusively and then to make love.
The boat seemed to sigh a little and pause,
Another bolt shot in its old warm flesh.

It was not to drop anchor, be master
Of when and where the voyage was over—
It was merely to mimic the flow of time,
Keeping the facts of history in steerage.

So it would seem, lover, that we put down
Our anecdotes, one peg at a time, the tent
Silken, invisible to passengers,
A skin the rippling wind cannot tear off.

Nothing like it till we hit a sandbar—
The needle jars from its close labia;
The zodiac spins its wheel of fortune,
The circuit of animals, jumped, jumbled.

One thing not foreseen—to modulate
The boat is far from easy. It pretends
To us all that it provides the slow, rich
Seductiveness of Cleopatra's barge.

It conceals that it has a nose for the shore
As if it smelled it in our warm embrace,
The swamps, the thickets, the phallic cities,
The bodies placed here, there, like paperweights.

You will remember then just how my hand
Rippled like the wind, your skirt, blouse, flowing—
The turnstile clicked shut at the threat of gale;
The zodiac tamped down its partitions.

Ah, clear night at last, so pick just one star—
We lie still as a slot machine together
We have outlasted the devious boat—
It drifts beneath us filled with shuffled signs.

PERISCOPE

Thinking hard and feeling threatened, that day
You went up and down in your own rapt mind,

Walking upright and yet so submarine—
Meeting the woman in the field swamped you:
You lay with her in a wash of flowers,
This roll in her soft arms of a beached thing,
Back and forth still so heavy with pressure.
You remembered the raised parabola,
How the sunlight like a vertical sea
Blinded you, how she towed you, so you thought,
To safety, her pearls the richest of ropes,
The old water coming back to the mass,
The feeling that you were missing its pull—
Therefore it may well be time to crash dive,
The heart a little waterlogged but sure
To respond to its own great pump once more.
There in your mother's womb, the periscope
Looked always everywhere for you, her eyes
Folding far horizons into the blood—
How the sea knows where the throat and mouth are,
How birth is the first coming up for air,
And then, levels of green, blue, forever—
There will be great, audacious, fluid days
When you fold in your fear like an instrument.
I have discussed this matter with lovers
Who ride each other's thighs like a pent ship.
We tell each other how it feels, how one
Does not mind, persuaded of invasion,
How we sway in a blue, hypnotic song
And rise to the rainbow spill overhead.

THE TORPEDO

The man of many pleasures standing on the luxurious ship
Never dreamed that the sleek torpedo was rapidly
   approaching him—

He had danced, drunk champagne, held the bediamonded
woman in his arms.

The wine sloshed a little, the woman swayed, but he braced
himself
As if he let down a virile pin into the ocean's depths:
If he had spat, it would have veered then hit the bright
spittoon.

Just the night before when he was a little drunk he had
pitched
In his berth but no more than a heavy sandbag stopping at
the edge—
He was too full of sex and satisfaction ever to quite fall.

All night the ring and watch which he religiously took off
Rolled in the tray but no more than a throw of dice,
Gleaming the comfortable suggestion that there would always
be a lighthouse somewhere.

The pool on board, the table for deck tennis, the shuffleboard
were his.
The salmon mousse lined him with his own kind of living,
The Captain saluted and acknowledged him as a genie of
good hope.

Everyone wanted to rub against him and produce the
exquisite day:
The boy worked his smile to arouse a better sort of father;
The dog looked at his stalwart leg and dreamed of a
lamppost.

Of course, the stowaway in the lifeboat has his doubts,
The one who peeped and saw him don the abdominal belt,
use the rouge—
Every man of pleasure in the world must have his imp.

And once in a while the woman in his arms became an
incubus.

Her roving hands would pause on his chest as if to pluck out
   the hairs;
Her sex was like a seal that meant to leave some lush tattoo.

Perhaps, too, the after-dinner movie might have alerted him:
A man riding a whale in deep water, holding on for dear life
As if somehow, together, they were headed toward land to
   bomb the earth.

It may have started also when the kid turned mean and hit
   him in the stomach—
A waitress spilled a scalding dragon's blood of soup upon his
   neck,
The purser gave him notice on the mounting bar bill.

I who am no expert in these devastating, universal wounds
Will always admire the final and immense sangfroid
Of the man who looks up and quiets the jangling chandelier.

He can be seen in his midnight blue evening jacket, smoking
   at the taffrail
As if he will always light a little fire in the face of fate,
A false signal at the very edge of the mass of things.

Live by him and you will feel the whoosh, the released,
   languorous shiver
As the torpedo passes by, or ride with him in exploding
   fragments everywhere
As if the star you harbored in your heart remembers how the
   world began.

THE REEF

It was thick, deep, and endless—that love and that belief—
The master in his spotless white, the mistress in her
   incomparable blue gown

Had discounted any possibility of ever coming on a reef.

Whitecaps did not inevitably suggest the possibility of storm:
The sea was fed and saturated with the sequins from her
    dress—
They had in perfect tact the most caressive sense of form.

Blue islands were forever along the seapath of their boat
Swirled round with that delectable meringue of cloud—
The mold of the sky maintained the *isle flottante* would always
    float.

If there were a lazy sense of something, somewhere, somehow,
    unpropitiated,
He could flick the blue ash of his rich, redolent cigar,
Or she would drop a sapphire—a final sequin in the sea
    whose appetite was not quite sated.

One likes this handsome pair rather more than we admit—
Unused to obstacles, they do not find them when they meet
    and kiss:
A sigh is heard around the world at just how perfectly they fit.

We hold if they will hold—no islands turning to volcanoes, no
    rocks, no screams—
When we wake, startled, sprawled, lying on our beds like
    ridges,
We turn and kiss and kiss and kiss as if to mend what parted
    at the seams.

THE ICEBERG

Perhaps it was the cool menthol cigarette,
The tear-drop candlesticks on the table,
That drew the enormous iceberg toward him,

A feeling of green and crystal looming—
He was one of those lost men who are found
Always at some awesome edge where break-offs
Drift in and shake the house, the table's edge—
The green cigarette, tears dropping in the glass.

These shatterable men always love icebergs
As if they contained enough bright splinters
To go on standing up to any grief:
The long bumping through the night, ice shavings
On the floor, an orgy in the morning—
With the first drink at noon, the dropped, square cube,
The slipped foot, are the first indication
Certain hard pieces move back to the mass.

So be it: an Alp upon the water,
Refreshing the blue sea for miles around,
Dwarfing at the same time it lures our range—
Those with the sea-colored veins and sad hearts
Gather their loose dreams into an ice pick:
The great block brought into the house in prongs,
A sound of the wagon, dripping, dripping—
How can one stab the home of every tear?

THE LOVE BOAT

He had heaped it with cushions, wine, grapes, pears:
Liquids and luscious shapes—the green canoe.
It was like putting a heavy jewel
On the water and expecting it to float.
Try that with your ring-loaded white hand;
The flesh will think itself buoyant, then sink.
The drag downward may be voluptuous,
Of course, but drowning is not quite the point.

So we toss the cushions, fruit, overboard,
Hands flutter like a pair of waterwings;
The breasts themselves are a form of ballast—
The man with the lean oar pushes off, cuts
The river like a dissolved jewel;
Naked to the waist, she seems to have tucked
Away a melon somewhere. The quick, mixed
Situation puts gloss upon some guile.

She learns to sit, uncushioned courtesan,
He lets the oar down deeper like a pole.
You have seen them come from the river mouth
There by the side of the white, gleaming ship
With just the fruit of their bodies for sale.
What did you expect?—Cleopatra's barge?—
The canoe shakes like a bed for barter:
The pole, the power, those planetary breasts.

SCREWDRIVER

Just because he meant for no one to put
The screws on him, the oarsman rowed so far,
So fast—The thick blue water resisting
Sometimes felt like wood close-grooved with lapis—
Back and forth in the scull as the hand does
When it turns and releases its grip,
No end to the river, no perfect fit
In the wood—the rest, an impasse always.
If lucky, you come on a scatter rug
Of water lilies, or, slow-drifting, see
A silver scab form on the rifted wake,
At least that much of the track smoothed over,
As vagary pulls and pulls the oarsman.
I have seen him bent over waiting,

Loaded with scrap iron, hands blue on the oars—
At the tip of the turn, a last idea,
As if a snake, stuck in the groove, shivered,
The backbone pushed by a screw propeller—
Perhaps no one will see the stained hands but you,
The whirling blades muffled in the world's mass
Of meanings—except, for you, no loose screws.
If the heart is a tomb of spirals, spurts,
We will forever summon out its ghosts
To plead the undelved day, the wood, the water—
I feel the driver in my flaccid pocket,
You twitch the drifting scull upon its line.

OUTRIGGER

How full, laden and lopsided, he is—
A flowering almond can swamp him with pink
As if he had been drinking rosé for hours—
Push him and he would slosh like a wine glass.
Or you might find him gorged on honeysuckle
As if Laocoön lent him a late myth
And he were entwined, tangled with sweetness.
Still, what a bold camouflage of cargo—
Not a pink drop spilled on his white shirt,
Not a rut mark on the wrist from the coils—
He does not sweat on the kitchen oilcloth
And leave a pink print for palmists to read.
He does not ask for sons to share his turmoil—
No plumber to rout the snakes from the pipes.
Strangely, it makes us think of the islands:
Calm sea, perhaps a boat loaded with spice—
Curious how we choose such serenity
For him when he's so stuffed, meant to stagger,
When he has told us often of his throes:

Too much drink—the rhododendron offers
Its bloom like a basin for his flushed face.
It may be last-ditch, left-over, longed-for,
A pink-poured stranger whom we take in tow,
Burdened with his basket of fragrant snakes—
You may have seen him weaving down the street
As if he knew a timber reamed the sea.

ARGONAUT

Sometimes one has to go beneath the sea
Only a moment when the race is lost,
Down and back, breathing and looking for sail,
The vague form of one's life slipping away.

It is an urgent and exacting argosy,
Arbitrating the two elements, lungs
Not easy in the water or the air,
A man tossed over, Jason's left-behind.

I dream sometimes the manta ray glides by,
This substitute for fleece, this floating cloak,
A pad, mattress, thick as a bloated sail—
One grasps at image pieces in the dream.

All this, mind you, only in fits and starts—
Jason racing in the vulva of the waves,
Even the shells on the shore, labia
Luring him onward to the golden pelt.

Those moments you will always call remora
When you lie for an instant piggyback

As if the parent body gave you breath,
Carried sweet as a papoose of the sea.

Sometimes even a shark may spare a ride,
But you must keep your sucking disk so tight
That you are a handle for another,
Some diver plucking at his fortune too.

It is much, much better on the soft side—
If you stay too long, the curling manta
May swaddle the child in you forever,
Little shrouded mummy of *mal de mer.*

Perhaps this wakes a kindred lust:
The voluptuous sea, your suction valve,
The down, the up, the deep, the blinding light,
The soul's unremitting remora.

I can feel this standing on the plush carpet,
A large bat beating against the ceiling
Like a residual dream of safe passage:
Just open the window—the sea comes in.

You have surely paused on another's fleece,
Felt the remiges of sail seethe and seethe,
Glad of the cigarette burns and mud tracks,
Remembering Medea murdering the offspring.

But if it is your fate to trail, to trim
The glorious canvas, lying illegal,
Rising to gulp in the bright, ravished world,
Take your catnap and then come up again.

Someone may even see you, wrapped radiant,
Put a mat at your door, curly and thick—
I meet these salesmen almost every day:
They brush and brush their feet and then walk in.

THE PIER

The fruit, the flowers were gone, and now the sea
Was the place to say good-bye to summer—
As far as he could get out on the pier
Dependent though it was on poles like roots
Of rotting teeth above the blue gum line.
It creaks, mutters, promises, and he longs
To extend himself as if a brown arm
Now flung out could be an estuary
Pouring from a warm mud river inland.
The oral cavity full of the blue sea
And his own body stocked with licorice:
It is too complex—he cannot convert
These images, swaying on the pilings
Where the blue mouthwash of the water
Does not clean out the old decaying smell,
The body will not leak its sweet, damp tar.
One thing at a time. The huge pile driver
Must put a pole in place, then another,
Out into the sea, the season forgotten.
What we have is a fresh human longing,
The licorice river-man, a footing,
The nerve in the sapphire socket,
A quick, blinding pain when the driver hits—
I can give you then the simple sadness:

Suddenly an exposed root in the air,
The props all gone, only the pier swaying—
Soon autumn with its overrich gold fillings
Will make some sort of tomb with each inlay.

THE WINGED EYE

I had come to the end of everything, the black sky,
The crows, red berries like a touch of blood,
When over the ship of death fluttered a winged eye.

For this is what it seemed, moving out, on, much too far,
The sense of a masked, red figure standing in the prow—
I have no other way to tell you what late autumns are.

It is as though the rose reneged, the fruits were all self-ravished—
One has these human but delusive ways of talking to the world:
How could the rose wish to die on whom my love was lavished?

Why did the fruit destined for my tongue dare to show a spot?—
It is as though a lover, fondled and fondled, claimed at last,
Said in a smoky, late-autumnal voice: I would rather not.

This is where—at least I think it does—the eye with wings
Hovers over red-draped figure and the falling leaves,
And says: You do not have a corner on all lovely things.

I am the one suspended in your dreams whether or not you know.
The ship was always full of fruits, flowers, now with leaves, men in red—
Here are wings. Look back into the mind again before you let the summer go.

III. A Retrospective of Swimmers

THE TRELLIS

So there I was lying in my breechcloth
While the scented trade winds blew over me,
Stripped clean of angst by a swim in the sea,
My skin air-brushed with the gold of the sun—
Somewhere, far off, the image abattoir
As I stretched out dreaming with open hands,
No hammer, no cleaver, no dripping club,
Blood in the eyes transferred to hibiscus—
One learns these extrapolations early,
The use of the salve and the saving grace,
The flinging oneself down at the day's end,
Calling amorini from the smogged air,
A woman's perfume floating a garden—
Done before, so we can do it again.
It is as though you harbor an ideal man
Who always waits like a nonpaying guest.
Give him a bed by the sea to flourish,
A sunset suit in the rich evening light.
Still one is struck with the fact that he is
Put down—a glancing blow of the hammer?—
The optic nerves in the thread of a flower,
In the soft hand, the ghost of a handle?—
He wants to pay his keep with your content,
Offering his chest to your late mistress,
Suggesting balneologies of blue,
How the demulcent trade winds treat the lips,
The *aequo animo* of his undress.
He is a trellis of the treasured life.
But one cannot quite get over the fact

That he is fallen, that some blow did tell,
His heart ravished with its own red roses,
The lattice of last resort, espaliered nerves.
One rests and rests—at last, supine success.
Whether it was wind, will, or wayward love,
You were pushed over in a pose—I come
Along the beach, stuffed with this fantasy:
No wonder it fell, no wonder it fell!—
Unless we finger forays one at a time,
Feeling the nerve faint in the golden man,
The cravings that cram from the crosspieces,
Even the lying down is too lonesome—
Who can say the tyrant of the trellis
Does not plan, pitch, a tower in the sand?

IN COLD BLOOD

You come up naked like something destined for a platter,
Some seaweed clinging, a trace of primal lettuce salad,
Stretch out, the sun's fresh meal, taken from deep-refrigerated water.

But you do not mean at all to really satisfy,
Repeating some atavistic ritual of the first Man-Fish
Who had no sacrificial thought of crawling on the land to die.

Self-cleaned of scales, you may indeed present the aspect of a feast,
A quiet creature breathing furtively against the ground,
Just beyond the grasp of that enormous blue-tongued beast.

Who shall have you is the question, cold or hot—
There are only two forthright primordial choices

Which promulgate cuisine—the conscious warmth, the gelid
   figure you forgot.

But, for a moment, lying comestibly upon the beach,
You are a deliriously delicious double creature,
Attractive to the sun and sea and flatly claimed by each.

A hand, an arm, a foot, is given to the sun
Much as you offer tidbits to a tender god:
The rest is blue-belonging fish quite sometimes upon the
   blazing sand may leave half done.

THE SUN SAYS GRACE

Lying naked on the long diving board,
You imagine the sun will nod to you,
That great, wondrous head without a body—
You are so simply and utterly there,
Semi-soft and ambiguously hard—
Suddenly your own head simmers, takes fire.
You rise and stand saluting the hot face;
You imagine how often that has occurred,
This intimate appeal for recognition,
A man lighting his oiled brain like a flare,
Writing a poem, a story, making love,
Looking first to that stark, cerebral glare
As if it loved a torso that it did not have—
Unless you believe that you have something
The sun loves, an utterance, an amorous hand,
You will not prosper long in this bright world—
Thus I can cast the young man upon the board,
Filled with his loose, relaxed recognitions;
Even his casuistry is commodious,
An intimacy so powerful and fine

The violation of a passing cloud
Cannot quite erase the warm, solar smile—
I have an enormous and worldwide sense
Of just what some such close rapport can do—
I lie on the board as if it were a stalled spit,
So much on this side—turn—so much on that,
A morsel for the manners of the sun.

WATER SNAKES

The young lovers met in the swimming pool,
Gliding toward each other like gold serpents
That had eaten the sun for days on end—
Open their mouths and their arched tongues would shine—
They wanted to be brilliant and yet supple.
The public pool is heaped with coils of them,
Her rings discarded like scales or squama,
His round watch an extra eye from Eden:
The suntan lotion marks a slithered trail—
One has every right to such an image;
We find our way around the world as best we can:
At this point, then, the shining water snakes.
They may sink, of course, to gold mosaic,
Figures to be walked on by hard, wet feet,
But not before, gloriously entwined,
They flicker on the surface of the pool.
Tell me if you have ever had this longing
To see love like a wick on the water?—
Bodies, oiled, clinging, an ignis fatuus,
Making the old, original nerves writhe,
Memory darting its dark, forked tongue—
We straighten our world in just a moment:

One burns these sinuous lovers sparingly,
A smell of incense smoking on the water.
Nevertheless, I strike a match by the pool,
And see two serpents kissing in the light.

VULCAN AT SUNRISE

It ebbs at night perhaps, but in the morning ego flows anew—
Green pajamas drop, peel off. The molten and metallic man
Goes down to the sea to do battle royal with that blue.

The fierce emotions are contained ironically in golden-glow.
It is as though a small volcano shaped like a suntanned man
Positioned itself at water's edge, ready with a lava-flow.

You know how full you can be of last night's left-over love or
 lust—
I have stood naked on the beach, and felt so golden, golden,
As if any minute I would erupt with sunflower-bright volcanic
 dust.

There is, of course, some sibilance in this—
The sea advances with its blue tongue curled:
You seethe, fume with your fantastic fire, the blue waves hiss.

One takes the first step forward, lined with brilliance and
 containing tons—
The sea, that enormous, everlasting cooling element,
Accepts the molten, manic foot, and makes it bronze.

Brushed with patina, a leg, a thigh, the chest, the head,
I love this beautiful, quiet, morning hour, cooling off,
No longer so disruptive—for liquid fire, this figure of a man instead.

QUICKSAND

Even among flowers his foot felt heavy,
The muscles like chains, the ball in the crotch—
The sea washed him in lapis lazuli,
A blue-gold man who dragged himself inland,
Dropping his rings like compressions of tears,
A secret gold tooth cached in the burden.
So you may wake even from love like this,
Only the mirror, a long-sought lagoon.

Why should those blue socks hold such terror,
The tie hang like the rope of an anchor,
The flaccid shirt look minatory, lulled?—
There is peace here, a perceptible calm.
Your feet are dangled, the lake is silver,
And yet one senses nearby a quagmire—
The razor that cuts away blue stubble
Could fall to the groin like a guillotine.

One foot down on the carpet, you have stepped
On the soft belly of the beloved.
Her scent, hair, liquid eye will suck you in.
It was the heavy man in you she loved,
The one who was chained to the sea's passion,
Entwined with vines and grapes of purple stone—
Just try to dip from the mirror a glass
Of water—it will turn to last night's wine.

Of course the finger will reline the ring,
You will put on the socks of silken web,
The lithe chest in the shirt will sail again.
The pen in the pocket harbors the javelin,
And the rude heart will hurl its hammer;
You will go forth well-laden from the lago.
It is our fabulous combination,
How we dress, undress, ourselves forever.

Nevertheless, just this curious note,
Learned of the hangover born in heaven:
The touch of blue stone in the lightest kiss,
The weight of a pendant in any grape,
The naked and the always bedizened.
Try to forget this over and over—
It will make you a man known to lovers,
The tailor retailored in sands so quick.

UP CLOSE AND PERSONAL

Pour water into the percolator
Filled with fine grounds of lapis lazuli:
Perhaps it will give you a cup of the sea.
Lance and peel the tightly wound golf ball—
Could it hold the final source of pictures,
The pure, packed message of the flight of birds?
Keep molten sunset, keep it in the heart:
Will you lie like an ingot in your bed?
Even a skewer run through raw meat
Drips into the ecstatic nerves of fire,
And the fat blazes up its reprisals.
I am saturated, impacted, impaled:
Sea-veined, gold in the flesh, a rich, stuck thing—
The loveliest silk woman at the cookout

Has no idea at all what she deals with,
Though her jeweled pin with its concealed, fine point
Contributes a subtle understatement—
The wine in her glass, the color of bruised sea,
Fondled white beads that could serve as a lifeline.
So one stands, stoked, stuck, with a long lifetime
Of longing, sensing a slow, blue dripping
In the ear, hearing the struck golf ball whirr,
Regretting the stiff, golden nights alone.
How can we stand so close to each other
Except that the point thrusts, and the fire flares,
And we hope for supple, sunset idols?—
I feel that pin on her breast, warm, pressing:
It is like fate that's still subtilizing,
Subtilizing—You never can quite say
If the crushed sea is coursing in her veins,
Or the fat fire has finished its suttee.

THE SPOOL

It may be hidden, of course, a blue spurt
In an hysterical vein when the sea
Makes an obscene, groping overture
And you are felt all over by the cold,
Afraid to be alone with nature.
It could be caterpillars dropped on your face
In the garden, excrement of the sky—
Do the trees waste such creatures on you?
Damage control sets in, and a warm hand
Woos the water—a support group of swimmers
Dive and give the cold sea their goldshots.
Though a personal sadness is inseminated,
Babies of ebullience are never blue.
A worm is better than egg on your face;

Lakes of the eyes shimmer futurity:
Leave life alone a bit, and wings may rise.
These little piercing dramas every day:
A stitch in the side means the universe
Is sewing, jaggedly perhaps, but keen.
Even sunset's glorious golden cloth runs
With red as if the needle always bleeds
As it pulls and pulls you toward the night.
So now you know that you must wet the thread,
Warn the sea, warm and warm the hapless worm.
It is no small thing to observe oneself
Making an eye of everything, ogives
Of regret and happiness. Drops of spit
Mellow in the mouth. It would take a dredge
To raise the projected pictures. So lie
At night, stuck, resting in a spool of silk.

THE TURN-ON

Just breaking the blue skin of the calm sea,
Using yourself as a gold swizzle stick
As if you meant to stir fresh concoction,
As though the world needed a deep blue cocktail,
The unsieved thing, swirling sand and gravel,
As if you had plated yourself in the sun
Just for this, undaunted dasher at dawn—
Why not say you have this dervish passion?

Why not speak of these extreme relations?—
How you stand bolt upright in a flower bed
And think what it is to mix earth's palette,
A coat of many colors as you turn,
This full, rich leaching-out of oils
So that a stone calls to you for lithograph—

You could follow the lead of the fountain
And gush forever with pentimenti.

Even your hand on the waist of a lover
Is the first signal to ravel the rose,
The sheath, the undergarments, the shedding,
As if sex itself were a centrifuge.
Why not say that you desire everything
And sorrow itself is a grindstone:
Something whetted every time you turn around,
The shimmer of dust, the shower of sparks.

This much and more this morning drips from you
As you stand from stirring the taste of the sea.
Inland, grapes are calling blue to brown feet:
Hitched up dresses, the circling in the vat—
You may have my grindstone as a discus—
I can see it whirling, whirling in the sun.

SUNBATHER IN AUTUMN

Somehow the summer did not penetrate
The screens of oil, the tilted umbrella—
In the hot days we are like steelworkers
In protective glasses working with fire.
Each day must be handled like an ingot,
The close, real touch of the thing is lost—
The worker is ready to be worked on;
He has a cool, empty mold inside him.

Now that it is finished with orchards, fields,
The sun acknowledges the waiting man,
The handler who wishes to be handled
At last in a natural relationship.

His chest that was a heat shield is a fan
Of muscles folded across a willing heart.
The moist genitals are heavy as fruit—
This is the cautious one from the hot shop.

It is curious but true that the love
Of a thing may be loveliest at the end.
The sun turns feminine, masculine, as the case may be:
The glasses are put down, the oil removed—
One is being looked for with the softest light.
In this case, a man will guide the warm hand.
Has one ever been touched like this before?—
How did we miss the fondler in the fire?

THE HINGE

In late summer these desires, back and forth,
Call up the subtlest of our scents and oils
As if one rutted with the rose in hand,
One last time touched the skin with golden glaze.
We look in the garden for its blood-drops,
Impatiens scattering red petals like stigmas,
The sun demanding the cross too often.
Someone with blue feet coming home from the sea
Jams the door of the bathing house to see
Us hanging wet suits on rusty nails,
The body-varnish showing its seams, cracks,
These versions clashing on a swinging door—
It is perfectly true the bee does not
Seek us out for nectar, nor wish
Even to sting us anymore. We lie
Bejeweled by the pool, and the mild sun
Has no lust to rob us of salt diamonds—
I do not wish to lead you at this time,

But let you linger here, there, this way, that:
The rose, the rough jumble of sea and pool,
The bee on missions exclusive of us,
The impatiens increasing stigmata.
So the season gives us split decisions—
The car comes back with some sand on the floor,
A few shells turned up like calcified ears
That still listen for the sea behind us.
Those cattails in a vase are the flails
Of the marsh to drive us back next summer,
All winter, a blue pennant in the mind.
One day here, one day there, a grab bag swings—
The shower pours down the chest like paint remover,
The feet grow tall into that new blue suit,
And the last rose falls to the greedy sea:
This heave of images is now unhinged—
It is time, at last, to oil the autumn.
I see the greased tools spread out in the sun.
The whetstone seems to tell us—Give me words:
Next time a lapidary in your mouth.

THE AFTERWORLD

Summer goes again, and you release its fable—
Tanned swimmers in blue pools, blue seas, the spectres of
 fading roses,
The glistening lust for life, the predator at table.

All the lovers, all the grapes and melons that you knew—
I kissed the girl, ate the fruit with her,
And fantasized that melon rind offered voyages of love in its
 canoe.

The thing we like the most is just the thing that keeps on
 coming after—

The caressive sun on skin made stringent by the pool,
The comic songs from sentimental ones, from those romantic
  tears the sparkling laughter.

This is what the fable says, this is what it does for us:
Pears come after peaches, melons. The hammock, packed with
  power,
Sways and sways—a basket for late pathos.

Or so it was, to me, in early June related.
Such relatives that came to picnic on my lawn!—
The muscled one looked like Apollo, the predator was never
  sated.

Still, in moonlight, comes a time for one last, rueful kiss:
Gold figures folded in the pool, blue worlds we fully
  occupied—
The afterthought is asking now if tales of autumn hold
  anything like this.

IV. Inland Waters

RIVER JOB

The man sitting by the smooth, blue tablecloth
Longed for summer, the rush of the river,
Wished that the cloth would make waves, show bruises
Of purple, dose the house with liquidity—
He gagged, swallowed hard from keeping so much back,
Lepered the surface with a few wine spots,
And then let it beg once more for bounty.
From such a source as this all rivers flow:
Blue flashes in the mind, the groin engorged,
Water-shadows shaking on the ceiling,
A strong need to swallow an emetic—
No deep current moves without this pressure,
Spends too fast, leaves only damp and mudstains
On the table, the thin trickle downstream,
Bathers stranded without a drop of blue.
Still, it may be an eternal question
Whether rivers do not rot when they rest,
Closed in the dark calyx of tight delta—
Let us suppose the man's symphonic best:
The house bulging and the great dam far off,
The moment when we first rumple forward,
The dried mud baking in the brilliant sun,
The nude bathers waiting in ecstasy.
I have had traffic with these river-gods
And let them ripple my life at will—
There is nowhere a massage quite like it,
Tense sinews, muscles, milked for miles of blue—
Then one rises, having been worked over,
And sits in the man who rolls the river up.

THE AQUARIUM

All of the fluid, it seemed, had been sucked from the room,
The spongy blue chairs, the shell-like objects on the desk were
   high and dry:
Nothing was left of the sea but the small aquarium.

The blue eyes of the man in the room could hardly wink.
Had he seen the sea into this subjection,
His bibulous art dependent on a hidden bottle of ink?

As though it might be home for silver fish, the mirror
Refuses to waver, becomes a monstrous oblong cenotaph:
One does not break and enter tombs without a certain ruffian
   sense of terror.

Still, the man can flounder just two steps and get a cramp.
Certain things extend the jagged, cruel touch of coral,
And fumbling with his shoes that seem enmired, he finds his
   socks are damp.

The aquarium, then, must be engaged head-on, clear-blind—
The lasciviously tinted shells, little turning wheel, arrogant
   bubbles,
Suggest crashing storms dehydrated almost too safely from
   the mind.

Curiously, rounding the wheel, the silver fish come on to
   thank
The man for standing there in silence like a pump,
As though an artifice could dread the large inclosure of a
   dried-up tank.

THE AQUAMARINE

When she put the ring in a velvet box,
The large aquamarine, the pressed seapiece,

She could smell the clinging salt all night long;
Her hair on the pillow felt like seaweed—
All day the intense blue concentration
Brought the slim brown men toward her like swimmers.
She cooled them in the ring's light, let them go,
Baffled by such clarity, their own damp feet.

And now the compressive lure put away,
She can breathe the night-fog and the sea-wet,
Wary of the thick tidal flow of dreams—
Would it have been better to drown someone,
Let him learn how deep the ring really was,
How it murmured and lapped within itself,
Casting blue reflections on the ceiling—
How it feared the flaws of human bodies?

One man, in fact, took heart and touched the stone—
In every gathering, perhaps one giant
Who blots the sun a moment from the sea—
The ring rippled, longed for a raging storm;
Then the woman dropped her hand like a wave—
He looked so small and sunken in her force.
At night, the poisonous pellet in the box,
The marsh-gas rising tells her where he rots.

THE SWAMP

That long summer the man was feeling somewhat damp—
There were roses, but they seemed to bloom from mists:
Was he living in a neighborhood rather like a swamp?

He did not want to think too ill of life, have thoughts too
    harsh
Of those who came to see him only in the moonlight
Just when the will-o-the-wisps were gathering on the marsh.

One woman, the very loveliest of them all,
Who brought him a rose with the chill of fog on it,
Seemed to say: I live this side, and you, beyond the pall.

In later years, would he see it as the most romantic summer ever?—
Moonlight, roses, and yet this fetor in the air,
As if gas were always rising, infecting him with something like swamp fever.

One must be an idealist, living near the spongy grass, the constant wet—
You cannot let the rose go silver in the head,
Or give the lovely woman nothing more than moonlight and regret.

One may not ever be quite rid of this estate,
The smell of gas, the sound in the trees like the sewing of a shroud,
But look again, oh look again—sunrise tints the rose, her hand is on the gate.

WALL FOUNTAIN

The imperial lion has lost his head
Flowing water instead of blood,
Green-mouthed as if he understood
The silent, virile things he might have said.

Perhaps a sickly moment but what verse
Would want this image gone forever,
The father-figure of a river
Which waits the lifting of a curse?

The rick-rack in the kitchen, the little hum
Of furtive lovers in the bower
Still simulate the finest hour
Of men who bring some monster to his doom.

We keep our images in trust—
The naked marble nymph for just that day
The satyr in us held at bay
Gleams like a sword redeemed from rust.

Thus, lovers who feel some sad lack
At last, missing some bright mountain,
May sit and hear the music of the fountain
As though a lion were roaring at their back.

WHITE LAKE

When he considered where to vacation,
He first constructed a lacustrine house,
Cool as a glass of iced water, yet bright,
Clear, as if lighted by a diamond,
Intermittent, blinking on a woman's hand.
His libido somewhere swallowed silver
And found expression in this broad expanse,
The lake going out to the horizon
As if drawn by white birds on noiseless wings,
Pulling this long, liquid, inner mirror
Into matrix of which it did not know.
He could lie in the house, eat *langue de chat*,
Smell the lilies, imagine lianas,
Since the white cottage could be anywhere,
Insisting on their lifting, slow embrace—
The kind of house where one can pad around
In drawers or nothing, a silver agent

At ease in little but a signet ring.
Those who have swallowed their share of those coins
Made from misapprehension's mother lode
Are glad to sit like Buddha argentine,
Knowing lake lotus has positioned them,
The cool navel chaliced for sweat
Should the sun work for vermeil through the slats.
Therefore, when you are making travel plans,
Consider the id, whether the lucent stretch,
Waterfalls, mountains, or the open sea—
Vacations, unless somewhat instinctive,
Bring the zombie into the harsh sunlight,
Waiting for silver leis beside the lake.

CLAWS

So there it was in my clear waking dream,
The rich nude struggling in a lobster's claw:
The mini-figure, minatory light.
One could see a little necklace dangling,
A bracelet—who was it tagged the tortured?
One has a sense of the tools of the trade,
Pliers, prods, and then this most natural thing,
The body caught in a claw like a finger.

I have nothing to say in my defense
When things like this well up into the mind:
The bruise on the thumb where the hammer struck,
The look of lacerations on the wrist—
This meat surfaced from the aquarium's murk
As if one went fishing with a phallus.
She dazzles in the light, those blinking tags:
How can a monster make a show of medals?

One could, of course, throw up a wry disguise,
Offering a crate of artificial eyes
That can be rolled to any point of view—
Here in isolation, let me enlarge
At least—the sharp grasp smoothed from my arms—
I dance with her, the imperious relieved.
She has him now, a man made up of tears:
How could that tiny sea contain such salt?

THE BLUE WINDOW

Push, tug, one could not make the ends meet,
It was at last a convulsive circle—
Is life made of imperfect blends, a mist,
A miasma? Even lovers fondling, kissing,
Could not bring it off, could not close.
They lay in blue light, two parts asunder;
They looked gassed, panting, spent, given over—
It was, as we say, voluptuous mischance,
Tending to those things that do connect, belts,
Buttons, beads, the sequiturs of sorrow:
Better the voyeur next time, just the view
Through the blue window and the gas rising.
A man on his way home from work, dreaming,
Sees in the foreground a break in the haze,
Just a keyhole now, a tight, pinched question:
Will the kiss hold, or can you reach around
The twilight loiterer to the blue window?
You can feel a safety pin give somewhere,
The tattoos are sliding down your sleek chest,
You cannot even save your sweat for sex,
Guess how loosely you are put together.
When you stop at the bar, the fire still burns,
The mounds of toothpicks make their wry voodoo:

They go on hatching up their latchings-on.
Once in a blue moon, you say, and return
To the much-observed, lamplit, unattached house.
She has had her day of splits and fissures,
The lust of entrapment lost from her arms.
How deep her rings are sinking in your back:
So far, so good, this is the place to pause.

WHIRLPOOL

At first so slow that you scarcely notice—
The foot of the snail as it barely curves,
Leaves on a stone an iridescent sleaze,
But somehow your own wetmarks begin to stir.

A drop of foamed spit spatters its caution,
Your damp socks begin to leach through your soles,
Armpits cannot solidify their diamonds,
The spiral in the navel overflows.

Is it then that you begin to decide
To toss in old love letters, locks of hair,
A ring to weight the head of the water,
Something she gave you that reminds you of her?

Smell of candy stirring in the kitchen,
So thick and slow, creates a *crise de nerfs*.
You could lie down with the brown dripping spoon
And rest, dreaming of a calm, straight river.

Upstairs, a toilet suddenly flushes,
Threatens an embolus unless instant
Passage is given through the constrained house—
The walls shake when a faucet is turned off.

Obsessed with the notion of a love imp,
That Priapus watches each meander,
That he sees how the screw pinches for blood,
You let hysteria mount before you heave.

Later, quite laconically, you admit
That you were building up the tight-packed thrill
Of the golden apple to give more head
To the water than the ring she gave you,

That you write down your doodles in vortex,
Your stickpin has the force of a cyclone—
If this does not tell the casual reader
Just how much you have thrown into the throes,

Let him stand in Priapus's varicolored shoes,
Let him leave out his laundry for the snail
To walk on—the god's wicked smile, wedges
That wander-wind, smear, and will not wipe off.

Let him put a scanner to the human skull
Itself where the feasting brain is crammed, flooded,
And drains its pictures toward the body's sink,
Even the blackest spout dripping its dross.

So what's to be said?—Some love letters dropped,
The rainbow sandals, the ripped-off rapture:
She turns her head and trips the vertigo—
A kink, a canker in Priapus's pool.

THE CRANE

You may have the egret if you will let me have the crane—
That symbol of good fortune and long life has been
For longer than I remember wading in my brain.

The little house surrounded by bamboo, the blue lake,
Need just this serious bird calmly stalking there
To tell me what I wanted all these years was no mistake.

In the house I really live in, really own and know,
I want a sometime refuge, drawn, perhaps, by Hokusai,
As if the heart were always beating round a secret cameo.

You have every right to chandelier, fan, plume, egret—
I love them too in many moods except this secret one
Which comes from moving in an aura, tone of the bird's-foot
    violet.

I like the rough-and-tumble, the rub of hardy fellows,
But in the twilight, I can feel the heart gathering, coalescing,
Its circular relief—the bird is standing in the shallows.

An hour, an evening, before *lex talionis* must assert its right—
Is this how we come at all to notions of good fortune, long
    life:
The plash, the long, slow steps in the water, until the crane
    takes flight?

THE TOWLINE

When you see a spectacle of nothing,
Be glad when something powerful obtrudes:
A stalk of lilies brought into the house,
The brilliant yellow throats and orange tongues,
These megaphones that mock the nihilist.
It is as though they had been lifted up
And out of life for just this stark meeting:
White vacant light everywhere—still, still life,
As if it offered no other refuge,

As though the flesh of the earth had been flailed,
Somewhere in the void the loose skin of things—
One bends, works up the world a bit from scent,
Sticks out the tongue toward the bright orange dust
As if language should be rolled in lavishness,
Impoverishment repaired in a mellow mouth.
Let me tell you lives can be built anew
On one such image. I have seen it happen
In a lonely room—the hostel, the hospice,
The powerful summoned and obtrusive thing.
I have seen the glorious sun coming back,
The skin returning moist and glistening—
First the musk of the marsh and then the sea.
I am perfectly aware the lily
Drops like a skin to the floor, shrivels, dies,
The orange is washed down by the mouthwater,
The lush word must wade on into shallows.
Still, give me lilies in a lonely room—
Each time we match a powerful obtrusion,
I think we twitch and tow the cosmos back.

THE SWAN AT SUNSET

It is late. Shall I have one long, last look at the swan
As it moves on the river, sluicing its purity,
Or simply say—never, never in this world will it be done?

One wants something else, another more exciting part—
A second nature to rise in the orange beak, stab
And stab again until a sunflower opens in the heart.

I have had this counter-urge perhaps more often than I know.
Wanting a thing to be itself yet come at me like a sunburst
As I stand on the banks, waiting for the powerful orange glow.

Once more, then, the impeccable purity and the brilliant
    skewer
Just as the image darkens, goes down to dross, detritus,
As though the brain of man, at last, floats on a sewer.

It is so late. Can one now, in fact, rethink—
The palace, the palm trees, the bird sowing on the river—
Must I let go, throw the ultimate sunflower down into the
    sink?

Or simply say: An orange glow. A swan has passed me by—
How many times have I felt so full as this, a face of seed,
As if I would go on, flowering and flowering, against the
    splendid sky?

THE HOUSE ON THE HILL

Was it the caged bird or the blue curtains
That we remember most?—that master scene:
The white bed with its rich, lace coverlet,
The pictures of nudes that looked like mirrors—
In another room the stored viscera,
The offal extracted from the absurd,
Ready to leach into the adored place.
This is simply to tell you that not all
Moments are "equal," that passion and power
May be divided, that a sorrow came
Into the world and we built our houses—
That we sort out our procedures
As soon as we take possession of the white
Room and the red, searching the spotless rug
For the first seam of blood, a reaching nerve,
Blotting the stain with a silk-stockinged foot.
So far, open house would be indecent

Unless you cram your friends in a tight space,
Some who favor the white, and some, the red.
We love those masterbuilders who permit
No compromise with a pervasive style
And who relegate the rest to closets,
The caged bird balancing the deep closure,
The sea wind pushing the blue curtains like sails,
The beautiful lovers happily enlaced.
Of course, some days the house will hang heavy
As if it wore a blood blister, a pouch
On its side ready to burst, flood outward
Into the city and into the news—
What are headlines for but lancing the soul?
Meanwhile, we may have conquered the ground plan:
That calm stroll from one room to another,
Somewhere, way in the back, a love story:
Remember those people who lived on the hill?

V. Blue Book

WATER WINGS

Too bad about the wax, but Icarus
Should have known his father was not perfect—
The sea is harder than it ever looks,
Pocked with meshing sapphires, secret boulders.

One needs in any case support systems:
A sense for landing where the waves are plush,
Someone in a canoe there just by chance,
Sea polyps standing in for water wings.

One or all of these unless you should have
A flawless nose for that daedal cunning.
For you will fall more than once—that for sure—
Even your dreams have warned you since childhood.

Smells of burnt jam call for the coiled hose:
The odor of an unwashed lover makes
You wonder if she set the house on fire—
Where are the exit stairs from this suttee?

Too bad when you had your first plunge you did
Not know the rock pools were sucking the sea,
The tit removed twice a day—While it flowed,
You could have floated in on mother's milk.

I know for I have seen Icarus walk
Away from it with just the sunburn marks
On his shoulder blades like bad memories
Of too much trust and those parental blunders.

I have seen him regroup his sore muscles,
Oiling and preening in the brilliant light,
Watching the bulging amniotic sac,
Still pregnant from his nearly fatal dive.

Ah, mother, mistress, the sliding sea
Cannot lay hands upon him any more
Or try to leave blue babies at his feet—
The condom on the sand is his congé.

It is time for cabana or kiosk,
The saline mouth washed out with pink fruit ice,
And the vendor tells you where the girls are,
Smiles, leers a little as he calls you, "Son."

For that predictable fall into bed,
One cannot ape the practice of our peers,
Those famous lovers and their bruises, salves,
Their arms printing and printing the moulting wings.

So shall I lie on the hard floor at least
And wish it might be richly sluiced with sweat?—
When nothing lifts up the heart, slip or slide
Back to the sea where once you learned to fall.

THE RECOVERY

He lies on the brown dune like a white scar,
A just-healed abdominal incision.
At a distance this is all that he seems,
A pearled oblong, a cartouche without name.
The man himself feels humiliated,

Stitched into warm belly under the sun,
Too reminiscent of operations,
Livid sutures paling beneath bandages.

He does not know that he will soon be gone
As far as the earth's belly is concerned,
Unnoticed, accommodated, old skin,
Or grown darker even than pubic hair—
But now his thoughts become much heavier,
An obelisk, a white monument,
Fallen by a sea of sensuous beauty,
An obsession settling for permanence.

Still the young man does not know his own mind,
Nor how monumentality is tipped,
Rolled by the sea, sun-baked, sanded over.
What begins as scar looms as cenotaph
And quite literally ends as weight forgotten—
There may be harder pavement underneath,
But for a while at least the young man walks
In a gold thought, twinned with a princess out of Egypt.

PICASSO'S EGG

A little oval painting, an egg lying on its side
Could roll over and over on the table, showing its transfers,
The most relaxed of all pictorial forms with nothing left to
  hide.

One may grow tired of stationary things, rigid in the frame,
But this bauble babbling of its images rocks back and forth—
One sees there is a signature, but cannot catch the artist's
  name.

This will proceed, even prosper, unless it runs into a spot of
   glue,
The most vivid curdling effect, the dasher in the brain—
A sudden pause, a smudge upon the hand, a maverick, pink
   tattoo.

This round, round world of brilliant miniatures
Promotes the notion of the palm inundated by blue sea,
Somewhat crazed, the finger pushing back, a shipwreck that
   endures.

One goes on and on—will it be forever?—gloriously
   deluded—
Not quite, not quite, there is a certain predication in that
   pause:
A native moisture, a stickiness in hands, is gradualy exuded.

Two dimensions stalk and stab the vacillating ovum—
You may feel blood spreading for a while like a red tree in
   heart and lungs:
There is nothing like a little sudden death to bring the
   shipwreck home.

LOOSE ENDS

Somehow he must relocate the center
Which would not hold—the sapphire dissolving
To blue sugar, the rose in the paperweight
Full-blown in his hand as he dashed it down,
A contrived thing in its tight crystal womb—
The chipped buttons sagging from his jacket,
A raveling thread in his thin underwear
As if, secretly, he were pulled apart.

But you can cite your own diaspora:
The cold wave drawing, sucking back from you
As if it took a ripe fruit from your groin,
The lover's head coming in like flotsam,
Rolling on your chest all kisses spent.
The flaming clouds, the skywriting, fade—
This, perhaps worst of all, such bold language,
With nothing graven except the gravestone.

Small wonder we take our knockout drops,
Overinhaling the rose so it will hold,
Remembering the glass splinters on the floor—
Drain glass after glass of wine for gem-silt—
Put a pin in the eye of the button,
Tie a loop in the head of the thread-worm—
I see you at sunset, hoping for star words
That blink in the trail of invisible ink.

I have no other comradeship to give
When the last diamond peels from the ring
And drops like a white seed in the darkness.
You hitch a ride one way, I another.
Somewhere the new garden will be centered;
It is not always autumn everywhere.
Even the flung paperweight makes compost,
Even the lolled head will be anchor-lulled.

You have bruised, purple night, I its splinters,
A string in the navel, a pulling hand—
At each new signpost, at least the flashlight.
I take this to be somewhat the answer:
The face at the lip of the undrained glass,
At my feet the sprouted diamond. We do
Not altogether fail to fling our foci,
Lifting syntax from letters on the grave.

THE WISTERIA SAILOR

Mentally, the man had come to the end of the road.
His mind felt like a mash of squashed dreams,
The succulence of disaster, a tumor of doubts accrued.

No wine, fermenting liquor, for it all lacked fire—
The silent hearer, who remembers inclosing cataracts,
Listens, drop by drop, to the climacteric of desire.

So this is the impacted life, the final, futile, hoard,
He is sick as a full ship without wind and water:
Subject to object cried, once too often, "Man overboard!"

And yet no one is more intent upon escape—
He resuits his dreams like costume-buccaneers,
Presses at each thought as if pumping a deflated grape,

Makes of himself an embattled literary situation, indulges in
    rhetoric.
What if he can remand the mutinous crew from cannibal
    islands
And the stuff of life around him is nowhere canvas-thick?

But spring acts as if it knows just what his malady entails:
Swathes of wisteria hung from brute pine staffs
Force the man on his back to take on purple sails.

THE FLING

Such a ferocious longing for the sea,
Gymnast that you are in sleek white suit,
Your hot head crammed only with blue hours,

Wanting a sea-smell under your armpits,
Hoping each package that comes in the mail
Is saltwater taffy pulled by veined hands—
You would like to lash the fountain with your tongue
If it would beg for mercy with blue wine.

So what can you say of yourself—that you
Have eaten and eaten diamond dust, slept
Between milk-white sheets, Atlas albinoed?—
That you wake, race to the indigo mouthwash,
Swear at the mangle for flattening the cloth
So that dreams could not pitch in a sea-swell?—
The shadows in the mirror as you shave confirm
The block of which you are a chip is blue.

Still, white underwear, knee bends, push-ups
Condone the desire at least to go out picking
Blueberries, write blue notes to a stranger,
The girl who would pass them on to the sea—
These appetites are seldom singular.
Therefore one makes way for the unassuaged
Offering their tongues to the doctor's paddle
As if it were a fathom—an anchor somewhere,
A ballast of bluestone in the belly.
We look for each other's fingernail disks
As if once in a blue moon we will find
The sea throwing its loose chips everywhere.

So in this great banter of obsessions,
I find these inland mornings do not pall
And do not pale in much comparison.
Our lips will have a trace of foam on them;
The cleaning lady with her slops is sure
She leaves a floor of sapphire in her wake.

Together, let us go today, next week—
The sea will be fulsome with our fragments
Because we put such chisels to our dreams.

ISLANDS BEYOND A

The man, Everyman's late, last, cousin felt trapped, walled up
    alive, interred—
You have seen him at the tombstone of his dictionary:
Where is the world that lies well beyond the Word?

How can one turn the heavy page among the Bs,
And find the blue that was the sea before we gave it any name,
Skip over toward the end and find our first perception of the
    trees?

Someone, of course, has saved up for this man a fruit
Which has not been through any funeral of the mind,
And smiles with its red lips as though, not having ever spoken,
    it is never mute.

Someone else has even hoarded up a human face,
Fresh as a flower, beyond all nomenclature:
No ethnic origin, no designated time, no master race.

She, if anyone, can make him throw away the book
And watch it, still unsinkable—the pages ruffled, a convulsive
    raft—
See some final word like love give back an agonizing look.

A fruit, a face, that language never touched informs the hand
Ambiguously to save and save, and throw away,
Clutching every shipwreck to the heart and pulling to another land.

DIPSTICK

He had wanted to be immersed in life:
Into the sea like a dipstick in blue,
Into the batter, a bloated raisin,
Into the cream, a lascivious tongue—
The nude in the choker—would she prefer
To be buried up to her neck in pearls?
The wine sop longs and longs for the weir,
A finger, pulled from the pudding, fevers.
One wants to enter, enter, not withdraw:
Fruits, heaped on the sideboard, all pies deep-dish.
The canoe is towed by the waterfall,
The naked skin cannot resist the kiss.
Into the morass and into the murk
To rescue a legend of the limpid:
The sea diaphanous to our desire,
The aurora held up in the wine glass,
The woman conceived as mother of pearl—
Just this morning, this thick, heady brew,
This slew, this great puncturing of pictures,
A wanting to come up somehow coated,
To center in the rising arabesque,
Shedding a shower of jonquils, hyacinths,
Drenched in the full, drawn-down, liquids of spring—
It is not every day that one can feel
This way, the pump somehow idle of all thrill—
The tongue dripping a single drop of cream,
The sea in its great, wide, blue flatulence

Unstirred by gold swan dives into its side,
The choker, a dog collar of desire.
Come, ecstasy, come, whenever you can:
The lips will swell to yielding cabochon,
Deep, deep, the stick is stable in the oil.

BODY BLOW

Like the Blue God's kidney, the pool
Lay there, an extraction, if you will,
Violence done upon a summer hill,
As though we must suffer to be beautiful.

It is hard to believe in shapes that simulate the dented lyre
If they are made of tangled, rusted strings,
And yet, underneath the perfect blue, the moanings
Were audible, bruised with feeling. Whose desire,

In aftermath, is this? The entrails
Of a god demand the highest price,
And we, today, command the very last device
For seeing, and seeing alone, divinity that fails.

Why not sometimes, if only in our leisure,
Posit a blue love in our loins again?—
The rusty lyre, of course, but before the god fell in such
   ambiguous pain
He gave and gave and gave himself to pleasure.

THE VISE

Remember that blue day by the full sea
When you wanted to match it with your love?—
The diapason of desire, the hand,

Then the gold body entering the water,
The jaws of the vise opening forever.
Somewhere out of sight, of course, the iron
Lies idle, the screw is tensing again—
The sea heaves as if pressed for some extract,
Even the rocks squeezed like balls in a sack.
Your last headache held hard without fenders—
Therefore this pushing is so passionate,
Like Atlas, akimbo, holding back harm,
The sun lifting its hammer from your head,
The lungs pneumatic, testicles floating—
I have long studied the vagaries of the vise,
How one side will seem to move first, bruising
The cheek, the iron wanting its lover,
A hard movement below as of leg irons—
Therefore whenever equal sides caress you,
Bathe, swim in an equilibrated sea,
Stretch out on the beach and suck a jujube,
The stuffed lockjaw delivered of its pearls,
The golden body supple as a chain.
I have told so many: Push, part, partake,
Use a chisel on the mouth if need be,
As if the first effusion were your blue rinse
And the sea loved the water of your tongue—
No matter if sunset finds you wriggling
At the hot touch of embrasure closing:
You will have learned such a turning technique
That somehow sea and summer match the heart.

THE ART OF QUOTATION

I quail, I do not really acquiesce, but still deliver shocks—
I remember when a powerful, pungent blue wave like volcanic
    undercurrent

Pushed me off my feet and, as if it had turned lighter-than-
  air, threw my body against the rocks.

I was proud of my metallic arms, the mettle in my brain,
Had even fantasized that I would stand, withstand,
If modern cities fell be one of those, when centuries passed,
  dredged up whole where I had lain.

The blue punch, the red blood flowing cured me of that
  trope—
Some rings appeared upon my hands, a red necklace snaked
  and snaked around my skin—
The sea struck again as if blue robbers never cease to
  interlope.

It gave me such a savage beating, so senseless that it had its
  sense.
It knew that it could take its full, sadistic toll,
And without a solid citizen in sight remove the evidence.

I did what Conrad might have done, advising me of fate,
Or how you must act hugged by the voracious bear:
Do not counterpunch just then. Do the impossible. Wait.
  Surrender as deadweight.

The blue hug, blasé at last, released me, cleaned, no longer
  bleeding, to myself.
I must get up, go down again, my mind a jar of images—
I do not write in red, nor live for shocks, but have a blue
  contained to sometimes ink the epigraph.

BLUE BLAZES

A long way to a garden or the sea,
An oasis tucked in behind some dunes—
Though it is hot as blue blazes, you walk,
Dreaming mirage, the sedan chair swaying.

Still, the heated mind leaches these notations:
A swing on a vine in the deep forest,
A waterfall, your own voluptuous chute,
The swoon when your bottom lands on thick moss.

I have seen men staggering in the sun,
Back, forth, hallucinating the floral censer,
The tongue curling in on its mouth water,
The picture of borne pallet, dehydrated man.

We cannot refrain, we must torch ourselves,
Calling to the nude girl to oil our way,
Cringe when the dry wind instead licks our skin—
The sand guards its brazier under the stars.

Comes laconic morning—the rope made of sheets,
The rushed escape down your cooling passions—
In the haze, the parked cars like sedan chairs:
You will be carried over simmering roads.

Still, the lighter on the dashboard flares up,
There's a glitter of sand on the floorboard.
The smudged sneakers belong to the firebrand,
Nothing but warm spit in last night's used flask.

I tell myself this fable on summer days:
The sliced melon ready to shoot the rapids,
My tongue let out to lavish a fresh world,
Aware of the heaped up, heaped in, conglomeration.

Clothes blow on the line, the spigot flumes,
Any minute I light a cigarette
As a signal of my depredation,
A sign to the blue flame in the distance.

Can we ever pull it out of the fire?—
One takes lip-salve from the rose, one simmers
In lucidity—the ignis fatuus:
I see it flashing in the swaying skull.

THE BOOK CLUB

In the Blue Book the wind goes right on turning pages—
The pool expands, becomes a sea, reduces to a sapphire:
With so much reading, back and forth, small wonder that the brain stem ages.

The white sail circles like a moth beyond, below,
The brilliant, liquid ring quivers on the lovely hand,
Day in, day out, responding, and responsive to, the immemorial glow.

Even our most rugged dreams follow it to bed,
Flicker black and white, flare vivid near the wick,
And flutter round the man with that lantern in his head.

Awake always, in part, for fear it languishes too soon,
I have seen these men and women with a blue-bound book in hand,
Reading some final, perfervid passage with a lamp at noon.

The glorious sea is somewhere pouring out its life;
Like fruit now petrified, the jewels drop from languid fingers
When light is surgically subjected to a brutal paring knife.

Some guard the glow and go on reading through the night,
The head stuck upon a brazen, brilliant pike, as if forever
Standing like a lighthouse in a place where might is right.

VI. The Cove

LAND'S END

If you follow the sunset long enough, you
Will come to land's end, a view of the sea.
Does anything remain of the old savage?—
This brilliant flare remembered from the caves,
How it spread and spread each day like the fan
Of your nature, the faculae of fate.
A man carries a torch toward sundown,
Lifting it up to see the painted world,
Having early a sense of afterglow
Like a peacock tail, sensation's bright trail—
Thus we wear our fine feathers to the end,
Or hope we do, moulting and moulting by torchlight,
Aware of inscribed pictures so far back,
The pulled, and pulled-out, inside of our life,
A walking fossil in the dying light.
If happiness is a kind of flourishing,
A flaring on and on toward sunset,
I need not even caution the cave man
In whose heart surely all ecstasy begins—
I know indeed the dropped and the drooped feather,
How the figure drawn with a burnt stick dims,
The folded fan of our fascination,
The broad sweep uncentered by a ruby light.
Before, I hope, the sunset of sunsets,
I come to the edge, stand like a colored stone,
The afterglow stalled and the future stilled,
The torchlight doused in a rich, deep dreaming—
Another picture shudders in the dusk.

THE MAN WITH THE BLUE SPINE

Not knowing what the day would bring, caring immensely, but fearful too,
He had a strange columnar, yet branching, sense of himself,
A secret psychosis of extension, as if his spine were blue.

Was it conspiracy or callousness that others did not stare?—
Here was a man hung from a stagy, startling, synaptic crux,
This shadowy thing, both stiff and supple, which holds him in the air.

The day might be warm, easy-sliding, to those in gold and tan—
In this way, most days are rather warm—We walk the beach,
Simmering our identities a little as they melt like butter in a pan.

But there in our straight and stricken man these azure mists
Which fall and fall like moisture of a multifoliate place
Where, so I am told, in the vagaries of a cistern, his body-tree persists.

Good God, we must permit somehow that image, essence, overlap—
We cannot have mere easy oil across a sliding picture,
And who would only settle for the blue, miasmal, spinal tap?

We live on a brilliant beach and in this forest of recessive trees,
Humped together: Wait a moment—the burn sinks beneath the butter,
And there is nothing cooling in the world but blue leaves falling in an arid breeze.

THE VIGNERON

The railing with its tendrils and black leaves,
Climbing vegetation stalled by the plague,
Wavers at least on the brilliant blue pool
As if the burnt chlorophyll awakened
Might capriciously bloom in the water,
Exquisite blue flowers on curled black stems—
The man on the balcony leans over,
Prepares to cultivate this blue garden.

The world must revere its wrought-iron fences,
Placing them near to lovers and graveyards,
Harsh cummerbunds for the living and dead.
One presses against them at groin level,
The vegetative lust between the legs,
A spike impaling the bluest love-ghost,
The cigarette smoke coughed up in anguish
From the deep innertube of indigo.

Nevertheless, wait for the vine to climb,
Teach the pool oceanic ambitions,
A hidden bag of sapphire for your seed—
Meanwhile, the modern fantasy arrives:
A circus man dives in a tank of fire,
In one fell swoon, the deep, fertile furrow—
I have seen these men wipe off flame like hair,
Depilated, heavy with natural fruit.

SQUEEZE PLAY

It may be the cold water of the sea
That leaves its blue tattoo upon the glans,

The charley horse that strikes the golden thigh
Just as the champion runner hits his stride—
Or the little, secret drama of desire
When the lover states her own conditions.
The pullback has the strange effect of pressure:
You feel naked, flattened against the wall,

Your fullness now totally espaliered.
The warning: Grow thinly and more sparely;
Don't look too rich, hung with fruits of pleasure,
A Giacometti man hides in us all.
I have seen the swimmer, blue in the light,
The cramped runner doubled over in grief,
The lover slapped around by the snapback
When the one pushed against the wall lets go.

We love the home stretch and the honing in
On contradictions of the lucid day:
The swimmer all flushed with the blood's revenge,
The winner finding breath for the victory lap,
The lovers' full, clutched, soaring monody—
Nevertheless, a last accordion note:
The stars tonight look pressed in perfect poise—
One falls, the phantom of a cosmic loss.

THE CHILD OF LIFE

So you have had enough and are filled, flooded,
Breast fed by the sea, rain infiltrated,
All those ruts and gulleys no one can see—
How can you hold that last cup of blue wine
Like a nipple of the sea stemmed on glass?
How can the creased groin manage the run-off,
The tongue take one more dewdrop from the lily?—

A look at the waves and your gorge rises.
The first signs could be cankers on your lips:
The ground water is rapidly climbing.
Then that luxurious sweat in the arms
Of a lover, the overplus of ardor,
At the end, to lie in a golden pool.
You rise, look at the mirror, all aglow
As though a solution of daffodils
Had been priming the power of contact.
Food after love, and the rapturous, ripe peach
Will drown, go under the mouth water,
The love-death swoon as the fruit slice slides down.
Ask yourself if this is not your first desire
That no sensation should ever escape you:
A copious spirit standing behind you,
Pouring and pouring over your shoulder,
The complexion of the jaundiced mirror clearing.
I say this, hating the blisters, skin-blight—
The pale orphan hiding in the mirror
Who never struggled from the silver swamp.

MESSAGE FROM METAMORPHOSIS

So they were still there, the blue mountains at noon,
Murmurous with mystery, saturated with deep, stained light:
It was a long time since he had basked on their flanks like a lizard in the sun.

He had sat sipping cola in the drugstore's blue gloam, of course,
Spent long evenings with lovers in twilight rooms,
A refugee, he thought, from something just a bit too brilliant at its source.

That deep, quiet, lizard pleasure in the lung!—
The cola brought a liquid shade into his throat,
The lover put a blue pastille upon his tongue.

But the lung itself could not forever take this musk—
The old, deeply buried, saurian bellows worked,
Puffing out, along with cigarettes, a blue revulsion to the dusk.

The store, the cooled-down lover—Something called him to
 the mountainside:
One has seen these men on the café terrace, smoking,
 drinking,
As if to prompt the sun in how deliciously it stroked the hide.

This light, this warmth, this wisdom, through and through!
One loves—one must teach the lover's fingers that exquisite
 touch
As if the Lizard Man she always longed for were not anyone
 but you.

THE GOBLET

It was sunset—an image prevailed:
The sky like a goblet holding the light,
A man standing there with enormous thirst
As if the day-long draft of the sea failed,
The wine at the table could not appease—
I know these days one should not say such things.
The world is set on the hard stuff, and "the real"
Seldom chokes on itself in the bottle—
A glimpse, a divot of sunset, quite enough.
But I love these expansive views that hold
A magnum for the megalomaniac
Who still wishes the world had its world view,

That a thing so simple as a sunset
Could still spread an immense saturation,
That one could come here with all one's daydreams
And imbibe, mouth and throat like an hourglass,
Infilled with light and then turned again.
It is not that days on the beach do not
Leave blotches, sunburn, the feet cold as lapis—
One brings these offerings to libation:
The scar where the flying whisky bottle struck,
The blue mole that needs electrolysis,
The doubts, cross purposes, and dissensions,
The raised welts of a Weltanshauung—
It is that one clears with the spreading light:
A hint of vine leaves, a kind of hero's bowl,
The lips almost carmined with rapture,
A splash of gold on the old canvas shoes.
Somewhere hidden in us, I do believe,
There's a desire for acute sensation
That does not linger on some dubious point
But flares and flares in a fast-fading sky:
The power, the proposition without pose,
The heart finding the great hourglass imbued—
We could discuss it for hours and hours,
But rather let us stand, sore and sea-soaked,
And drink and drink until our rims are one.

WILD OATS

Perhaps it came down to that—the lover,
The lemon trees, a view of the blue sea,
And somewhere blowing in the wind wild oats
Like seed to keep you young forever.
It is something you must take from the air,
It makes the eyes smart, leaves musk in the nose—

All because she lies naked beside you
Like the warm subject for a work of art.

Therefore we practice these gestures over
And over in secret, the casting out
And the reining in, youth not being half
Long enough for the crop you have in mind:
The inseminated fact, the furrows
That open everywhere until the stone
On her hand looks like a swollen grain,
The citrine of parthenogenesis.

No doubt, you choose the jacaranda tree,
The purple blossoms and the amethyst,
The dark lady lying by a river.
Arrange the subject, and the seed will fall.
The water, perhaps, has turned dark as black grapes,
And you will feel fertile with fatality—
In a dark hall, the throes, a dangerous mood,
The old torn overcoat sagging with groats.

I can tell you that it never passes,
The performance before the fact that counts.
It is the only way: Expose yourself—
This is where the seed touched down, took root.
All of those mornings of the outflung hand,
And the curving and the swift reining in—
Stay out on night patrol if need be—Feel
And smell the wild oats blowing through the world.

BLUE DANCERS

In the midst of crises, the insolence of fortune and appetite,
One tends to summon something that moves freely on its own:
Dry your tears. There are blue dancers in a soft blue light.

Love has made you this once more a plaything and a fool:
Hot palms, hot feet, dry tongue, the parched lips of longing—
Apply the poultice of a picture, dancers in blue tulle.

I know it pulls away even from your magnifying glass,
Devolves into the very vortex you despise—
Drama is jealous of pictures, and pictures say: This, too, will pass.

What have we here?—The world withdrawn, the world is moving faster,
The day destroys philosophy as hard as you can tug the scene:
Blue clown, admit that you must be a dupe before you are a master.

I have these scumbled pictures on my hands—
One would think that I had dipped them in a vat of blue,
But, in fact, I have stacked them up against—how many days' demands?

It is a powerful sensuous surge, another taking over—
Master, tap your cane, tell them how and where to move:
Blue dancers educate the fool and elevate the lover.

THE POND

Do you remember those days we went fishing in the pond,
Wore cut-off jeans, no underwear,
Drank cola in the sun, and did not think that we must share
With anyone a having to ourselves the Great Beyond?

This is a focus filled with jeweled light—
We stripped, tanned beneath its magnifying glass,
Felt the prism in the blood, the rainbows pass,

Their colors, like a Dance of Seven Veils, unite.

For naked boys, the shimmering gauze—
I take some comfort that it comes to me so late
The most alive of us can lie in state
And break the rigid pattern of eternal laws.

I smile to see the old man in the mirror
As though he saw the pond in morning glow,
And knows in unforgotten places time is very slow,
Waits in grave attendance at the edges of an error.

An error with the most imposing truth in it—
A jeweled ring that dazzles on my finger
The rich belabored dance of those who linger
Yields as little to attendance as those edges still permit.

THE TRUSS

Just that pad on a special belt—a touch
Of something firm, and a sea wall rises:
The blue, adored and feared, is held in check.
Still one shakes, shivers, spits out a bit of foam.
There is a blue rocking in your shoes,
An hallucinatory desire for puttees,
Their low, supportive signals to the truss,
Warning the pad to harden like sapphire.

Furthermore, you are advised not to lie
Languidly in a hammock's slumped canvas,
For all your strength will seem heavy and bagged.
It is being held, helped, upright that counts,
The exoskeletons of your legs chiding
The raised head to find the sacred river,

To answer the full sea with source-waters,
To have a hummock, a hill, for yourself.

There will be time for violets at your feet,
Indeed, low-slung hammocks that do not pinch,
A supple jewel holding a healed place,
But when that time will ever be, who knows?—
I hear old men mumbling of golden years,
And want to break off a headland for them.
Meanwhile, one gains, gathers a kind of youth,
Feeling these tremors of a tightening world.

THE PREMISE

Hawk-shaped, the shadows of the diver fall
Into the way the pool argues out its blue.
The body, some do not know, can be a harsh thought too—
Consider, in larger terms, the weighted parachute's bolder
    universal.

An umbrella collapsed, a plummeting bird—
These are the facts of fall on which to trade.
One could set up a metaphysical racket with the aid
Of any two of these that mutually concurred.

I offer, however, a beaked shadow, the chute
Of an unknown body, quite merciless to ground.
But even here we range the world too wide, confound
The issue of the swimmer, half figment in a feathered suit.

Let us close in on fall, believe the pool
Which cleanses hawks and gives us man—
Surely we flicker in doubt, and no one can
Be sure he knows what went into the beautiful.

LAST WORD

It was as though the sea rose up and stuck
Out its blue tongue at him with the last word—
Was it a kind of lump sum of language,
Would it come crashing down on him at last?
Was he, in fact, the last of a lost tribe
Who had tried to face down the mammoth mouth?—
It was only one of those immensities
That loom some days in towering regard.

I must keep a civil tongue in my head
When the extravagant sunset insists
That a rapt plethora pervades the world,
A rich, pink wine pouring into the sea,
The blue lips engorged, engulfed, backing off—
You have seen that pulled and placid water
When the end of the day has had its way
And a gull floats like phlegm in the great throat.

Then the blue night comes on like a numen,
And you are asked for prayer and evensong:
No stepping back, feeling for the night latch
Though the sudden lamp looms like a loophole—
One thinks of warm thighs, the lodestone of love,

The retreat to a place where nothing matters:
Two people, jammed, lying by a wicket,
Speechless, counting on dawn to let them through.

THE COVE

Was it a new or a remembered place—
Too calm to hold his life's rough history?—
His boat had lost its calligraphic power,
The placid water like a vast blue mirror
That swallowed all his spoken sentences.
Only the touch of glittering dragonfly
Flitted, here, there, across the stalled morning
As though punctuating a vacuous page.
Even the sun looked bald from spreading out
Its light, and the hazy, violet hills,
By contrast, looked mad, savage with dyed locks.
Of course, no litterbugs were on the beach,
No village and no steeples to push down—
Was it time to weigh anchor or reminisce?
A compulsive image kept coming back:
A girl in a canoe, the parasol,
His face tanned, his shoulders hard as topaz,
The incredible intaglio they cut,
The shape of a love-knot in the water,
A figure repeated on soft, inland grass—
As if the crotch always preceded the cross,
Her purse like a silk pouch, stretched out, crammed
With the makings of the bird of paradise,
His moist straw hat beside them like a nest.
Of course, one can throttle the manic fly,
And the story ends, the sun grown senile.
The savages have lost their appetite,
The flesh long marinated in the pot.

Only ants carry their wafers of the world
As if an enormous, brisk sense of wings
Had been grounded in their green desires—
Perhaps it is just the iridescent buzzing:
A fish leaps like a phallus from the water
And lands gasping, quivering in the boat,
Perhaps your loaded, lounging hand picks up
Luxuriant blue tattoos from the warm water
As if the sun were needling you again,
As though senility simmers, then sears—
I have had so many idle summers
With the last anchor hung between my thighs,
Words no more than wisps of smoke in the mouth,
Feeling the cove has come for me at last—
No inland foot, no shadow on the ants,
The purse rifled, the hat singed by a brushfire.
Perhaps it is nothing but pictorial surge—
I feel the topaz leaching from my arms,
And I study all my old incisions.
If she could read me like a book, it would
Be lurid with just this love of living—
So tell your children's children where the cove
Will lie, waiting well below the cross.
We go on inland, upward—there it is—
Save that lasting image for the very last,
But loll until you lavish in the sun,
And give your final kiss to what may be.